Praise for
Mama Still Got It!

'I adore how honest this is – Louise finds the funniest
moments in the smallest everyday occurrences.
I loved it.'

Fearne Cotton

'Utterly heartfelt and blimmin' hilarious – Louise has
created that perfect cocktail of laughter and tears.
It's like a bosomy maternal hug in a book.'

Anna Whitehouse

'This book is for anyone who, like me, has watched
Louise's reels on repeat and wanted more more more
– it's bloody hilarious!'

Katie Piper

'Beautifully observed, wickedly funny, expertly told.
BRILLIANT!'

Giovanna Fletcher

'A brilliantly funny, and more importantly, realistic take
on the joys and woes of parenting. From nappies to nits,
soft play to screen time, we've all been there and you
have to laugh, or you'll cry.'

Gill Sims

'Louise is a genius. This is a brilliant, hilarious and refreshing perspective on parenthood that isn't often expressed. I'm going to buy a copy for every mother I know!'

Alex Light

'Utterly brilliant! I laughed out loud from start to finish. Full of messy, real life parenting stories which I'm so grateful for, because let's be honest, it's not all sunshine and rainbows. Louise's comedic and self-deprecating narration, even around the more serious parental decisions, made me feel like I wasn't alone or doing a terrible job. This book should be a pocket guide for all parents to remind us to stop giving ourselves a hard time!'

Millie Mackintosh

LOUISE BOYCE

Mama still got *it!*

HOW TO MAKE IT THROUGH THE CALPOL YEARS WITHOUT LOSING YOURSELF

HarperCollins*Publishers*

HarperCollins*Publishers*
1 London Bridge Street
London SE1 9GF

www.harpercollins.co.uk

HarperCollins*Publishers*
Macken House, 39/40 Mayor Street Upper
Dublin 1, D01 C9W8, Ireland

First published by HarperCollins*Publishers* 2023

1 3 5 7 9 10 8 6 4 2

A catalogue record of this book is
available from the British Library

ISBN 978-0-00-856184-0

Printed and bound in the UK using 100%
renewable electricity at CPI Group (UK) Ltd

This book is produced from independently certified FSC™ paper
to ensure responsible forest management.

For more information visit: www.harpercollins.co.uk/green

To Jesse, Basil, Sonny and Inca.
You are my Magic.
<m m>

Sonny, Basil and Inca by Sonny, age 7.
Notice Inca's devil horns and Basil's angry face.

Contents

Contents

This is us, by Sonny. The Boyce's. Sonny, Jesse, Inca, me and Basil.
Our family slogan is 'team work makes the dream work'.
Two out of the three kids hate being in teams.

Introduction

Hello, I'm so happy you're here, and thank you for picking up my book. I wonder if you did that because you're a parent looking for some light-hearted writing about motherhood, or if you're looking for a gift for a friend who's in this area of life at the moment? Perhaps you were drawn towards this beautiful book cover, or perhaps you recognise the title and have seen the videos on social media. Or maybe you're pregnant and about to enter into the parenting world (many congratulations). Either way, welcome to my book! I hope you like it. For the record, in writing the majority of this book, it's been stop, start, stop, sta —

Smell the pages … take it all in!

Before we dive in, I thought it best to have an introduction – most books have one, and even as a novice writer this seems to be the norm. And the clever people at HarperCollins said it was OK to do it … so I guess this is the part where I introduce myself and tell you why I wanted to write this book.

When I first became a mother, like many others, I really felt like I was thrown in at the deep end: I was the first of my close friends to have a baby; I wasn't on social media as I am today – nor was I looking at any parenting social media account; and initially I didn't gel with my NCT group. I was searching for a really honest approach to motherhood that didn't sound all doom and gloom, or equally wasn't all 'practically perfect' in every way. I thought I was doing everything wrong.

Being a mother is hard.

This is no joke.

The way I found out I was going to be a mother wasn't how I had expected it to be. I had just turned 31 and was at the doctor waiting for a prescription for cystitis, casually scrolling through Facebook, when 'Dr Insensitive' told me what bus to get home. Sorry, excuse me, my mistake – he actually told me I was *pregnant* ... but he may as well have told me about the bus, such was his cavalier approach to letting me know my world was about to change forever.

Perhaps my reaction wasn't what he was expecting either and, in hindsight, I think I could have handled it differently, but alas at the time I was in shock. My body became very hot, as if I had suddenly stepped off an aeroplane in a hot country, but the ARE YOU KIDDING ME? heat was too much. So I stripped down to my bra and knickers and stood in front of Dr Insensitive in my mismatched undies and with a massive sweat on.

'There are options,' he said, not making eye contact and checking his watch – not surprising really.

'No, there aren't,' I corrected him. I knew this was my baby.

I cycled home feeling like a different person, like I was having an out-of-body experience. *How can this be happening? Is this real? How far along am I? Am I ready? Does anyone ever feel ready? What will my boyfriend think?*

My boyfriend Jesse and I had only just moved in together, and he had deliberately only applied for a parking permit for six months (and not a year), just in case our living situation didn't work out.

Romantic, right?

That evening, when Jesse came home from work, I was waiting anxiously, face pressed against the back of the front door, looking through the peephole. I swung open the door before he could use his key and greeted him with a fake smile and a sweaty brow. 'Hi!'

'Hi. What's going on?'

Jesse hadn't even taken his jacket, bag or cycle helmet off as I urgently ushered him into the living room and told him to sit down. 'Brace yourself.'

'OK.'

'We're having a baby. I'm pregnant.'

Luckily, he was thrilled!

A good friendship is being able to open up and speak the truth about all sorts of things. Sometimes the best release we can have is to be able to sit and rant to your friend. My best friend Jessie (yes, my husband, best mate, sister-in-law and neighbour are all called Jessie/Jesse) and I even have a name for our version of the kind of excellent friendship where we can speak the truth about all sorts of things. We'll say: 'Fancy a BWC drink?' This stands for 'Better Wives Club.' Ranting to each other over wine makes our worries and stresses lift, which inevitably makes us not 'nag' our partners so much. It's nice to know we aren't alone. And everyone wins!

The trouble is, I find there are lots of women who sugar-coat everything which, afterwards, makes you question yourself and feel like you're failing when you're not.

My NCT group was a perfect example of this. We all met when we were about four or five months pregnant and endured classes (including husband Jesse putting a nappy on a doll – hilarious to watch), all the way through to giving birth and beyond. Although we had all been through birth at the same time, I felt a lack of 'in this together'. We all met up when our babies were around five weeks old. Four of the mothers were gushing about how amazingly well their babies were sleeping, how much they loved their partners, and how everything was marvellous. I was envious that they were all doing so well in this new life we were expected to adjust to so magnificently.

I could have lied and said how well I was doing too, but instead I decided to lay all my (exhausted) cards on the table. 'My baby doesn't sleep and my husband is driving me insane!'

There, I'd said it!

And it felt good.

But it was also a release – as much as I tried to fight it, I could feel my eyes starting to fill with tears as the tiredness and 'failure' dread started to seep out from my soul.

The other mothers stopped in their tracks, peering at me over the rims of their coffee cups with furrowed brows …

Had I said the wrong thing?

Then, one by one, all the coffee cups were planted back into saucers with a clatter, coffee spilling onto the table as the whole group gave a collective sigh of relief. Then these wonderful new mothers said, in unison, 'Yeah, me too.'

It was an amazing feeling to know I wasn't alone. This openness sparked a brand new lease of friendship – and has continued throughout all the years of motherhood.

My children are fortunately (or unfortunately) past the baby phase now, but along have come new issues such as finicky eating habits and not finishing homework. But I know these too shall pass and we'll learn and grow from it all with the help and support from other mothers.

This is why I am so pleased to write this book. Because motherhood *is* messy and challenging, and we have to laugh along the way and take inspiration from the difficult moments. I want this book to make you feel 'normal'. That's how I've coped with the day-to-day challenges of motherhood.

*   *   *

So why 'Mama Still Got It'? Before I was a mother I was (and still am) a fashion model. From 1995 to 2011 I worked in front of the camera – before social media, before the internet, before diversity inclusion of models of colour, size and ability. It was a very tough time to be in the business if you didn't fit in. In 1995, when I was 15, I took part in a modelling competition with Highland Spring Water, which introduced me to a prestigious London-based modelling agency; I went from science class in school to being interviewed on TV's *This Morning* with Richard and Judy, to then having lunch with Richard Branson, Carla Bruni and Jeff Banks (a TV fashion guru back in the nineties), all in the space of a few days. Shortly after this I was entered into another competition called 'European New Face Model of the Year.' I flew to Greece to represent England. This was a time before mobile phones, and I even remember people were smoking on the plane. I have no idea how my mum ever let me go! Still, I won the competition.

Back in the UK, I didn't have much time to celebrate – I was told by my agency that I was too fat and needed to lose weight. I was a UK size 10, maybe even smaller: I remember buying a pair of black satin trousers from Miss Selfridge in Kingston and they were a size 8; I had to prove to my agency what size they were by showing them the label.

But it wasn't just them. In Paris, meeting a different agency, they took one look at my figure when I walked in and rolled their eyes. I wasn't thin enough, and I was sent home. Back in London my agency, furious with me, pulled me into a meeting room, told me to strip down and a measuring tape was lassoed around my skinny body. I was told I had two weeks to lose three inches off my hips.

By 16 I was bulimic. Like so many girls in the business, I tried to lose weight for other people, silently punishing and judging myself. I was miserable and a shell of the real me. I looked awful, I lacked energy, my periods stopped and I was told I wouldn't be able to have children.

When I was 17, I went to Sydney to model there for six months. I didn't take care of myself. The bulimia continued to a point where it was the norm, and without my mum's watchful eye I could do it more often – and add strong laxatives to the mix. When I returned to London in November 1998 my family were shocked by my appearance – my sister burst into tears when I walked through the arrivals lounge at Heathrow airport. They all knew I was sick.

It was my family that got me through my illness, which I'll be forever grateful for.

I took a step back from the business and from 1998 to 2000, I worked in an office as a receptionist and PA. And I loved it! I started to get back the confidence that had been stripped away.

As fate would have it, in May 2000, my boss suddenly left the company and I found myself at a loose end at my desk. I literally had nothing to do. I would spend my mornings emailing my best mate, Laura (I'm talking essays). I needed something to change. A former model mate of mine told me about a new agency that catered for 'plus size' models – those starting at a UK size 12. (Ridiculous, I know, to think of 'plus size' and size 12. You'll be pleased to know it's no longer called 'plus size' and just 'curve' ...) I sent some photos into the agency thinking nothing of it, but two days later a new agency was calling me non-stop, asking me to join them. Completely unsure about getting back into the business, I made a decision: I would quit my job and give it six months.

From 2000 to 2011 I worked only as a curve model. I travelled the world, met wonderful people, made a small fortune and felt confident in my own skin. I was the model in a bikini you'd see that hadn't been airbrushed, and you'd see stretch marks and cellulite. It was a little daunting at the time as no one else was doing it, and I wasn't sure how the general public would accept it.

Luckily, this is something you see more and more now on social media and fashion campaigns, thank goodness.

In 2011 I became pregnant with my first child, and my modelling work stopped. I had known it would. When I became a mother in 2012 I was told by my former agent that my career was over. In addition, I felt like I had lost my identity and I wasn't prepared for the stigma that can come with being labelled 'mum'.

So I started an Instagram account with the name 'Mama Still Got It' as a reminder to all mothers (and women) that regardless of your age, profession or life choices, we all still love and deserve to look and feel good.

My passion for beauty and fashion has evolved, like I have. I'm not the same girl I was when I was 21 – and thank goodness for that!

With my determination to make women feel good about themselves, my account started to get noticed and my modelling work picked up again. I shot campaigns for Max Factor and secured a contract with L'Oréal Paris.

By the time I was pregnant with my third child, I had a small following on my 'Mama Still Got It' Instagram account. Maternity clothes are not always modelled by actual pregnant models, so I started a campaign called 'Push It Out', asking for more honesty in maternity advertising, making it clear to the consumer if the model showing off the maternity clothes was pregnant or not. Why? Because all bumps are different; because pregnant women were comparing themselves to models online (who weren't pregnant) and starting to diet; and because so many women (including myself) were pushed out of a job.

My campaign was shared, and brands listened. I made a small difference. Hurrah. Then Covid hit, and everything stopped. I felt anxious about the idea of home schooling an eight- and five-year-old, plus caring for a one-year-old whilst the husband was locked away in our bedroom office (I'm sure you can relate). So I started making light-hearted videos.

I have a lot to thank social media for: having a platform where I can be silly, making up characters representing my children and husband playing out everyday, mundane situations has evolved into this book. And if you're familiar with these videos, then I want to thank YOU for your support. Your likes, comments and shares have given me the opportunity to reach other parents out there who have perhaps felt alone, overwhelmed or anxious about being a mum, a dad, a carer. I receive hundreds of messages from people all over the world thanking me for making them smile, or making them realise their kid is 'normal' – or that they are 'normal' – and that their partner is not the only one doing all those annoying things. And that is why I keep making more videos – and now this book – because of your encouragement, and knowing that maybe this is a form of therapy, a way to unwind, a chance to let off steam.

Laughter is the best tonic to any crappy day. I get asked a lot about the 'little hands' and how I make my videos. When my third baby was born, my friend Jenny came over to meet my daughter and gave me a gift. This gift was a pair of small plastic hands.

I must have looked perplexed as I unwrapped them.

'Thought you may need an extra pair of hands, now that you're a mum of three.'

I'll be honest, these small plastic hands were quickly thrown into the back of my 'everything drawer' and I wasn't expecting to see them ever again. To be fair, they are quite odd!

It was during home schooling, when my son asked me to watch him over and over: 'Mummy, watch …' that I realised this was a video I wanted to portray on my account. I asked my son to re-enact this irritating habit. He refused. Naturally. I still wanted to make the video – but how could I look like a kid? You guessed it – I fished out the small, plastic hands from my drawer and the rest is history.

I never thought I'd be known as the 'little hands' lady. Yet here we are.

This book won't necessarily give you any tips or advice on being a parent – but it will give you stories you can relate to that will raise a smile or LOL, and make you realise you're not alone on this journey. It makes the stressful days ease up a little. My mum has always said that when life gives you lemons, make a gin and tonic. I hope this book is your tonic when you need it.

The book works around the academic school year because we all know that New Year's Day for us is September (you *know* you celebrate a little bit as you drop-kick your kid into the school gates after six to eight weeks of high-performance parenting), meaning the final chapter of this book is August when, let's face it, we are exhausted after a year of parenting events, whether it's play dates, football practice or sodding World Book Day – (isn't there ALWAYS something going on? Don't get me started on the copious amount of WhatsApp chat ...)

From swimming lessons to meltdown sessions, flying with kids to crying at gigs, this book will cover it all – and then some. This is also my opportunity to bash my husband, Jesse (just a bit), but I have made space within this book for his 'right of reply' too, to make it fair (eye roll – if it was fair, men would have nipples that could also produce milk). My mum has also written her experience of becoming a grandmother for the first time too: an excellent, honest and somewhat *interesting* read (oh, how times have changed since the eighties, when she was first a mother).

I also understand that busy parents may not always have time to read a full book, so for your convenience (we all love convenience), I have written this book in such a way that you can open it at any page and start reading, and it will make sense – you

What's with my nose and boobs? This is me. By Sonny.

don't have to read it from start to finish. Pick it up as you go along or, if you prefer, you can listen to this as an audio book, perhaps even in the dead of night when someone small isn't sleeping.

A final thought has struck me: this book is almost like my fourth child – it's felt like a writing pregnancy: I've had three trimesters growing and building this book; I've had ups and downs with it; worries about it; joy about it; and been so over the writing and just wanting to get it out there …! But just like any other child I've had, the end result has been totally worth all the hard work (and less painful, hurrah).

I suppose you holding this book is the fourth trimester. Please be careful with my baby!

(Just for the record, my kid said: 'Mummy, Mummy, watch!' on loop whilst I was writing this introduction. And I was very much watching him. Thank goodness I can touch-type with my eyes on him and not my keyboksa$%^.)

September

New school year

Ahhh, the smell of new beginnings is in the air ... perhaps your child is starting school for the first time, or you're a seasoned mother hauling your child into the next school year. Either way, a hint of autumn is upon us – no need to include sunscreen on the kids in the morning routine, and with the nights starting to draw in, the challenge of bedtime will start to get easier. Parents everywhere rejoice and, like any new start to the year, a sense of change and excitement circulates.

It's also time to fish out the school uniform from the bottom of the laundry bin, book in mandatory kids' haircuts, and purchase a new pair of school shoes.

Note to self: leaving this until the beginning of September means little stock will be left for school shoes at Clarks ...

The shop was packed with other last-minute, panicked mothers all trying to get the same decent-looking shoes, all having the same conversations with their children, trying to remain as patient as possible.

'Just try them on and see how they feel.'

'I don't like them!'

'Just try them on and we can go and get a snack afterwards.'

I felt beads of sweat building up around my brow as I helped shove shoes onto my son's uninterested and limp feet, as well as restraining my toddler from touching EVERY SINGLE SHOE on the shelves, and trying to convince her not to run out of the shop.

It's safe to say it was an outing I'd have liked to have been over as soon as possible.

The 'back to school' hair appointments at the local kids' hairdressers – where they play CBeebies on loop on a TV attached to a sit-in toy car that is surrounded by lollipops – was fully booked. *Drat.* We had no choice but to go to the local dodgy barbers on the high street, who basically sheered their heads like sheep getting ready for summer.

The gangster haircuts and panic-buy girls' orthopaedic shoes weren't the back-to-school look I was hoping for, but it was better than putting them back in their old shoes from last July with open flaps exposing their toes.

What on earth do they *do* in the playground?

The first day of school, all parents and carers wake up like a Disney princess from a movie: blue skies, birds singing, I'm singing. Full of energy, we dance into the kitchen and pour cereal into the breakfast bowls with a spring in our step, glancing over to the perfectly laid-out school uniform.

Please note that in the first week of September you'll be feeling so on top of school life, smug with your organisation, you will *not* be rushing to get to the school gates as you do the rest of the year. The night before you will probably have planned out the backwards school run because you've totally forgotten your usual routine: *we need to get to the school gates at 8.45, so we need to leave at 8.30, which means we have to wake up at 7.45 latest.* (Madness, really, as my toddler gets us out of bed at 6 a.m., so all this backwards maths is pretty pointless. Yet I play on the hope that maybe one day I can sleep to 7.45 a.m.)

During the summer holidays, my two boys Basil and Sonny woke up before 7 a.m., but they are at least now at an age (ten and seven) where they are pretty much self-sufficient in the mornings. I would leave the breakfast bowls and cereal out on the table and they'd sort themselves out. This was very helpful, as by then I'd be trying to negotiate with Inca, my toddler daughter, about what to wear.

Who ever said girls were easy – THIS IS A LIE. Girls just sit around and play tea parties and draw? Umm, no, they don't! We had a girl after having two boys and very naively I assumed it wouldn't be a challenging journey: *She's my third child so I know what I'm doing, don't I?* I always thought boys were the difficult ones but, oh, how wrong I was. Inca is Miranda Priestley from *The Devil Wears Prada* with regard to fashion: just trying to get her dressed we go through three outfits before leaving the house. She also treats pyjamas as an actual outfit that needs accessories – she must have a handbag next to her when she sleeps.

Naturally, as it is the first day of school, the boys have their first lie-in in six weeks and I realise getting them out of bed in the morning can be even more tedious than putting them into bed in the evenings.

I am always the first parent out of bed in the morning, whereas my husband Jesse will relax into the school morning with a casual Twitter scroll and sometimes even join in a debate at 7 a.m. with strangers online, usually regarding our government and/or football. This will also coincide with his morning 'turbo poo' – for a good 20 minutes – whilst I get everyone ready.

But it's September, and everything is so very organised and nothing, NOTHING, is going to get me in a bad mood on the first day back at school – I am so very much looking forward to my morning coffee *alone* at the local coffee shop after drop-off.

School uniform

September is the only month of the year when school uniform and shoes (albeit dodgy-looking ones) look their absolute best: ironed shirts, polished shoes, matching socks, updated PE kit (the school added a hoodie over the summer), shiny water bottle standing to attention, and backpacks that are crumb-free.

(I've even name-tagged every single item! I was planning on sewing name tags onto the uniform, but this idea quickly turned into the iron-on name tags, which then morphed into just using a black Sharpie pen on the clothes' washing labels. My rationale for this is that name tags can be cut off, but a Sharpie pen is permanent, thus quickly reframing the narrative from me being lazy to being extra vigilant.)

During the school year, however, this will all change. By July, the uniform looks like it's been through a prison break, shoes have open toe flaps displaying mismatched socks … one year I didn't even realise that my kid had in fact swapped shoes with his best mate, who is a size smaller than him. And his backpack contained remnants of a packed lunch from a school trip taken back in March, rogue bits of paper, a spoon (?), while last year I found a snail in the front pocket.

School shoes

Oh my word. If I'd had a pound for every time I say 'SHOES!' before leaving the house to get to school I'd be a millionaire by the end of the first week back. Bloody shoes. Why do we have to repeat ourselves? I've even made it simple for the kids – they have their own basket and all they have to do it put their shoes in their basket. Does it happen? No. There they are, flung across the living room floor, or under the sofa, or even in the bathroom by the toilet. Putting on shoes is one of the most stressful parts of the day. And it happens five days a week! Actually, sod that – it's seven days a week, 365 days a year, and sometimes there are shoe changes in the day too – don't get me started on getting wellies on. Not just for the kids but me too. And then, of course, we have the toddler who won't keep still whilst trying to apply the sodding shoes to their suddenly transformed Michael Flatley feet, resulting in a rugby scrum type 'cuddle' to force the shoes on. Naturally you win the battle and finally secure the buckle with a sweaty forehead and gritted teeth, only for the toddler to kick the shoes off in the car.

Back-to-school photo

This is also the day to take that obligatory school photo up against your front door for all to see before you head to school. This can and will add time and stress onto your already tightly timed schedule to get to school, and some negotiating/bargaining with your children is essential. (Isn't it always?)

'OK, look at me and smile … smile!'

'Oh, come on, this is the best day ever! Smile!'

'OK, put your arm around your brother and smile.'

'OK, don't smile.'

'Don't even think about smiling.'

'No smiling.'

'If you don't smile then we can get extra snacks after school.'

Got it.

My mum has always said to me: 'If you want something done, you have three options: do it yourself, pay someone to do it or tell your kids *not* to do it.'

This photo is later uploaded to social media or shared with family members over WhatsApp for all to see the school uniform cuteness, regardless of the kids protesting and me whispering to myself 'for fucks sake'. You know you've said this one too many times when your two-year-old starts saying 'bus sake' at any given frustrated moment – which in our experience is a lot.

Parents should also have a back-to-school photo at the front door too. If we did, Jesse would be holding his fishing gear heading off for the day, and I would be in my dressing gown with a face mask on, holding a glass of wine.

The first-day-back walk to school

As we walk to school, I have a broad smile on my face. My two boys don't have such a smile on their face and, as predicted, here come the pre-school chants: 'Mummy, I don't want to go to school.'

'I don't want to go to schooooooool, Mummy.'

'Mummy!'

'I don't want to go to schoooooooooooooooool!' Notice the emphasis on 'school' and how every time this word is repeated it gains an extra amount of 'oooo', and sounds equally as annoying as it is to read it. This broken record chant isn't going to tire so I take control of the situation and give them some encouragement before we get to the school gates.

'School is wonderful! You're so lucky to go to school! I miss my school days so much, because I didn't realise how good they were! *And* you're hanging out with your friends all day!'

I smile to myself on the school run as I reminisce about some of my school-day memories. I remember bunking off art class and feeling so bad about it I came back halfway through the class and told the teacher what I had done. Another time I drew red pen on my hand and told the teacher I was bleeding – he excused me from the classroom to get it stitched up. I remember my fingers getting caught in the fire doors and having to go to hospital, or when friends and I stole 12 bottles of champagne from the home economics classroom. They had been put there to chill for a teachers' drinks evening after school. We turned up to geography class half cut. I didn't ever think the first time I'd be tipsy would be at school …

'Mummy, school is Six Cruel Hours Of Our Lives.'

It takes me a while to figure this out. 'Actually, it's Six *Cool* Hours Of Our Lives,' I correct them.

I greet other mothers on the way to school who are also smiling, and we give each other a silent but knowing nod, knowing that we all danced around the kitchen this morning.

We arrive and wait for the gates to be unlocked. A murmur of polite chit-chat spills out as you see other families that you haven't seen in six weeks, all looking fresh and ready for the day ahead.

'Did you have a nice summer?'

'Yes, thank you! It was great!'

What we actually mean is: 'No, it was a juggling, expensive mess and I don't want to enter another Pizza Express for a good six months. It rained the entire time on our camping holiday; I cannot hear the word, 'Canihaveasnack?' without wanting to throw food at my kids' heads; my work Zoom calls were constantly interrupted with my kid asking me to 'Mummy, watch'; my husband was unusually busy in the office for the entirety of August; my in-laws very conveniently were away when we were here and here when we were away; I inadvertently became a qualified lifeguard; and it was hotter in the UK when we were away in Spain.'

'How was your summer?'

'Really wonderful – the weeks just flew!'

The very first day of school

'My little one is starting school for the first time and I'm so not ready.'

Ah, yes, the first-time mum with a kid going to school. First of all, many congratulations on having navigated the eAdmissions system to apply to the school and wait an agonising six months to find out if you a) filled out the form correctly, b) chose the right school and c) uploaded the documents needed.

This is definitely a huge milestone for any family, whether it's school or nursery ... and college too, of course. When our eldest, Basil, first started nursery both Jesse and I were so nervous, we treated it like he was off to university. He was only seven months old, bless him. We were both tearful when we dropped him off for the first time, questioning if we were doing the right thing. I spent that day overthinking everything, calling the nursery for an update, asking for the manager's name and number in case we wanted to WhatsApp them, googling the nursery teacher's name, scrolling through photos of Basil on my phone, and drafting my letter of resignation to the modelling agency I was working for at the time, as an agent. I counted down the hours, minutes and seconds until we could go and pick him up.

Second child: there was not a wet eye between us. But we looked forward to coming back to get him.

Third child: basically drop-kicked into nursery. (Especially after lockdown.)

The same goes for starting school. Although I was slightly more jubilant knowing that I no longer had to pay nursery fees, and it was much cuter seeing my son in school uniform looking like a miniature business man, the mum anxiety and guilt still crept in. *Is he ready?*

What if he gets lost in the school?
What if he needs help cutting up his lunch?
What if he doesn't like the lunch?
What if someone is mean to him?
What if he accidently wees himself?

After this particular drop-off, back at home, I remember sitting still and trying to take in all my emotions. *Am I sad? Am I happy? Why isn't Jesse feeling anything? How can he just carry on as normal?* Cue argument over who cared more about Basil starting school. Great start.

Picking Basil up from his first day at school was really quite magical. I genuinely couldn't wait to see him. Whilst my arms were tightly around him, I asked a million questions, all of which were responded to with: 'Fine' and 'Good' and 'Canihaveasnack?'

Sonny started school in September 2020, during Covid and after six months of lockdown. His first day was on my fortieth birthday, and it was possibly the best gift ever.

The gates open and I wish my children well. As they head off to their new classroom chatting to friends in the playground, I get a pang of love and feel an ache in my heart – but quickly pull myself together and join the other parents dancing the conga out of the school playground. I head off to get that well-deserved coffee in peace.

WhatsApp chats

September is also the month the school mums' WhatsApp chat starts up again. This consists of a copious amount of messages regarding the cupcake sale after school, messages asking you to join the PTA or Friends Association, homework questions, worried mothers losing their child's school uniform, birthday parties and, of course (and my favourite), the arranging of nights out that only amount to messages saying, 'Sorry, I can't make it' on the day.

If I may, can I suggest a universal rule for any school WhatsApp group chats? If a parent or career asks in the chat: 'Has anyone picked up Olivia's cardigan?' could we all agree to answer only if we actually have the sodding cardigan?

'No sorry!'
'Hope it turns up soon'
'Not me, sorry xxxxx'
'Have you asked lost property?'
'Nope xx'
'No x'
'Nada'
'Nicht'
'Nothing over here'
'Did you put her name in it?'
'Nope sorry'
'No xxxxx'
'I had the same last week'
'Sorry babes no'
'Oh no!'
'I'm sure it will turn up'
'Sorry nothing'
'Jumper or cardigan?'
'Nothing here'
'I'll take a look'
'no'
'no sorry'
'nope'

However, it's therefore easy to put some personality behind the parents on the WhatsApp group:

The stressed-out mum
The organised mum
The scatty mum who never has any idea what's going on
The gossip mum
The know-it-all mum
The head of the PTA mum
The secret-lurker mum
The mum who only replies with emojis
The mum only there for wine
The mum who never reads the newsletter or school emails
     and only comes on to WhatsApp for updates.

On top of the WhatsApp messages we have the school emails – and the text messages, and the app, and the screen grabs of the app that are now also in the WhatsApp chat. Honestly, school admin is a job in itself … our parents never had all this shit and they got on fine. I remember getting letters to take home for my mum once a month and even then I don't think I gave her half of them.

Then, outside the main class WhatsApp chats, are the smaller groups of parenting WhatsApp chats that are curated specifically for certain people.

'How did you get into that WhatsApp group?' I asked my friend, Anna, who was currently chatting away with six other very cool mothers. I found myself inconspicuously side-eyeing her phone screen and oddly really wanting to get involved in the chat. They had drinks and coffee together, and arranged play dates.

I wondered if I could be part of their club. (Turns out I, too, am back at school, metaphorically speaking.)

'We're all at the same gym,' Anna replied.

'You mean the gym that I go to as well?' I replied.

'Oh, yes. Let me ask Joanna – she's the one who started the chat.'

I sensed that Joanna was the alpha female in this group.

I felt quite excited at the idea of being in the chat, but two weeks went by, and I still hadn't been added.

'I did ask her, but Joanna said she's not sure how to add you into the group,' Anna told me.

Hmmm. I found that hard to believe considering Joanna was the one who started the group in the first place, and had managed to add other people. By this point I *really* wanted to join this chat – it had become my obsession. So much so, that I found myself waving at Joanna across the school play-ground more than I should have done, and even agreed to attend a fund-raising ideas evening knowing that she might be there.

In my twenties it was all about getting into the best night-clubs; in my forties, it was all about getting into WhatsApp chats. Rock 'n' roll.

A few agonising weeks later, a notification pinged up; I recog-nised the group photo profile picture of all the ladies in the chat. I had been added to the chat called 'Gym & Tonics'! I had been accepted! I had been declared worthy – I WAS COOL!

I am going to create some great banter in this chat. They'll not regret asking me to join.

Ten minutes later, I decided to make my first opening message in the chat but was rudely welcomed with the notifica-tion: *Louise has been removed from this group.*

WTF just happened? I'd been removed already?? I hadn't even got the chance to show my best gifs or one-liners! How could I be removed? Maybe there had been some mistake. Or had it been deliberate?

That afternoon I went to soft play and spotted Joanna there. Before I could approach her she hid inside the bouncy castle right at the back, behind an inflatable beam that protruded from the bouncy castle floor. She was deliberately avoiding me.

So, that was my answer. She never did see my humour in my WhatsApp messages. She can just read them all here in my book instead.

Nits

Of course, there is always one WhatsApp chat that no parent EVER wants to receive:

'Just to inform you, a child in your class has been confirmed with nits, so please check your child's hair and as a precautionary measure, please use treatment.'

Bloody nits. And they're taken as seriously as Covid was – parents reminding you to self-isolate if you have been affected, to stay at home and not to be super spreaders; being frowned on if you don't treat your child – avoiding certain children who seem to be scratching their heads too often, and skipping birthday parties just in case you may get it.

And then there's the absolutely DISGUSTING agony of applying the nit treatment, followed by the combing through of the hair for the entire family. I'd rather deal with several poonami explosions than treat sodding nits. The MELTDOWNS from both myself and the kids is beyond my parenting capability. I think I'd rather they have nits than deal with the lengthy negotiations and bribery needed to have the 'special' shampoo applied. One time I think I paid them to sit still and be treated (which works by the way). We once had back to back nits three times. THREE TIMES – by the third time I was broke and the boys actually enjoyed looking at the nits that had been caught on the comb (making me retch and question why I didn't just give them skin-head haircuts). For the record, Jesse has not once treated the kids for nits – nor has he ever had them. Nor does he catch the children's colds, whereas I will pick up everything the kids have – colds, stomach bugs, nits, meltdowns … Whatever they have I have too, but no one looks after me (cue the violins).

When I was a kid at school, we had a 'nit lady' who would come to our classroom and check our hair. You were sent home if you had them which was a rollercoaster of emotions. On the one hand you could go home early (if the school could reach your parent to pick you up), but on the other hand all the kids in the class knew you had nits and would spread this gossip around the school. I remember shouting a lot when my mum treated me for nits. The 1980s toxic nit shampoo STANK, making it utterly obvious you had had treatment (embarrassing for kids, smug-making for parents), and that dreaded metal comb that may as well have been teethed with knives being scraped over my sensitive scalp, already burnt by the toxic shampoo, hair getting tangled up along the way causing an impromptu home haircut … I would kick and scream whilst Mum held me down making sure she got every single louse and their eggs.

It's not a fond memory at all, so when I was reintroduced to them years later as a mother, a multitude of emotions came flooding back. Which was why, first time around, I held off the treatment for my son. He was selected to sing in a choir at the Royal Festival Hall with his school, and he was the only child continuously scratching his head throughout the entire concert. It was so obvious he had nits, even the other kids were shuffling away from him to a point where I thought he may be singing a solo in the concert.

'I think you need to treat your son for nits,' a fellow mother from the school leaned over during the concert and whispered into my ear. Ugh, she was right and my mum guilt went off the chart, but I reminded myself that as nits only like clean hair (urban myth?), at least he was clean, right?

And another WhatsApp chat we don't want to receive (or perhaps we do) is the announcement of chicken pox. There's usually a mix of messages back, which will show that you're either a parent whose child has already had chicken pox, is therefore immune and is slightly smug and complacent in announcing that this doesn't affect your child; you stay away from everyone; or you're desperate for your kids to have it to 'get it out of the way' and encourage the kids to play closely together in the hope they may pick it up. A chicken pox party if you will. I wonder if there are party invitations one can buy to the event. Perhaps chicken is on the menu, followed by lollipops. (I called it chicken POPS until I was well into my thirties, not really knowing the correct wording until I had children and started being active on these WhatsApp chats!)

Of course, it's not all about parent WhatsApps, either …

Monday morning. A message pings from my WhatsApp chat called 'Pennies'. For whatever reason, my closest friends and I have always called each other 'Penny'. I can't remember where it stemmed from but even though we are all called the same name, when we're all together we all know which 'Penny' is being spoken to – a bit like being able to single out your baby's cry from other babies' cries.

The message is from Laura, a girl I met at secondary school during Science, when we were 13 years old. It reads: 'I started the week in reverse cowgirl – happy Monday!' (Laura is embracing not having children. Can you tell?)

To which I replied: 'I started the week wiping up shit off the hallway landing. Happy Monday!'

My toddler, Inca, had decided to, once again, take off her nappy and use it as a shopping basket. Using her small pellets of poo as vegetables that she placed into her nappy basket, she

missed most of the time, thereby leaving a trail of poo for me
on this particular Monday morning.

I screenshotted the message, made Laura anonymous and,
with her permission, added it to my Instagram stories. It got a
few laughs but the joke was on me when my mother called me
to ask me what 'reverse cowgirl' was. Once explained, she said,
'Well, it wasn't called that back in my day.'

I wasn't sure which was more mortifying – talking to my
mum about a sex position or knowing she had once upon a time
done it herself!

Note to self: block Mum from all social media channels.

The husbanned

It's also around this time – with the kids out of the house but
with your husband working from home (thanks, Covid) – you
realise you still have an extra child to deal with.

I refer to my husband regularly as 'my husbanned' due to all
the vacuous rhetorical questions he asks that I have now banned
him from asking. Thirty-six months (and counting) of us both
working from home has given me such rage, it has convinced
me on the idea that perhaps my husband is indeed from Mars,
after all. *'Are these dry?'*

Clothes horse full of washed laundry and there he is, standing in extremely close proximity to clothes in question, and
pointing at them. I politely point out that in such an instance, it
would be an idea to just reach out and touch the clothes to see
if they feel dry.

'Is this on?'

The radiator. My husband asks if it is on, whilst standing in
front of it and pointing at it. 'Feel it, dear,' I say, through a
bemused and irate grimace.

'*Is this off?*'

Fridge door open, holding up a bottle of milk with legitimate uncertainty. 'Smell it, dear!'

(This was when I realised it was my duty as a wife and mother to make public service announcements for women everywhere to reassure them that they are not alone in their husbanneds.)

'*Is it raining outside?*'

I'm asleep and this particular morning he's up early to go fishing. Did I mention I was asleep? And that I'm not Carol Kirkwood? Did he think I had been outside before him this morning to check for him, then got back into bed? 'Look out of the window, dear.'

And the questions keep rolling in. '*Who's at the door?*' (when the doorbell goes). '*Do I need a coat?*', '*What time shall I put the kids to bed?*', '*Where do we keep the ice?*'

Home schooling

A quick sidebar: I'm truly grateful to see the back of home schooling. The first episode of home schooling back in March 2020 was actually quite fun and we embraced our own rules (mainly inset days and TikTok training). I remember emailing the school asking for some structure LIKE A TWAT, but at the time I felt like I wasn't doing enough. Like I was failing my kids and the anxiety of them not being educated properly overwhelmed me. Little did I know at the time I was living the home-schooling dream.

When we were thrown into home schooling again in Jan 2021 the schools (and a brand new school for us) were well prepared and I remember emailing the school asking for less structure LIKE A TWAT.

From 4 January to 8 March 2021 we had SIXTY-THREE whole days of the kids at home, trying to teach them maths which, by the way, is now taught in a TOTALLY different way to when I was at school. The usual long multiplication where you put the three-digit number on top of the two digit number and work from the right over to the left, multiplying, carrying the zero and then add up —? Makes sense to me (perhaps you too, if you were born in the wonderful eighties) but no, no, no – not anymore. The new way of teaching maths is a MINEFIELD. They split the numbers up, cross-dress them, multiply their roots (nothing to do with highlights), carry the number somewhere else, erase all the above method, subtract something else and add a partridge in a pear tree – they do all sorts of some shite, *et voila*, there is your answer.

It completely beat me. I was trying to teach maths that I didn't understand with an eight-year-old, a five-year-old and an 18-month-old … and a 42-year-old husband, who asked for snacks as much as my kids did.

The ironic thing is, when I was at school, I very vividly remember my maths teacher, Ms Shanai, at Waldegrave School for Girls, telling me how important long multiplication was because (and I quote): 'You'll never carry a calculator around with you all the time.'

Hullo, smartphones. (Just saying!)

Anyone home schooling during the pandemic scaled the height of all motherhood challenges. Many congratulations to you for coping so well with the hideous tasks of trying to work at home and also play teacher, remembering to log into ALL the Teams meetings with two different classes and one laptop. You too may also have had a toddler who wanted your attention ALL THE TIME, and a not-so hands-on husband around all day, every day.

In his defence, he did have to work. (Sense the sarcasm.)

I have never missed soft play so much – which is something I never actually thought I would say. Turns out I missed the deafening, high-pitched, excited screams; the random raisins wedged in the bouncy castle inflatable panels; and the disgusted side-glances from other parents when your kid demonstrated Hulk Hogan's iconic leg drop wrestling move on children half their size. I also have a new-found respect for all teachers, especially those who teach small children. I mean, WOW – these teachers either have the patience of a saint or those coffee flasks are filled with something a little stronger.

I remember, at the height of home schooling, trying to answer emails or to professionally engage in Zoom calls in between the breaks that the kids got, when they would enter the room and say, 'Mummy! Mummy, watch!'

Actually, it was more like:

'Mummy, watch!

'Mummy, watch!

'Mummy, watch!

Sonny asking me to watch him and Inca on loop.
I think he's captured my expression quite well.

'Mummy, watch!
'Mummy, watch!
'Mummy, watch!
'Mummy, watch!
'Mummy, watch!
'Mummy, watch!
'Mummy, watch!
'Mummy, watch!
'Mummy, watch!
'Mummy, watch!
'Mummy, watch!
'Mummy, watch!
'Mummy, watch!
'Mummy, watch!
'Mummy, watch!
'Mummy, watch!
'Mummy watch!'

And, of course, whilst the child is repeatedly asking me to watch, I am indeed watching. So much so I have given up blinking and enlarged my eyeball stare just to show my dedication to watching. I am very much watching my child gear up to some magnificent never-been-seen-before demonstration.

The child pauses. Then the child does a little and quite pathetic hop from one leg to the other that is quite frankly not that impressive at all, followed by the child celebrating with a triumphant chuckle. Well, that was two minutes of my work day I'll never get back. Cute? Yes, of course. But after three months of home schooling and this happening nine or ten times a day it becomes extremely irritating, and I don't see my husband being expected to partake in these demonstrations from the kids. Perhaps this is why he spends so much time on the loo?

Post pandemic, schools opened again on 8 March 2021 – a date I'll never forget. The school uniform was looking its best and you could see your reflection in the over-polished school shoes. That morning, even more than in any normal September, I definitely woke up as a Disney princess character in my own movie, while the energy from all the parents at the school gates was so palpable you could almost feel a choreographed street dance about to unfold, like a scene from *The Blues Brothers* or *Fame*.

Home after drop-off (or drop-kick-off), I had never appreciated the sound of silence so much. I found myself standing in my hallway, coat still on, keys still in hand, staring into space with an enormous grin on my face. It was a euphoric moment. Absolute silence. *They're. Back. At. School.*

I must have been standing there looking like a creepy mime artist from Covent Garden for a good five minutes when I was rudely awakened by a WhatsApp message from a worried parent: *'If Harry was exposed to Covid on Tuesday and had no symptoms for four days but he got it from his sister Isabell who caught it from a party three days before Harry did and tested positive five days later, how likely is it that Harry's little brother is going to test positive on an antigen test if he tests two days after Harry tests positive?'*

They should teach these calculations in KS3 maths. Thank goodness for the mute option on WhatsApp.

Phone calls

Your day ahead is looking great until your phone rings and you see that dreaded word on your screen: SCHOOL or NURSERY. My heart sinks as I am usually about to enter a meeting, am in the middle of a yoga class, enjoying a coffee or perhaps taking a nice, long, hot, bubble bath. When you get *that* call you know it's either game over for the day, or it's a very pointless phone call that raises your blood pressure for absolutely no reason whatsoever.

For example – I was in the middle of writing this book. I had a deadline to meet and I was behind massively. (Don't worry, editor Katya, we got there in the end! This is the proof in your hands.) I sat down to write but as soon as I was on a writing roll, the words flowing, my phone rang.

NURSERY.

'FUCK!'

I considered not answering so that they called my husband instead, but then reminded myself that he was in the next room, working from home, and would pass the phone over to me anyway. Grrr.

I answered with caution. 'Hello —?'

'Hello, is this Inca's mummy?'

'Yes, speaking.'

'Oh, hello, ummm … just a quick call.'

GET TO THE POINT – WHAT IS IT?

'There is nothing to worry about, Inca is fine —'

THEN WHY ARE YOU CALLING ME?

'I just wanted to let you know she has a small graze on her hand from playing in the garden. She's absolutely fine, but we thought we'd let you know.'

WHAT THE ACTUAL FUCK? I stay the calm, professional mother. 'Thank you for letting me know – is there anything else?

'No, that's all, and there is nothing to worry about.'

EXACTLY! I KNOW THERE IS NOTHING TO WORRY ABOUT! SO WHY ARE YOU CALLING ME?

There have been other pointless interruptions from the nursery too. I was waiting for a train to depart from Euston station to Manchester for a work trip once, when 'Nursery' flashed up on my phone screen.

Shit. Please please pleeeeeeease don't be anything too serious … I can't get out of this trip to Manchester.

'Inca has a very small red spot … a spot on her … on her … ummm, on her …'

I deliberately waited for the nursery teacher to say the correct word. The feminist in me was enraged that not only was she calling me over something so trivial, but there she was, a professional care worker who changed nappies every day, and couldn't say the correct word. '… on her lady garden.'

Oh, wow. OK.

'Inca doesn't have a lady garden, she has a vulva and Sudocrem will sort it out. All OK?'

'Ah, yes. Well, Inca has also been saying the word "penis" a lot.'

'She has two older brothers who claim their penis is their best toy.' (And the more Inca said 'penis' the more the boys would laugh, inevitably provoking her to say it over and over.)

It turned out that Inca had taught her entire class the word 'penis', to a point where at pick-up time a class full of three-year-olds would all chorus 'Goodbye, penis!' and 'Goodbye, smelly bums!' ('smelly bums' was not from us but from another family, who I'm sure were equally as concerned by the choice of words. Of course we discourage this use of the word, but as we know – you tell a child not to do something and they will do the total opposite.

When I was at primary school I got three fingers trapped in the fire door: a girl called Sally had been holding open the door in the corridor that led to the hall and I thought it would be a good idea to put my fingers in the hinges. Sally let go of the door and I screamed the school down. My mum wasn't called, however: I was left sitting in the first aid room with a cold towel wrapped around my fingers and was given a hard-boiled egg to suck on. Gotta love the eighties.

To add to this, in the school canteen at my kids' school there are signs everywhere with positive messages:

'Be the best you can be.'
'Make good decisions.'
'Believe in your dreams.'
And so forth.

In my school canteen there was one sign. Just one. It read, 'No flicking peas.'

School pick-up

Six hours of blissful school time may seem long enough for anyone to get lots of work done, but blink and the day is gone. I always find myself racing to the school gates to make it in time – the panic, the sweaty upper lip, the slightly weak pelvic floor starting to show its true colours as you race to the school gates. Triumphantly, you make it, albeit feeling like you've participated in a 5k tough mudder, and you're breathing much more heavily than you'd like whilst catching up with the other mums at the school gates who are discussing the weather and ignoring the repeated lip- and brow-sweat wipes.

And then, with a sinking heart and a drying mouth, you real-ise you are snackless. You spy your kids across the playground and you know they'll hand over their backpacks and before they even say hello they'll be saying: 'CANIHAVEASNACK?'

Snacks. The word we as parents have heard one too many times. The word I have verbally blinkered and even tried to rename as 'bite' or 'light refreshment'. (Neither worked.) Is it my fault this blasphemous word is so commonly used in our household? And why do they ask for snacks at the most incon-venient times? Like straight after a meal, or when I'm on the loo, in the shower or on a work Zoom call?

Once when I was away on a work shoot in Portugal, my ten-year-old called me, asking if he could have a snack. I was in another country. His father was in another room in the same house, and yet I was called.

Before I could shamelessly announce that Mummy didn't have a snack that day, but more importantly had made it on time to pick them up, the teacher beckoned me over to have a chat.

The walk of shame. I nonchalantly walked over to the teacher but I could tell by the way she was looking at me that my kid was in trouble. I could feel the weight of other parents in my year group's stares, watching me as I walked over to the teacher.

Here we go …

'Your son told another child to fuck off today,' the teacher said, sternly.

I was waiting for her to crack a smile and brush it off but she didn't, and I found myself fighting with every ounce of my soul to not smirk and laugh. Nervous laughter, perhaps?

I always find it both odd and humorous hearing someone you don't know well, and who, in this case, is a classic primary school teacher (think Ms Honey from *Matilda*), uttering a swear word that is not in the context of a great gossip story, road rage or a cocktail lounge.

Ms Honey didn't smile or didn't seem to think it was funny, and was looking at me for an explanation as I waved to other mums in the playground and mouthed the words, 'I'll be five minutes.' A couple of mums at the school, gave me an 'Oh, shit' kinda look, mixed with a 'Don't worry about it' energy.

At first I was quite relieved – he'd been telling his older brother all week to 'Suck my balls', so 'fuck off' didn't seem so bad. Naturally, I stood to attention, like a good mother. 'We have a non-swearing policy in our house,' I said. *Do we fuck.* 'I have no idea why he's using that word.'

'He also wrote "fuck off" on a piece of paper and handed it to another child in his class,' Ms Honey informed me. I paused

and asked, with complete sincerity: 'Did he spell it correctly?'
To be honest, the kids know better than to swear at home
because they know we'll take away the Wi-Fi, which makes life
harder for the parents. And therefore for them.

As I looked at my son, who was mutinously staring at his
not-so-shiny shoes, I suddenly realised this was the perfect
excuse for not giving him a snack after school ... thank you, Ms
Honey, for saving the day with our chat! Mummy was no longer
the bad guy!

Yes, you must learn to take your victories where you can get
them. Even if they're 100 per cent undeserved. I've noticed my
eldest son no longer kisses me hello or goodbye at the school
gates – 10 years old seems to be the new teenager. A 'tenager',
perhaps. He's at that point where I am on the cusp of not being
cool, even though his mates think I'm cool because I have a blue
tick on TikTok. Instead, he gestures his head towards me, like a
headbutt. So I get to kiss the hood on his jacket most drop-offs
and pick-ups. We do, however, have a secret hand signal that
means 'I love you'. We'll do the hand signal at the gates and
only we know what it means. And it works in all situations – it's
literally our own sign language for love for embarrassed kids.
Jesse and I even do it to each other from across the pub on a
night out. (Although generally I'd rather be sending the universal gesture for, 'You're designated driver' and, 'A white wine,
please.')

After-school clubs

New terms means new clubs to throw your kids into in the
hope they may become the next David Beckham or Rebecca
Adlington. Most of the time, as you watch your kids partaking

in an after-school activity, you realise they are actually shit, yet you cheer them on with an abundance of enthusiasm whilst slightly dying inside and without wanting to compare your child to others in the same class.

On one occasion, we took our eldest son to a football kick-around with the school. Whilst all the other kids were tackling, scoring and generally had a true love for the game, my son stood on the pitch day-dreaming. He was eventually passed the ball (by the teacher) – cue my over-amplified words of encouragement whilst side-galloping down the pitch with him. But then, all of a sudden, he stopped in his tracks, the ball got tackled and his teammates groaned with exasperation as they watched my son bend down, pick a daisy from the pitch and walk over to give it to me. Very cute, but I'm pretty sure David Beckham didn't do this in training.

Swimming lessons, although very necessary, are up there as possibly the most hideous activity to do with your kids. A public swimming pool is generally a place where you have to undress and redress your kids (including shoes and socks) whilst getting them dry; apply the rubber swimming cap that, if not on properly, can cause a major meltdown and usually does because, let's face it, they have hair that is pulled; and feed them a snack; all in a tiny cubicle, dodging stray hairs and used plasters on the wet floor. And all this next to strangers so you have to be mindful of your language, all whilst overheating. It's a place of true patience-testing. Add a baby and another kid to the equation, and it's pretty much mental and physical parenting abuse.

And then, after all the trouble of getting the kids in the water on time for their lesson, it's abruptly stopped when a kid takes a poo in the water.

You pray that it's not your child.

It's my child.

All out and lesson cancelled. By the end of if you're pretty shell-shocked and need a few moments in the car to assess what's just happened, through the sound of children bickering in the back seat.

I've realised we have to do what we can to survive in these situations. There was one swimming lesson incident shortly after I had given birth where I found myself in a pickle. I was three-kids deep in a changing room doing the usual frenzied pre- and post-swimming juggling act when I realised I needed the loo. My bladder was full and my pelvic floor was weak. I needed to go, but couldn't make a run for it as that would involve leaving all three of my kids (under the age of seven) in a changing room alone. And getting them to the loo with me would take too long, resulting in a possible wet-yourself-in-public scenario.

My bladder was starting to win this fight, so I did what any mother would have done: I took a nappy out of the nappy bag, demonstrated a perfect ballet plié in second position – and peed into it whilst overheating, one hand holding the nappy in place and the other hand firmly on the changing room door, stopping my middle child from trying to unlock it, surrounded by my half-naked kids in a small square cubicle.

Naturally, my sons start laughing and pointing, trying to have a go themselves with another nappy while I fought them off in mid flow. All the while they were shouting out for all to hear: 'Mummy's weeing in a nappy!'

My calm reply: 'I'm just seeing that it works properly'. (Which it does, by the way.)

It was a low moment, but I've never been so grateful to the inventor of disposable nappies.

We all go swimming as a family on the weekends. It's slightly more relaxed without having time against us dashing from school, and I have an extra pair of hands – my husband (although there are times – most times – where I have to tell Jesse to 'Stop it!' and 'Calm down' as he and the boys play Sharks, It or Noodle Train). Families tend to vacate the kids' swimming area when we are there. Goodness knows what they think as they watch my seven-year-old try and drown Jesse by climbing on his head, and my youngest running out of the pool whenever she can, resulting in me running after her and getting a telling-off whistle from the lifeguard. This results in the toddler running around the pool and me following at a fast walk-waddle feeling very much like an ad for contraception.

It's great and also awful when you bump into a family you know in the pool. It's wonderful to socialise albeit in a pee-infused swimming pool whilst accidentally swallowing water mid conversation, very conscious that the couple you usually greet with just a 'Hello' or 'Goodbye' at the nursery are now half-naked in front of you. Naturally my youngest child decided to pull down my swimming costume one day in front of a dad from the same nursery, and since then we've both done our best to avoid the fact that he's seen my deflated and lopsided boobs by carrying on talking about house renovations and the cost of living without making eye contact.

One time, with my sister and her children, we went to an overcrowded, over-stimulating and very tired-looking swimming baths where the main idea seemed not to swim at all, but instead navigate yourself around different-coloured water slides.

It didn't help that my sister has a very real and strong phobia of changing room floors (yes, I agree, this is weird), which introduced a whole new level of adulting-with-children chaos. Imagine all the stress you usually get changing your kids into their swimming things in the TINY 'family' changing rooms (including putting on a swimming cap – THERE ARE NO WORDS FOR THIS UNNECESSARY ACT OF PARENTING) and retching at the sight, feel and smell of the floor you are standing on. That is my sister.

Finally, we headed into the swimming trenches – after spending an agonising extra seven minutes asking other parents if they could break a £2 coin into two £1 coins for the sodding 'family' locker. (It's times like these where you question what is so wrong with kids watching iPads on the sofa.)

We cracked on with it because the kids were really excited to ride the slides, and just a dose of their excitement distinguished any doubt in being there.

Let's embrace this and DO IT!

As I looked around the centre, all I could see were kids smiling and adults grimacing. Everywhere echoed with the high-decibel shrieks of children of all ages, whilst mums desperately tried to avoid the 13-year-old boys with goggles on, who swum around their perimeters like sharks, checking out tits underwater.

Such a joy.

The kids loved it, of course, but by the end of it all, I was dying inside a little bit and could not wait to get out, sort out my running mascara and get the hell home. To add to which, Jesse as ever, managed to get a shower ALONE after it all, whereas I was back in the overheated cube of hell dressing and taming three kids.

And it was only as I closed the door to the cube that I looked down and realised I had somehow managed to expose my left tit for the last five minutes or so.

Baby classes

And of course, the precursor to clubs are the baby classes. I go to these special one-on-one sessions with my youngest, now that my oldest two are at school.

I say 'special' time, but it doesn't feel too special when I'm doing things with her that bring out the worst in my impatience. Has anyone ever been to a baby sign language class? Where you teach your child to sign for things, before they can talk? It's not for me. Totally respect for those out there who can tolerate the lessons but for us it didn't quite work. In fact, it was an eye-opening situation of WHAT AM I DOING HERE? Tell me what you think ...

We arrived in a cold church hall with other tired mothers and small children – nobody knew anyone else. We all smiled and asked about each other's children; we compared notes on the size of the kids and how advanced they were with walking/talking, and made excuses for our young children not playing ball (polite way of saying having a screaming meltdown): 'She's tired/she's hungry/she's teething/she was up earlier this morning than usual.'

Nobody will ever say what they're actually thinking, which is, *She's being a twat and I'm on my last legs of parenting patience.*

The room was full of toys for the kids that even I wanted to play with: electric cars that you could sit in and actually drive, instruments that turned into robots ... incredible!

But the thing was, when we were trying to teach our babies how to ask for milk or say thank you in sign, the last thing we wanted was anything that was going to distract them from paying attention.

A circle of overwhelmed and exhausted mothers and the odd dad was formed and we all sat crossed-legged with our children on our laps. The teacher began talking to us in sign language and we all stared at her as if she had three heads. Finally she spoke, and taught us how to say 'thank you' in sign. We also learnt how to say 'food', 'milk', 'poo' etc. Really helpful stuff – but the class very quickly went from being parents and children to just parents: the kids had all diverted their attention to the toys. So, there we all were – tired strangers in a circle signing to each other, wondering what on earth we were doing.

It got worse, too. One exercise was to choose someone to sit opposite, look into their eyes and try to communicate through eye contact. As I was gazing into the stranger's eyes, trying to figure out what she was communicating, all the while very conscious that my child could be shoving something into a plug socket, I was wondering if the person opposite was thinking the same as me. *Pub?* Or was she looking at my dodgy mascara that had been applied at the quickest of speeds that morning?

Either way, the class wasn't for me. I made a dash for it when my daughter brilliantly started to cry. That's the great thing about kids – they can be used as a reason to leave and no one questions it. I've learnt the hard way when it comes to mother and baby activities. With my first child I managed to convince myself that I needed to fill my days with classes. I took Basil to swimming lessons when he was three months old, even though the only slot the class had available was during his nap time. And I went ahead with it because HE NEEDS TO LEARN HOW TO SWIM (please read that with a slightly hysterical tone), even though he wasn't old enough to eat solids. Of course the entire time he was a screaming mess and I was a lactating one. AND YET we continued to go, and even made a sodding Christmas card of me, Jesse and Basil underwater with Basil wearing a Christmas hat. WHAT??? (It's included in the book for your pleasure, and is a reminder to me of some very stressful moments thinking I was doing the right thing.)

We tried out football when Basil could just about walk; we went to a music class which made me partially deaf in my right ear; I even tried out a chess club when he could just about hold his head up.

When Sonny was born I took a much more relaxed approach to mother and baby classes. I basically didn't do them. Instead I had 'play dates' that usually consisted of staying at home with a bottle of Prosecco with other mothers. And everyone was happy.

My third child, Inca, was thrown into lockdown when she was six months old. I really wanted to go to mother and baby classes when life started to open up again and was excited at the idea of this. I took her to a sensory class in a room in which you wouldn't have been able to swing a cat. And, once again, it was overheated and led by a 19-year-old boy who hummed sounds and played some peculiar instruments. I genuinely think he was high at the time of 'teaching'. I called it a day when Inca and another baby started to grab each other's toys off each other, resulting in dramatic crying.

I like to call this gradual wising-up the 'evolution of mother-hood'. Take the nappy bag on an outing to the park as an example.

First baby: the nappy bag is filled with nappies, wipes, nappy bags, muslins, more muslins, extra clothes, rattle, a book, snacks, milk, water, more clothes, dummy, nappy cream, your slippers, a phone charger, a book on how to wean your baby, cuddly toys, nipple pads, spare top for mum, bottle of water, decaf coffee pods, vitamins, baby food.

Second baby: nappies, wipes, snacks, water.

Third baby: I genuinely don't think I had a nappy bag for my third child. If I did, it was an orange 'for life' Sainsburys bag that possibly had something in it for the baby ...?

The park

Going to the park on the weekend, as a family, is always a great idea for us all. The kids can run wild, we are outside getting fresh air, it's free, and it's totally fine to hide behind sunglasses that are covering up the tiredness and stress caused by the expe-rience of actually getting to the park.

The kids all decide they want to ride on their scooters and yet refuse to wear the helmets and refuse to wear their wellies. We negotiate with these small dictators and silently celebrate when we have won the battle – with bribery.

'If you don't wear your helmet we can't go to the park.'

'If you wear your helmet to the park you can have a snack.'

'Peppa Pig wears her wellies so she can jump in muddy puddles so you must do the same – or we can't go to the park.'

In fact, getting kids out of the house usually takes longer than the time you actually spend at the park.

It's also very likely you'll bump into other parents and children you know, making the experience a social one for the parents too. Social for the dads, anyway, so it seems. Myself and the other mum will chit-chat but spend the entire time constantly watching the children in case they fall over, eat dirt, throw dirt, push a child over, get pushed over, get hit by a swing, take their coat/wellies/hat/dress off, wee themselves, or run into the woods they're not supposed to go in. Even though I am in conversation I am always switched on and ready to save my child from any park situation and usually end a conversation by running off to restrain my child/children from doing any of the above mentioned.

The dads, however, when they're in conversation, seem to have forgotten they're at the park with their kids at all – as the following beautifully illustrates …

It started off well – Jesse was pushing Inca on the swing when a dad friend came over. They shook hands and dived into non-child-related conversations – probably football, fishing and where to buy the best beef. A couple of minutes later, Inca demanded to get out of the swing so Jesse took her out, still in conversation and not realising one of her wellies had got stuck in the swing's seat. He was tugging away at her, to get her out of the swing, in the meantime disconnecting a welly from her foot.

'Daddy, my boot!'

'Yes, very nice, darling.'

'DADDY, MY BOOT!'

I was watching this unfold as I tried to listen to my mum friend. She was in the middle of talking about a new recipe when I was forced to shout over her: 'JESSE! INCA'S BOOT!'

There was relative calm for 20 minutes. The dads were still at the swings chatting away, even though none of their children were actually on the swings, and were completely unaware of a drama unfolding in the park.

Sonny wanted to climb up the slide at the same time another child wanted to slide down it. The slide stand-off.

'Sonny, sweetheart, get down, please. Don't climb up the slide.'

'But I was here first.'

'It doesn't matter. Slides aren't for climbing up.'

The mum of the slide child appeared and tried to help: 'Oh, don't worry about it – my son can wait.'

Very kind of her, but we all know a child going the wrong way up the slide whilst another one wants to come down the sodding slide is really infuriating and telling them over and over is exhausting.

It's all exhausting.

We end up going home carrying the scooters we came with. Standard.

Homework

Fucking phonics. Even the word 'phonics' isn't spelt phonetically. A classic example of how the English language doesn't make any sense, especially to a six-year-old in year one. Yes, it makes sense at first: C-A-T sounds like 'cat' and D-O-G sounds like 'dog.' Simple. Then you get words like 'said.' Your kids spell it phonetically S-E-D and you have to tell your child, 'Good job but WRONG. It's S-A-I-D,' and they look at you like you have three heads. And don't get me started on trying to help explain a noun, a pronoun, a proper noun, a common noun, a sodding noun first removed (probably), a verb, adverb, The Verve, Veuve Clicquot (slightly off track), an adjective, conjunction, connective, preposition, quantifier, graphemes ... What is the point in me trying to help with homework when I don't have a pissing clue what the hell this is myself? Have I used any of these things in writing this book? Dear Katya (my editor), please tell me – I am intrigued!

[Ed: Louise, I can confirm that you've correctly used a number of these grammatical forms while writing the book, most notably 'Veuve Clicquot' which has structured and underpinned your narrative flow most pleasingly ...]

I didn't get homework when I was at primary school, and a lot of my friends say the same thing, yet here is my six-year-old in year one having to write a paragraph on how they think Britain has changed since women had the right to vote. Umm, what? Seriously, *what*? Or how about build your own eco house and explain what materials you have used and why and demonstrate how it works —? Cue an overload of WhatsApp message from exasperated parents.

Homework for kids under nine in primary school is basically more work for us parents – just to add to the already enormous workload we have, we have to enthusiastically engage with homework with kids who are doing everything in their power not to. I love how the teacher says, 'Just spend ten minutes on it', then they question why your son hasn't finished their homework. Well, it took three minutes for him to sit down properly, two minutes for him to choose a pencil, another minute to actually pick up the pencil and engage with the idea of homework, and we spent the remaining three minutes writing out phonics, or subphonics, or whatever they are called like 'ao' and 'ai' and 'ay' ...

My patience wears thin rapidly when I see the state of his handwriting ... Arlo and Albie, his best mates in his class, have much better handwriting. (Must not compare, must not compare.) I encourage him to improve his handwriting and try again, which results in a full body-slide down the chair and under the table as if his limbs have turned to jelly and his mind has turned into mush. That's quite enough for one day.

I'll be honest – there have been a couple of times where I've taken matters into my own hands (literally) and done my son's homework for him. If you ever want to try this, I highly recommend using the hand you don't usually write in and close your eyes as you put pencil to paper. *Et voila.* Homework is done by your child. (I'd actually love to know how many parents have done this. Please tell me I'm not alone.)

Nursery homework

Let's not forget the homework from the nursery too.

For crying out loud.

I dread the week we are given the nursery bear called 'Ted the Teddy', who has to spend the weekend with us. The bear also comes hand in hand with a scrapbook to demonstrate and decorate the weekend we have had with Ted. I look through the scrapbook of all the previous children who have already experienced a weekend with Ted and quickly realise this is a 'who does the most at the weekend' book. Some kids have taken Ted to the zoo, the VIP area at Legoland and even bloody Disneyland!

A pang of competitiveness compels me, and I quickly have to change our usual weekend plans of park and possible pub to keep up: 'We need to do more this weekend so we can add it to the Ted scrapbook,' I say to Jesse.

A serious case of pointless anxiety hits me as I try to book a last-minute city break. I'm sure Ted has never been on an aeroplane. This would look great in the scrapbook!

But it's not just the photoshoot around the world with this sodding teddy – it's the presentation in the scrapbook afterwards. For a start you need to print out the photos, which means a trip to your local Snappy Snaps; then you have to write a description under said photo about your fabulous weekend; and on top of that properly decorate said photo with ribbons and stickers and fucking doodles made to look like your two-year-old has done them. Mums always end up dealing with it – like we don't have enough on our plates. And who is it even for?

One time I asked Jesse to take control of the weekend with the toy. It was nice to hand over the baton and see what he came up with for the book. Well, he lost the fucking cuddly toy who was spending the weekend with us. Left it on the train. It had gone through the entire nursery class (slightly disappointed we were the last family to be asked), and yet we were the ones who lost it.

Jesse, clever as he is, found the exact same teddy on Amazon Prime. As I said – pointless anxiety.

PTA/Friends Association

To raise money for the school, the Parent Teacher Association (huge respect for anyone in the PTA) comes up with all sorts of ideas to raise money for the school to pay for school trips, musical instruments, school equipment etc. Cake sales is a big one. I must say I am really impressed with the amount of money that can be made from cake sales. I guess this is the perfect snack at school pick-up, and if you forget snacks like I have, many times, this is a perfect 'get out of jail' card – AND now we can pay for a 50p cake using Apple Pay. Genius.

Generally, it's us parents who are the utter mugs in this fund-raising event … well, it is for me, anyway. I don't bake cakes because I don't have the time – I'm writing a book, for crying out loud – but I will buy a box of Mr Kipling cakes from the local shop near the school for £1.59 for a box of six, hand them over to the brilliant PTA staff at 3.15 p.m., just before the end of day bell goes, then buy three of those cakes back at 50p each at 3.20 p.m. (Oh my gosh, this sounds like a maths home-work problem …) Ugh, let's move on from this! But you get my drift. One day I will actually bake the cakes … I promise I will!

Another PTA fave of mine is the evening parents-only quiz night: a chance for the parents to bond, have some wine and make perfect fools of ourselves whilst doing a good deed raising money for the school. In the past we have wrapped ourselves up in loo roll, tried to see how quickly we can eat cheese crackers, slid melting After Eights down our faces and into our mouths (Jesse was a pro at this game, while one dad was so dedicated to the game he ended up face-down on the assembly hall floor, tongue out, determined to get that After Eight in his mouth.) One dad at our previous primary school was a stand-up come-dian. He would host the most fantastic stand-up shows, often roping his comedy mates in too. It was odd, though, being in a school hall filled with positive-affirmation paintings and decora-tions from the children, and hearing the word 'cunt' several times.

The head teacher of this previous school was always up for a laugh on these nights. Possibly too much of a laugh? One day at school pick-up, letters were being distributed in the play-ground:

> Dear parents and carers,
> Due to unforeseen circumstances, as of today Ms Chapstick (*fake name, but am using some Chapstick whilst writing*) will no longer be head teacher of our school. We are working on a replacement and will have more information for you shortly. Thank you for your understanding.

The parents' WhatsApp chat went crazy.

> What happened?
> Is she ok?
> She was fine last week
> Can you find out?

Turns out Ms Chapstick was our very own Ms Hannigan from *Annie*. And it got me thinking. When I watched *Annie* as a child I thought Ms Hannigan was the baddy. I found her frightening and vile. Now, I actually think we'd get on really well; I'd like to be friends with her, and think she is totally misunderstood. So, thank you, Ms Chapstick, genuinely, for all your help and dedication towards the kids. And who knows – maybe all the bottles of wine in your office were just gifts from us parents from last Christmas?

There can definitely be some competitiveness within the PTA committee – it's as if there's a hierarchy of importance within the committed parents. The mothers all naturally fall into line and play the part they have been given, taking joy in talking with the PTA queen bee at the local coffee shop after a two-hour meeting on how many days a year there can be a cake sale. (I'll be doing the school run for twelve years throughout my three children's school careers. I have calculated that to be around 720 cake sales.)

Being on the PTA is like having a full-time job. It's basically marketing, advertising, fundraising, recruitment and PR all rolled into one. Incredible dedication from the parents who take on such a role, and I have so much respect for this. Until you get that one person who makes it all too serious and you end up thinking they're a dick. One mother was the new head of PTA and was organising the Christmas school fair. There were a number of meetings and unnecessary WhatsApp messages – anyone would have thought she was organising Winter Wonderland in Hyde Park.

I thought I'd like to help out for once so piped up and said I wanted to have a stall with a 'wishing tree' – I'd seen it at Kew Gardens the year before. You write a wish on a tag and hang it on the tree. The head of the PTA agreed to this but had no faith in it whatsoever and made that very clear. So much so she wanted my stall to be totally out of the way of all the rest of the other activities. I could be wrong but I don't think she liked me very much. Turns out my wishing tree made more money than most that day, AND one boy's wish was to win his football match later that day AND HE DID!

I may have also donated a wedge of my own money to the stall to make a point but don't tell anyone. It's all for a good cause, right? (The school and my ego.)

Water bottles

I don't think anyone was interested in my hydration when I was at primary school. I had a flask, but it was kept inside my lunch box – I may have taken a sip, but I also remember my head under the school toilet taps. I'd take a sip, completely bypassing the washing of my hands, and wipe away the water residue running from my chin on the back of my jumper sleeve. Wiping a runny nose at the same time was an extra bonus. And guess what? I survived school!

It's now almost a competition to see who has the best, the fanciest, the frilliest water bottle at school, slotted into the bottle holder on the side of an oversized backpack with a ton of trinkets attached to the zip for all to see. There are all sorts of catches and flip top lids that my seven year old can't figure out how to open, or even worse, doesn't close properly, leaving his homework book and reading log a soggy, smudgy mess.

And oh, the guilt for not remembering to fill up the water bottle and pack it for school! I've actually dropped off a water bottle into reception after registration so my child can still have water throughout the day. Regardless of the fact they have water fountains all over the school, water handed out liberally mid morning, lunch and mid afternoon, and of course, toilet taps to drink from. But they must have their own water bottle!

'Basil! You haven't drunk enough water today. Quick have some now! Are you ok?'

'Bruh' followed by an eye roll.

(If you're unfamiliar with this term, it means 'for crying out loud' in preteen language. This seems to be Basil's favourite word at the moment.)

I open the lid of the water bottle by unfastening a multitude of snaps and pops until the straw finally makes an appearance as if to say 'I've arrived!' and hastily hand it to Basil, who I am convinced is dehydrated.

'Bruh, I've had loads of water today, I'm fine.'

Where does this water obsession come from?

And, naturally, their water bottle is still full at the end of the day.

October

Just when you're back into the swing of your kids being at school – enjoying finishing that hot coffee, managing to work a half-day of 9 to 3 without any interruptions and bravely thinking, at times, that you have life nailed and you can easily juggle kids and work – the murmur of half-term starts seeping into the WhatsApp chats.

Didn't they just go back to school?!

The excitement for Halloween is also bubbling as shop windows start being decorated with all sorts of scary shenanigans, and supermarkets are fully stocked with frighteningly synthetic costumes and party-sized bags of Haribo.

The best part of this month – apart from bribing your kids to dress as Kevin and Perry from *Harry Enfield and Friends* – are the darker skies at night. Halle-fucking-lujah. After months of summer evenings and still-bright skies at 9 p.m., and having to convince my kids it IS actually bedtime, all the while demonstrating this by passionately pointing to the clock on the kitchen wall that my youngest two children can't read yet – the nights are starting to draw in. This makes the bedtime routine slightly more bearable and believable, and I find myself having more of an evening to myself.

Halloween

Halloween is the one day a year where you have to unparent all the things you've ever taught your kids: knock on strangers' doors, accept sweets, eat way too much sugar, stay up late, bludgeon my red lipstick and scare your siblings.

If choosing a Halloween costume from the selection they have at the supermarket, it's best not to buy one before 20 October if you can help it. From my experience, if you choose

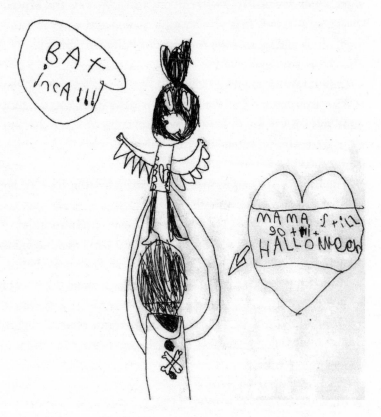

Inca dressed as a bat last Halloween. She did a great job
of getting caught in my hair.

an outfit at the beginning of October – one that took hours of loitering in said supermarket with a toddler who wouldn't sit still in her pram and perfectly demonstrated the back plank routine whilst trying to grab whatever was in her sight and screaming over my six-year-old's whinging about what outfit he wanted to wear (deep breath) – come the 31st, it'll not be what they want to wear … They'll have changed their mind – and I'm about to lose mine.

We also buy all the other totally nonsense paraphernalia, including a plastic pumpkin basket for all your sweets (when I was a kid I used my mum's handbag); some face paints *and* masks; some skeleton candles (I mean, why?); the pumpkin carving kit that isn't robust enough to carve a sponge; and more sweets than you actually need in case someone knocks on your door (but chances are you're already out Trick or Treating yourself).

When I was a kid the phrase 'Trick or Treat' actually meant something. It was so exciting to knock on the door (with or without a lit pumpkin outside) and wait for someone to answer – hoping they may be dressed up too, or be horrified by my outfit. I'd hope they'd say, 'Trick!' so you could show off a magic trick you had learnt, or tell a joke you'd practised all day.

For those of you wondering, my joke was – and still is – the same:

Knock knock.

Who's there?

Dunnup.

Dunnup who?

Ewwwwww!

Ha, it still gets me – my kids love this joke too. (It can also work with 'Europe' if you want to mix it up a bit – I mean, I've been saying the same joke for 35 years. Maybe time for some new material.)

Nowadays, nobody cares about the trick. Some houses even just leave sweets outside the front door with a notice that says, 'Take snacks'. Where has the Halloween magic gone? Kids go bonkers for this! I don't even think the kids know what they're saying. 'Trickletreeeat' is what my kids think it is – where has the trick gone?

One year, when I was ten, my friend Hermione and I decided to go Trick or Treating as a two-headed monster. We had no other option than to make our own outfit (Amazon and YouTube tutorials weren't around then, and there was no way Mum would spend money on a costume that you could design yourself). We thought it would be a brilliant idea to cut two holes in a large white sheet and walk together with our heads popping out. Mum wasn't too pleased when she saw her bed sheet missing and massacred that evening. Sorry, Mum – but it was a great costume!

Trick or Treating with the kids can feel like you're in your own parenting battlefield: throwing yourself in front of cars so the kids can cross the street, surreptitiously hiding sweets or eating them along the way to protect your kids' teeth, the constant panic of losing a child who has run on ahead and has blended in with all the other children who are all wearing black, and keeping them from arguing with their siblings when competitively counting how many sweets they each have. This is then followed by trying to remove fake blood from their faces, clothes, your clothes (how did that even happen?); vigorously brush their teeth and threaten a trip to the dentist; and deal with the bedtime chaos when they're high on sugar. It's the witching hour (literally) on speed. And let's not forget an hour later, when they wake up having a nightmare or throw up from all the sugar.

It's such a magical time.

And, of course, us mums also need an outfit or some make-up to make us look like we are part of the Halloween festivities. The truth is I do love Halloween! Before being a mother, my Halloween 'trick or treating' included dressing up as the sexy nurse from *Kill Bill* and heading out to fabulous fancy-dress parties, and dancing until the early hours. As a mother, my make-up for Halloween has changed somewhat.

Ideally you want something easy and fuss-free – cat ears, a witch's hat – or, in my case, a single dribble of fake blood coming out of one nostril. I thought this was a great idea until other parents pointed it out and offered me a tissue. Turns out trying to look subtle during Halloween actually looks like you have a drug problem instead. Won't be doing that again in a hurry.

Here is a great Halloween make-up hack that takes 30 seconds to do, and is very effective.

You will need:
A bag of flour (self-raising or plain)
Black liquid eye liner
Black eye shadow

Instructions:
Pick up bag of flour and pour over face (make sure your
    eyes and mouth are closed).
Lick fingers and scoop out a good amount of eye shadow
    from palette.
Rub eyes with fingers.
Draw stich lines vertically to your lips with liquid eyeliner.
Draw on cheek bones with liquid eyeliner to make you look
    more gaunt than you are already feeling. If you have an
    extra couple of seconds to spare, blend with your finger,
    making it look like black contouring.

Et voila! Job done. I can guarantee you will look shite but that's the whole point, right?

Carving pumpkins is fun, isn't it? (Sense the sarcasm.) One year there was talk about town that pumpkins were scarce and we were advised to pick one up as soon as they hit the shelves. Competitive parents everywhere scrambled to buy one.

Said competitive parents fall over themselves trying to produce the perfect pumpkin, only too happy to end up carving it themselves when their kids lose interest after five minutes as they're refused the use of the carving knife.

Pumpkin dissecting is another great job to give the kids (again, sense it). Their complete revulsion at the insides of the pumpkin and the work that is needed to take it all out (and the mess) will always result with me doing it. Of course, every year I find a pumpkin soup recipe – and every year I end up not doing it.

It's always when I'm hand-scooping-out the insides of a pumpkin that a child calls to me from the other room:

'Mummy, Mummy, watch!'

'Mummy …!'

'Mummy, Mummy, *watch*!'

'Hang on, darling, I've just got my hand inside a pumpkin and —'

'Mummy, watch! WATCH!'

Oh, for crying out loud.

You know they're not going to tire so the best thing to do is go and watch your child do the thing that they so much want to show you, and cannot wait for.

'OK, coming!' I say, grumpily washing my hands and wrists of the pumpkin's internal organs.

This takes a few seconds longer than my child can handle …

'MUMMY, *WATCH*!'

This had better be good.

My child is showing me how he can blink his eyes and press the remote control at the same time, pretending he is controlling the TV with his eyes. Creative, I suppose, but also two minutes of my life I'll never get back. Nor am I allowed to take my eyes off his eye magic until he has done it about 25 times. Naturally, later on, when I finally collapse in front of the TV, the remote is missing.

The kids' school has a pumpkin carving competition, but we all know it's the parents who are the driving forces behind them. And you can sense the slight competitive streak within certain parents when their six-year-old arrives with a pumpkin that has been carved to look like a scene from *The Addams Family*. One year a poem had been carved into a pumpkin. I mean, seriously impressive stuff – but just sod off. Sod off with your pumpkin carving that you probably kept your child far away from so it wouldn't get ruined.

Most years I am ahead of myself and carve the pumpkin a week or two before I actually really need it. By the time 31 October has arrived, my pumpkin is covered in fruit flies and has caved in on itself. To be fair it looks the part, but it also looks (and smells) like utter shite.

As someone who suffers with arachnophobia, Halloween decorations and accessories can be a hazard for me. The black plastic fake spiders are a bastard – especially when you find them in your kid's school bag and end up screaming and throwing the bag to the other side of the room, knocking over drinks. They're everywhere, and usually in those fake webs that hang above your head when you walk into a shop. I really struggle to walk into a shop with this decoration. I just can't. I am such an embarrassment to my kids when they see me walk into Poundland with them. Crouching down, my hood up protecting my head, looking like the Hunchback of Notre Dame, I quickly squat-walk into the shop, grab all the party-sized Haribo packets (my husband ate the first batch), and do the same pathetic squatted walk on the way out.

There is a reason behind this. My fear of spiders grew into a full-on phobia after a night at Jessie's (friend not husband) house. It was pre kids. I was in the car the morning after the night before, on the way home from a late, boozy night and was sitting at a red light when I thought I'd check my hair in the mirror. It was there I saw a HUGE spider crawling through my hair.

I lost it.

I actually *lost* it.

I screamed and started head-banging in the car, running my hands through my hair as if I was washing it at 100 miles per hour. I slammed my foot on the accelerator (luckily the lights had just changed), and took the first left – down a no-entry road.

I scrabbled, still screaming, out of the car whilst stripping off my T-shirt (exposing a very sexy black bra that showed my pre-breast-feeding nipples off perfectly), crouching down behind a parked car, apparently hiding from said spider.

It was then that I realised I had left the engine on and the handbrake off, as I could see my car starting to roll back into the main road.

SHIT.

As I hid behind a parked car, essentially topless, watching my car roll away and still not sure where the spider had got to, adrenaline on an all-time high, I heard footsteps coming towards me …

'Was it a bee?'

Oh, great. It was a man, and I was pretty sure he was on last week's *Crimewatch*, but I didn't care as he was my way out of this mess.

'STOP MY CAR!' I barked at him.

He ripped off his shirt to expose a Superman T-shirt underneath and ran to my car. (Just kidding, but he did stop my car.)

I could sense he was intrigued as to what was going on. Or was it just my bra that he was interested in? But he came back.

'GET MY T-SHIRT!' A second bark at this poor stranger as I pointed to my crumpled white T-shirt lying on the other side of the road in a pile of autumn leaves.

He walked across the road, picked it up, then looked both ways up and down the road, presumably to see if this was some kind of joke and if cameras were about to jump out of the bushes and surprise him Jeremy Beadle-style (if you don't know who this is, I am really showing my age).

He handed me the T-shirt engulfed with gook 'n' stuff, but I demanded, 'PAT IT DOWN!'

And he did. This stranger who, moments earlier, had been minding his own business, and who had stopped a rolling car, was now shaking leaves off a T-shirt that belonged to a girl showing her nipples and hiding behind a car.

I mean, you would be intrigued to stick around, right?

'PAT IT DOWN MORE!'

I could see the T-shirt was clear of any spiders and I felt safe enough to take it off him and cover myself up.

'Thank you – now, can you please help me check my car for a spider?' 'It was a *spider*?' The man was obviously disappointed it wasn't anything more sinister, as he turned to me and said, 'You need help.'

I never saw him or the spider again, but I'd like to thank him for saving my car – and for being the catalyst for getting hypnotherapy for my fear.

I am still paranoid about getting spiders in my hair in the car and regularly look at my hair in the rear-view mirror just to check. Passers-by must conclude I am vain and need to get over myself, when in fact I'm just terrified.

As parents we don't want to show our phobias to our kids and give them a phobia too. One day, on the school run, a spider was running riot in our car and Basil was screaming away, causing all sorts of stress and commotion. My heart pounding and every ounce of my soul telling me to scream and run, I managed to calmly capture the spider and put it out of the window using soft words like, 'Poor little thing,' and 'He's trying to find his mummy'. Gotta say I was really proud of myself – perhaps the hypnotherapy worked? UNTIL my middle child was messing around with Snapchat filters one day. Every now and then he would ask me to look at the phone to see my face distorted with a huge jaw or massive eyes. It was all fun and games until he showed me one where spiders crawl all over your face.

Cue hysteria.

Luckily, my kids don't have a huge fear of spiders – but they do seem to have a fear of healthy green food.

One Halloween I'll never forget was 2011. Jesse and I had invited my mum, my sister Bonnie and her boyfriend Steve, and my brother George over for dinner. It was a time before having children – you remember, when you could actually have a conversation with your guests, and not a haphazard one where you stare behind the person you are talking to, eyes fixed on your toddler about to do something they shouldn't, followed by a quick dash to the toddler and then back again, pretending all the while that you're taking in what the person you're talking to is saying, and repeating this scenario three or four times before you both give up on the conversation and decide to text each other at 9 p.m. instead. Right?

So we'd all sat down and were talking about Halloween and had I got sweets ready at the door for kids coming by etc etc.

Wine was poured and I looked over to Jesse, who gave me a wink and a nod.

'Speaking of Halloween,' I said, 'we've got something spooky to tell you ...'

Everyone looked at me.

'Jesse and I are having a baby.' My smile and eyes welling up with happy tears was a sure-fire sign that I was not kidding. We too were still processing the news as we had only found out two weeks prior to our 12-week scan. Saying it out loud to our families made it official. It was really happening!

'WHHAAATTTTTTTT?????' My sister Bonnie was never one for holding back what she is really thinking.

A mixture of emotions swept over their faces, ranging from disbelief, to shock, to joy, to love, and they all ended up crying.

I reached for the 12-week sonograph image that I had hidden on the coffee table under some books, ready to show to the family.

'WHAATTT? OH MY GOSH, YOU HAVE A SCAN ALREADY?' My sister again. She turned to her boyfriend, Steve: 'We need a baby.'

Steve rolled his eyes and turned to Jesse. 'Nice one, mate.'

Half-term

So, half-term – it's arrived, with all its Halloween-themed cake sale crescendo, and we are thrown into the abyss of 'What will I do with the kids when I am working?' mode.

A week off school doesn't seem so bad as I plan to make sure they are all occupied with clubs, various activities or seeing grandparents as I juggle work, which always seems to step up a notch and be busier than usual during ANY school holiday. Classic.

As a freelancer and working in an industry that has no guarantee, it's important to say yes to work when it presents itself.

One October half-term I was confirmed to shoot a TV commercial for a fashion brand with a celebrity that we all know and love. When I arrived at the studio my eyes immediately went to the Olympic-sized trampoline that was being decorated by a team of props stylists.

I was handed my outfit by the stylist and thought half of it was missing – it was a bra and knickers set. And it soon transpired that during filming I would be jumping on the trampoline. Wearing said bra and knickers. Riiiiigggggghhhht.

'Mother of three', 'lingerie set' and 'trampoline' should never be in the same sentence, and definitely not in the same creative brief, yet there it was, in all its glory.

I immediately started working on my pelvic floor muscles, thinking that a few pulses before I jumped would sort me out and counteract pushing three babies out of my vagina. (I bet you're doing your pelvic floor exercises now … good job!)

I decided it was a good idea to not drink anything until after I had done my trampolining, and took a few toilet trips just to make sure I had completely emptied my bladder. I felt confident with my ability to not pee myself in front of fifty people with cameras on me.

I won't drag this out as we probably all know where this is going. Somehow I had urine stored in a place that I didn't know existed and ended up peeing myself in my underwear on that enormous trampoline for all to see. Ultimately, they switched my outfit for a dress that I could wear a Tena Lady pad underneath, and the swimsuit I also had to shoot with was very cleverly styled with a sarong.

I came home just in time for supper and took over from Jesse, who quickly headed off to the gym. He had managed to take a good 40 minutes to heat up fish fingers, chips and peas.

Kids' meal times

Kids and eating is one of the hardest and most frustrating parts of parenting. Before I became a parent I thought I'd be one of those mothers that only cooked from scratch with organic ingredients, and that my children would eat all sorts of dishes without complaining, and all with perfect table manners.

What on *earth* was I thinking?

You cook a meal – for example, fish fingers, chips and peas – believing full well they will eat it. You present it to them nicely laid out on the plate (making sure it is the correct plate for my toddler – the only one she will eat from that week). Perhaps you get super creative and make a face out of the food you've heated up?

But this can go either way, depending on the temperament your child has decided to have on this particular hour of the day. One mealtime I made a brilliant (if I do say so myself) portrait of the kids using noodles (hair), chicken goujons as a head and ears, cucumbers as eyes and tomatoes as lips. My boys shrugged at it and started eating. My toddler? Utter disgust, and sheer hatred towards me and my food art. How dare I even *think* to make this fun for her! Food was thrown across the floor, screams were high-pitched, and I was the chump on my hands and knees picking up the food (five-second rule and third child) and asking my toddler what art she wanted on her plate.

'I want Basil's face!'

Deep breath and eye roll.

I reconstructed the EXACT same portrait as before, handed it to her and said it was Basil and not her.

Inca was satisfied with this change of artwork and deemed it acceptable.

FFS. Tonight it's a fish-finger smile, pea eyes and chip hair, and I'm confident they'll lap it up, eat nicely, not argue and generally prove to me they have listened to all my table manners tuition over the years.

Sonny, my middle child, looks disgusted both with the meal and me. 'What is this?' he asks, grimacing.

'It's fish fingers, chips and peas …' Why is he asking me this? It's quite obvious what it is – he's been eating it pretty much twice a week for the last six years.

He prods it with his fork and fingers. 'Is it dead?

'Yes, it's dead, darling.' *WHAT????* You know when you are so tired and mentally exhausted you can't even piece a sentence together and you hope that the expression on your face is doing the talking for you?

'This is the most disgusting meal I've ever seen.'

'Darling, you've had the same meal twice a week for the last six years!'

'I don't like it!' he says, matter-of-factly.

'I don't lliiiikkkkkkkeeee it!' echoes my toddler.

By this point I am close to motheruption and have to use the kitchen towel to bite down on to gag myself, shielding my darlings from the rage that is building up inside me. ('Gentle parenting' requires a lot of rough and ready behind the scenes – my kitchen towel always takes the wrath.)

As well as deciding they no longer like a certain meal, there's often the added frustration of the children not sitting still during the course of the meal. I'm sure it's where the expression 'Ants in your pants' came from (which, for the record, I don't recommend you saying to your child, as mine took it quite literally and ran off to the bathroom in hysteria whilst pulling down his pants, head between his legs, looking for ants in his bum).

Mealtimes at the table will consist of the kids climbing, falling, spinning, kneeling, kicking and even licking the chair and table, coupled with full plastic cups falling and ricocheting off the kitchen floor (several times), spilt drinks, fighting over food, over the plate they want, the spoon they use, the chair they want to sit on ... Then there is the reluctance to use their knives and forks and instead use fingers, and then wipe their hands all over their clothes.

And this is every meal time.

No matter how many times I remind the kids about proper table manners, I still find myself saying the same things over and over. So here's a script for you, or your partner, friend, grandparent, babysitter or a passer-by who may happen to come along in the line of supper fire.

Sit up at the table
Don't touch that
Knees down
No toys at the table
I'll do the ketchup
Eat up
Sit up
Don't use your fingers
You liked it last week
No pudding if you don't eat up
Santa is watching (optional – depending on how dire the
    situation is and what month of the year it is)
Don't throw food
How dare you throw food?
Pick it up
Quick, help me clear this up
Sit still
How dare you?
Close your mouth when you're eating
You are not a cement mixer – close your mouth

Stop doing that

Why did you do that?

Pick up your fork

Close your mouth whilst you eat

Don't tease your brother/sister/cat/dog/ (pick whichever
   is relevant to the situation)

One more mouthful

Almost done – you can do it

What do you say?

Stop jumping around

You shouldn't have had so many snacks

Two bites of vegetables

OK, one bite

Just lick the broccoli then

You're welcome.

Feeding time at the zoo is over and you calculate how much
they have actually eaten by looking at the food on the plate vs
the food on the floor, and you know full well just before they go
to bed they'll ask the dreaded 'CANIHAVEASNACK?'

My toddler has already picked up on this phrase, thanks to
her two older brothers, and she's usually the first to pipe up.

Be cool. Beeeeeee coooooooool.

'Mummy, canihaveasnack?'

'Do you want a banana?'

'No banana.'

I put the banana away.

Toddler cries: 'I want my banana!'

I got it again. 'Here you go.'

Toddler: 'I don't like it.'

Me: 'Do you want me to cut it up?'

Toddler: 'Yes.'

I cut up the banana.

Toddler, disgusted: 'I don't like it,' and she threw it on the floor.

I muttered 'FFS!' under my breath, picked up the sodding banana and put it to one side.

'I WANT MY BANANA!'

At this point my imagination had picked up the banana and smeared it all over my toddler's face whilst shouting, 'YOU

Inca pretty much summed up, especially when asking for a banana,
by Basil.

WANT THE BANANA? HAVE THE BLOODY BANANA!' In
my mind, of course.

Instead, I calmly gave her the choice of both the cut-up
banana or a new banana on a plate.

'Not that plate.' She was disgusted.

I offered another plate.

'NOT THAT PLATE!'

She was livid.

I was livid.

'What plate?' It took all my soul to stay calm and collected.

'This one.' She picked up the one I offered her first.

Is it wine o'clock yet?

But my fridge was empty of wine. I walked out of the room,
cursing, and ordered a bottle of wine on Deliveroo.

Once again, in the height of my parenting feeding stress and
with the husband conveniently out of the house (possibly at the
tip, gym, pub or perhaps work), I really fancied a glass of wine
and had to rely on Deliveroo to bring it to me. I was stressed.
The witching hour was more hideous than usual; and had even
turned me into a witch, as I found myself calling the Tombliboos
from *In the Night Garden* a bunch of cunts. That irritating music
when the birds sing, rocking backwards and forwards on the
tree, was what took me over the edge. I was also pre-menstrual.
(Can you tell?)

It's times like these that I really love apps and how technology has evolved. I clicked on my local wine bar within the app
and chose the cheapest bottle of Sauvignon Blanc – at £18.99. I
wouldn't even spend that going to a fancy dinner party but I
justified to myself that it was what I needed and deserved. The
app informed me the wine would be with me in 25 minutes.
TWENTY-FIVE MINUTES? It would have been quicker if I'd
gone to New Zealand to get the wine myself! I contemplated
leaving the house to walk to the wine bar at the end of my road

to collect the bottle of wine, then very quickly decided to stay put as I glanced over at my kids, who were making a den out of my previously neat bed, that I purposely make every day to look perfect, as a gift to myself at the end of the day.

Within the twenty-five minutes of waiting for my wine, the kids knocked over every item on my bedside table, shouted at each other, and wiped their snotty noses on my white duvet cover. (Actually, it used to be white – now it's some kind of hideous, off-white colour. Underpants Grey, perhaps?)

By this point I was pacing the floor, waiting for the doorbell to ring.

My driver arrived and I opened the door channelling Cruella de Vil when she lost all the puppies.

'How are you?' asked the polite driver.

'I'M THIRSTY!' I exclaimed, as I grabbed the bottle of wine out of his grip.

The driver was still standing at the door and I wondered if I owed him money, or perhaps he wanted to see my ID? A hint of joy materialised at the idea that perhaps I looked 25 or under, but was then quickly replaced with absurdity and embarrassment.

'It's me, Louise.'

The driver took off his motorcycle helmet and I instantly recognised the man before me, whom I had been unnecessarily short and grumpy with. *Shit.*

Shit.

Shit.

It was the father of a kid in my son's class. We had had a play date recently at their flat, and my son had done a poo in his pants and the dad had very kindly washed him down and given him a change of clothes.

I was mortified. Not only did it look like my six-year-old child was incontinent, but I looked like a rude, drunk mentalist.

Moral of the story: always keep your cool, even in stressful situations. And buy wine in advance.

Sleep

Sleep, or lack of it, is a killer when you first become a parent. And FYI, telling a woman she looks tired is like telling a man they have a small penis. Just don't do it.

The expression 'to sleep like a baby' is codswallop, and what's more codswallop is my husband Jesse not hearing the baby cry. For years I thought he couldn't hear the shrieks in the early hours of the morning – ones that literally sent shockwaves up and down my entire body. I'd grimace at him as I realised I would be the one getting out of bed AGAIN and dealing with it. But I'd like to point out that Jesse will ALWAYS wake up to the sound of the garbage men, who arrive at 5.30 a.m. on a Wednesday morning, to see if they have emptied the bin that we haven't registered with the council. So, selective hearing is confirmed ...

When I was doing the night feeds, Jesse, right on cue, would start snoring as soon as the baby latched on my nipple – almost like he was rubbing in my face that he was asleep and I was awake. One night, with Basil, when I was in the height of sleep deprivation, and after changing a soiled nappy, I realised I had a tiny bit of baby poo on my finger. I visualised wiping it off under his nose so he smelt the poo for the rest of the night, and then continued to come up with all sorts of devious, revenge-based scenarios that revolved around Jesse's sleep being disrupted in the night: honking my son's very offensive-sounding bike horn in his ear, shaving off his eyebrows, putting a peg on the end of his penis, sticking him to the bed with duct tape and so forth. (These imaginary situations actually saved me a fortune from my usual middle-of-the-night Amazon shopping.)

Suffice to say, the poo was washed off my hands, and my husband was not disturbed in any way.

In the mornings, he'd wake from his slumbers. Naturally, I would already be awake with a child feeding from my body.

Once the littles ones reach a certain age, when they realise they have the capability and freedom to get out of their cots and greet you in the middle of the night with a small slap in the face, a wet nappy or a bogie, they will do so. Almost every night. If you're reading this thinking to yourself 'well my child didn't do that' I applaud you and please can you let me know how – HOW? – you managed to do this.

The truth is, I quite like the idea of snuggles in the early hours of the morning and feeling that bond between us, stroking each other's faces and kissing each other's noses. But this isn't how it goes, *is it*? Quite the opposite. When my daughter gets into our bed she bypasses my husband altogether even though he sleeps closer to the bedroom door and is much easier to get to. To get to my side of the bed you need to take part in an obstacle course of dodging boxes and stepping over clothes that I mean to put away and somehow never get around to. Perhaps it's subconsciously a boobie trap to keep the kids away. She reaches my side of the bed and I am woken with a 'Mummy!'

I wonder what would happen if I pretend I am still asleep. Maybe she'll wake up Jesse? Maybe she'll go back to her own bed? Maybe she'll slap me on the cheek to show her presence.

SLAP 'Mummy!'

I was suddenly very awake and very put out.

'What's going on?' Stupid question; I know exactly what's going on. We did this last night too.

'Can I sleep with you?' She looks so cute and so innocent.

'Darling it's very late and —'

'Shhhhhhhhhhhhhhhh mummy!' Her hand is again slapped over my mouth to stop me from talking. 'Don't wake daddy.'

ARE YOU KIDDING ME. Why? WHY? I curse in my mind.

'Ok, but straight back to sleep.'

Inca is thrilled and I help manoeuvre her into our bed hoping that her swinging legs might whack Jesse's head and then he, too, can be awake.

It definitely isn't back to sleep. For me anyway. My daughter sleeping is like being in a fitness class. The wriggling, the squirming, the sleeping sideways so her foot is on my face, the kicking off the covers and refusing to put them back on, the constant coughing directly into my face … after three hours of this commotion I decide it's time to call for back up.

'Darling, why don't you snuggle with daddy?' My hair is in disarray, I am beyond irritated and oh so tired. Daddy taking over now would be great.

'No mummy!' She looks at me in disgust. 'Daddy's asleep!'

'YES HE IS!' I agree through gritted teeth and bloodshot eyes.

At 7 a.m. Jesse is woken up by his alarm, has a nice stretch and looks over to my side of the bed where he sees me looking like I've been in the toddler trenches, and Inca finally fast asleep.

'When did you get into our bed?' He snuggles into Inca who immediately hugs Jesse and they have a really beautiful embrace. Kiss each other's noses and even share what dreams they both had. Really? REALLY?!

Jesse looks up at me. 'You know, I didn't sleep that well last night.'

To add more fuel to the fire, the neighbours who lived above us were young, single, twenty-something-year-old brothers who partied every Thursday, Friday and Saturday night; whilst breastfeeding in the early hours I would have the duet of my husband snoring, and party neighbours listening to something

Jesse asleep whilst I'm kept awake with a foot in my face. By Sonny.

that didn't even sound like music – it was just noise. (I KNOW I sound like my mother!)

Shortly after they moved in it was clear there was a noise battle between us. They would play awful party music until about 3 or 4 a.m. and I would play hideous kids' TV programmes like *Little Baby Bum* as loud as I could below their bedrooms from 6 a.m., in the meantime talking pleasantries to each other when passing in the communal hallway. So British!

To stay sane and get more sleep, I realised I had to hatch a plan to stop all the noise … so I did what any sleep-deprived, crack-nippled mother would do. I broke into their flat. (For clarity and to not sound like a criminal, I should say I was their landlady and had keys to their flat.) A plumber came and on the same day I got their Wi-Fi password and logged into their Sonos sound system …

In the early hours of the morning, like a lioness about to pounce, I would watch the Sonos app on my phone, counting the seconds down to when the song would end – and right at that moment, I would turn the music down. After around five songs it would all go quiet – I would victoriously roll over and get some much-needed, smug shut eye.

It was a moment of brilliance if I do say so myself ...

My devious yet necessary plan was working well until one morning my husband used my phone to play *The Gruffalo* audio book (one of the kids' favourites) on our Sonos system, not realising he was logged in to the wrong Wi-Fi and wrong Sonos system. Alas, my twenty-year-old party boys were awoken by a mouse saying he wasn't afraid of the Gruffalo. The audio book continued to rise in volume as Jesse continued to think our speakers weren't working properly.

Needless to say, the party boys clocked what I was doing, changed their Wi-Fi password and continued to play ridiculously loud music at night, while I continued to play hideous baby music on repeat at full volume (once I left the flat for hours, deliberately leaving it on). And yet it was *still* pleasant to chat to each other in the communal hallway as if nothing had happened, and we even exchanged Christmas gifts.

November

Bonfire Night

Just after we pack away all the witches' cackle, we embark on the bonfire crackle, as parents and children everywhere start the build-up to celebrating a near-massacre by burning a man on a massive bonfire. *Remember, remember, the fifth of November ...*

Now, call me crazy, but if this storyline was in a YouTube video that my kids watched or in a game of Fortnite, I'm pretty certain I would ban my kids from ever viewing it again. However, taking my kids to a live bonfire evening where a life-sized stuffed guy is placed on an enormous bonfire with crowds of adults and kids chanting with anticipation for the barbarian act of lighting him on fire is totally fine ... because it's EDUCATIONAL. It's a history lesson, right? And I love that this story is quintessentially British and a reason for parents to meet up with other families and really enjoy the festivities.

But, generally, as a rule, when you have sparklers and small children you can rule out a peaceful evening ...

Of course, there was a drama even before the sparklers were out of the packaging. All the kids scuffled around me like hungry dogs, sniffing for the best (identical) sparkler:

'I want that one!'

'No, I want that one!'

'That one's mine.'

'I already said that one is mine!'

'Mummy, Basil said I can't have that one.'

'Stop pushing me – I was here first.'

'Mummy, where's my one?'

'Mummy, can I light it?'

'Can I have two?'

'Sonny, I was here first!'

SHUT UPPPPPPPPPPPPPP!

As there were other parents around I put on my best 'patient parenting' hat and asked the kids to all line up as I dished out the sparklers. Trying to light them in the wind was interesting – it immediately extinguished my match, and blew off my patience hat as well, so we all shuffled back inside for a bit, and the sparkler commentary from the kids had a round 2. Using sparklers will ignite a whole new personality within children (and parents, so it seems), that we won't have hitherto known, showing their true colours: are they sadistic or sympathetic? So, was the evening a success? On one hand (literally), the kids were transfixed – eyes wide, hypnotised almost in disbelief – that we, the responsible parents, had given them something 'dangerous' and on fire; on the other hand, we, the parents, who thought buying a pack of ten sparklers from the local pound shop would be great fun, turned out to be greatly mistaken. We had envisioned having a glass of Prosecco in the garden, watching the kids play safely and normally with their sparklers ... yes, it all sounds lovely, doesn't it?

In reality, the kids used their sparklers as swords, light sabres or Harry Potter wands, flailing them in front of each other's faces, scaring their younger siblings, petrifying the cat and giving the mothers a run for their money as we tried to hold conversations clutching said glass of Prosecco, which didn't get sipped but instead gulped back in two large swallows whilst husbands were totally unaware of what was going on.

I wanted to be on *their* night out.

Naturally there were shrieks too. There were some kids who were absolutely terrified of the sparklers, yet we still *encouraged* them to use them as a wand or light sabre, and *helped* them do it by standing behind them and becoming a puppeteer, manoeuvring the kid's arm this way and that way to demonstrate how fun it could be – at the same time hollering over to the other, more confident children to 'Stop it!' as they waved their sparkler in the next-door neighbour's face, or started a sparkler sword fight with an invisible person whilst moving closer and closer to my not-so-confident child's flammable winter coat.

'Careful!'

'Don't hold it too close!'

'Stop it!'

'Keep it away from you!'

'Don't scare your sister/brother/cat/dog!'

'Stop shouting!'

'Stay away from each other!'

'Don't touch it!'

And then, for one wonderful moment, the kids were behaving themselves. They had taken on board our stern words about how dangerous sparklers could be. (I had decided to ignore Basil's smart-Alec question of 'Then why give them to us?' as, to be fair, he had a point.) Finally the other mums and I joined in with the adult conversation and topped up our glasses of Prosecco (as we hadn't quite enjoyed the first one). The kids stood with their arms out like little statues, watching the sparklers dance down the retired sword, light sabre or wand until it reached the bottom and extinguished itself with a depressing fizz.

'AGAIN! MUMMY, AGAIN!'

We agreed to give them another chance (and sparkler), and set them a challenge, which I immediately regretted.

'Why don't you write your name or draw a circle with it?'

Their enthusiasm returned.

'LUMOS!' they yelled, swirling their sparklers around and around, creating the perfect circle. Things seemed to be calm ... until ...

'Mummy, watch!'

'Mummy, Mummy, watch!'

'Mummy, *watch*!'

'Mummy, Mummy, Mummy, Mummy, Mummy, watch!'

'Mummy, *WATCH*!'

I watched. I watched so hard that I too became mesmerised by the bloody sparkler and I wondered if the fluorescent circle I saw before me in the night sky was in fact a door to another dimension that I could jump into and be spat out in a place where '*Daddy*, watch!' was something my kids actually said ...

The sparklers were left burnt out on a wooden table in the garden, that still has the faint burn lines left from them.

Note to self: put the old sparklers in a bucket of water like it explains on the packet. (But does anyone actually do this?)

There are always various bonfire and firework events to choose from around 5 November. We usually prefer to go to the family one instead of the pyromania club one for people under 30 who dance around like extras from The Prodigy's 'Firestarter' video.

Getting the bonfire started took way longer than it should. I could feel the energy from ALL the kids in the field (not just ours) waning. They were cold, it was dark and we couldn't let them out of our sight for fear of losing them in the abyss of darkness. A sea of kids echoed the same words:

'Mummy, has it started yet?'

'Mum, I'm bored.'

'Can I have your phone?'

'Canihaveasnack?'

'Mummy, I'm cold.'

'When will it start?'

'Mummy, when can we go home?'

Please note – Daddy was also present, but Daddy didn't get asked very many questions because the kids already knew the answer he'd give: 'Ask Mummy.'

Finally, the bonfire was lit. And about five minutes later, the standard procession of families who were smug at first, getting front-row standing spots, started to back away from the over-powering heat, dodging fire particles that came shooting out from all angles like burning shrapnel.

'Mummy, it's too hot.'

'Mummy, hold my jacket.'

'Mum, can I film it?' (aka 'Can I have your phone?')

'Mummy, I don't like it.'

'Mum, can we go home now?'

'Mummy, I'm bored.'

'Mummy, why is there a man on the fire?'

'Canihaveasnack?'

I gazed into the dancing flames, trying to tune out the noise of the 'fun blockers' and instead listened to the crackling sounds of the bonfire, using it as a form of self-care as I too shuffled backwards away from the bonfire. Just two minutes of staring meditation was better than none, and I told myself the kids would be happy when the fireworks started.

And when they did, the kids were silent and totally into it. All parents were aware of this and wanted the moment to last for as long as possible so, as if by agreement with something out of a parenting manual, we all said in unison: 'Oooooooooohhhhhhhh' as they took flight into the sky with a sizzling, whistling sound.

Nothing.

Then, BANG!

And 'Aaaaaaaaaaaaaahhhhhhhhhh' as the flying dot transformed into a beautiful work of gunpowder art.

The fireworks were incredible and for a moment everyone was still and looking up. I reached for Jesse's hand and together we watched the night sky light up and I actually felt a sense of calm …

Until our toddler kicked off and it was game over.

This was our daughter's first experience of fireworks and it was, as suspected, extremely stressful. Toddlers, as we know, are a handful on any given day, so add loud noise, weird things in the sky, crowds of people and having to sit on your dad's shoulders during the witching hour when you'd prefer to escape is a recipe for disaster.

Jesse has always loved the kids sitting on his shoulders and chooses this form of transport whenever he can – probably because the kids can't run away – but this shoulder seat very quickly became aware that our toddler was not having it. I'm not even sure if the fireworks were annoying her; I genuinely think she saw Mummy, Daddy and her two brothers having a nice time and she wanted to ruin the vibe.

Cue the tantrum toddler who, whilst climbing Jesse's head – using it basically as a cat's scratching post to claw her way off his shoulders – was grabbing what was left of his hair, also sliced the silence of the crowd around us into pieces with her screams of sheer disgust. People looked at us as if to say 'Shut her up' or 'Thank goodness that's not our child' and we looked back giving a knowing shrug and eye roll as if to say, 'We've got this, don't worry.' But the truth was we didn't, and we had no idea what her next move would be.

Toddlers and the terrible twos warning – this part of the book may cause anxiety, reduce you to needing a glass of wine, or will act as a really good contraceptive. Toddlers.

Wow.

Breathe. If this part of my book-writing journey were being filmed, you'd see a shot of me staring blankly into space, fingertips poised over my keyboard, not knowing where to start, mentally flicking through the 'toddler files' in my head from all my three children. When I started writing this book my youngest was a two-year-old and definitely my most demanding child

An evening at the fireworks. Inca on Jesse's shoulders having a meltdown and the crowds around us moving away.

to date, to a point where I felt like I was new-parenting all over again, using different tactics and skills.

Maybe this is a girl thing? Maybe it's a third-child thing?

Jerry Seinfeld was right, having a toddler is like turning on a food blender without the lid. It's their mind games, the constant need to destroy everything in their path and the mood swings that give me whiplash. But actually, the worst bit is not being able to predict when or what will make them finally erupt – it could be the way you open a zip on a bag, the way you point the remote control at the TV, or how you open a yoghurt pot.

Once my daughter didn't like the way I was breathing. 'Mummy, stop the noise! Stop the air noise!'

Is she telling me to die? It wouldn't have surprised me.

I can guarantee the most common four words a toddler will say on a daily basis is 'I don't like it.'

But really they do like it. And you know it. And they know it. So you end up having a cowboy stand-off and you let them win because you're practising gentle parenting, and at the same time having to listen to unasked-for advice from your mother and mother-in-law, who seem to know all about parenting and what I should do.

Shortly after a session of unwanted advice was offered, my kids stayed at my mum's house for the night. When she dropped the kids back the next day, Mum army-crawled into my house looking like she'd been in the toddler trenches. Inca arrived in only her knickers. And I wasn't surprised. I was actually happy that it wasn't just me.

'I couldn't get her dressed, Louise. She just wouldn't have it!'

I nodded knowingly, patted her on the back and offered a cup of tea.

'Have you got anything stronger?' she asked.

* * *

Trying to get my toddler dressed is a mental and physical challenge that requires the utmost amount of patience and decorum, especially when I'm up against the clock for the school run and have to leave the house at a certain time. Clothes are thrown across the room, she only wants to wear her 'Elsa' shoes from *Frozen* (which aren't allowed in the nursery – not surprisingly, as the soles have been made of something as slippery as butter) BUT SHE WON'T LISTEN and I don't have time to negotiate, so I send her into nursery with the damn shoes and a pair of sensible shoes in her bag and wait for the call from the nursery telling me she's not allowed the sodding shoes. AND YET SHE LISTENS TO THE TEACHERS AT NURSERY.

I pick her up from nursery and she runs towards me, so happy to see me. She hugs and kisses me and listens to what her key worker is telling me with a smile on her face.

'We had a great day today, didn't we?'

'YESSSSSS!'

'We played with cars, played with our new bikes in the garden, we painted with our hands and we made some gluten-free bread. She has also eaten really well – ate steamed salmon, cous cous, runner beans – and asked for more. A really great day. Inca is a delight to be around.'

Errr, who the fuck are you talking about?

Is this a script that all teachers say to parents for a quick exit at the of the day, or are you seriously talking about my child? Because I have *no* idea who you're talking about. But I lap it up anyway and play the *Yes She Is, Isn't She* card and head to the car.

I praise her all the way to the car and keep going as I plug her into her car seat … but I know what's coming.

As soon as the engine is on and we're off out of the nursery car park, she erupts, having apparently saved all her tantrums and shite for me after a long, stressful day at work.

Still, I continue to talk to her calmly and try to reason with her, offering her a snack – some melon that she throws across the car. So I offer up some music she usually likes, but this just serves to raise her screams a few decibels louder.

She stops.

'Darling, are you —?'

'ARGHHHHHHHHHHH!' She screams over me.

'Who did —?'

'NOOOOOOOOOOOOOOO!'

'Shall we —?'

'SHUT THE FUCK UP, BITCH!'

For the record she doesn't say this (yet), but am pretty sure she would if she knew the words.

The next morning, when I drop her off at nursery, she's full of smiles again and tells her teacher: 'My mummy has a big *bagina*.'

Awkward silence that I break with: 'Well, I have had three kids!'

When I pick Inca up later that day, the same teacher beckons me over.

Shit. What now?

'Many congratulations! Inca told us everything!'

I look blankly at her.

'About the baby? And it's a girl?'

Fuck's sake. 'No, no, definitely no. That's just cake.'

'Are you sure?'

Er. Yes. This shop is CLOSED and I think I would know if I was pregnant or not. Thanks, Inca, for spreading rumours.

Which reminded me that when Basil was a toddler he had this sixth sense, which apparently most children under the age of five have. They see things we don't.

One day, when he was two, he came up to me, put his hand on my tummy and said: 'Baby.'

Jesse and I looked at each other. We had been trying to conceive. My period wasn't due for a few days but I did actually have a feeling I might be pregnant.

I took a pregnancy test the day my period was due and there it was, in all its beautiful glory – a message from my Clear Blue pregnancy test: 'Pregnant 1–2 weeks.'

WOW!!!

How had Basil known?

Two months later, Basil came up to me again out of the blue, put his hand on my tummy and said: 'Baby gone.' (Just writing this gives me the shivers and brings tears to my eyes.)

For peace of mind I booked in a private scan on Harley Street, but I already knew. I knew in my heart Basil was right, I knew my baby was gone.

I had miscarried at ten weeks. But I was grateful my son told me before a stranger in a white coat did.

I wasn't going to write about this, but it's part of my motherhood journey and something that means so much to me. She meant something to me. I had never met her, but I knew her and I loved her so much.

So when Inca told her teacher I was pregnant I actually *did* do a pregnancy test to make very sure I was without child – despite being on the coil and not having had sex in a while.

It was negative. Obvs.

Other things to look out for with a toddler, on a daily basis:

Opening the dishwasher
Touching the washing machine buttons
Playing with and ruining your make-up
Smearing yoghurt on your work laptop
Throwing clothes out of the wardrobe and cupboards
Putting finger and toys in plug sockets

Messing with the oven settings

Touching a lit candle that is out of reach, but manages it

Pressing buttons on your laptop

Drawing on the walls of your home

Reaching for a pair of scissors – also out of reach, but manages it

Knocking your tea over whilst it's in your hand

Throwing pasta across the room

Putting hand inside a yoghurt pot and finding something to smear it on

Pushing all cosmetics on the side of your bath tub into the bath tub

Stamping on your mobile phone and other precious objects

Rummaging through the bins

Pulling your glasses off your face

Stamping on (and breaking) the TV remote control

Spilling coffee

Putting a toy down the loo

Pulling loo roll off the roll

Putting toothpaste down the loo

Putting shampoo down the loo

Putting nappies down the loo

Pulling more loo roll off the roll

Throwing plates off the table

Ripping pages out of a favourite book

Smearing Sudocrem all over the walls and floors

Running with a carving knife

Pushing over photo frames

Throwing food

Throwing toys at your head

Opening and closing doors continuously

Squashing banana into absolutely anything

And this is all before 9 a.m.

Then, of course, at the end of the day, thrilled it's bedtime, and after all the bedtime routine madness (including my dear friends, the Tombliboos), I tuck her into bed and do a small celebratory dance to myself as I step out of her bedroom without her calling my name. I settle into the sofa still sightly damp from the thrashing-around-in-the-bath protest against getting her hair washed (I mean, seriously, the neighbours must think I am trying to torture her) …

Aaaaaand, relax.

Until my little one realises she has the power and free will to climb out of her cot: 'Hi, Mummy.'

The shock of seeing her out of her cot, and being so gorgeous, caught me off guard and I managed to spill my red wine over my pale pink jumper. 'What are you doing out of bed?'

'I wanted to kiss you again.'

At first I embraced this beautifully polite child standing demurely before me. *Look at what I have created – isn't she an angel?* I was enjoying her cuteness and we had a lovely bonding session, until I put her back to bed. And then this routine of her popping her head around the door and being polite was getting more and more irritating as she asked for water, a wee, medicine, a banana, Daddy (who wasn't there). I gave her all these things to hurry up the bedtime relay but when I couldn't produce Daddy she used this as an excuse to have a meltdown.

It quickly became a battle between us both. Who will win? Who has the most staying power? Kicking and screaming and having the ability to make her body feel twice as heavy, I tried to carry what felt like a plank of wood back to bed. This continued throughout my entire episode of *Stranger Things*. To the point where I wondered if she was actually Eleven, slightly possessed.

Did you know that 16 November is the International Day of Tolerance? Hmm. I wonder if the idea for one was thought up by a mother? We require a ton of tolerance – how many times have we tolerated all the daily crap? And how many times have our buttons been pressed the wrong way ... and how are children so good at doing it? Here are a few things that I have learnt to tolerate over the years of being a mother:

The lack of sleep
My cracked nipples
My sore vagina
My weaker pelvic floor
My postpartum hair loss
My lack of sex drive
My tiredness
My brain fog
Going to mum and baby classes
Being spoken down to because I don't have a job
Being spoken down to because I have a job
Lack of social life
Lack of pay
Being pooed on, peed on, thrown up on
Being slapped by toddler
Having hair pulled by toddler
Having a messier home cluttered by primary-coloured
    plastic
Asking kids to put their shoes on
Asking kids to brush teeth
Asking kids to do their homework
Asking kids to put their shoes on again
And again
Asking kids to eat up, to not eat with fingers, to sit up, to
    not lick the walls when at dinner table

To stop hiding the remote control

To stop taking my phone charger

To stop taking my phone

To put on their coat

To stop messing around in the car

To stop fighting with their sibling

To stop asking me to watch, *watch*, WATCH. ALL THE TIME.

And this is what makes us superhumans.

Self-care

Even superhumans, however, need some time and space to themselves to remember that life isn't just CBeebies, baby vomit, wiping bottoms, homework and being a taxi driver to and from after-school activities. We have our own identity too, and it's normal to crave and need independence and time away from the monotonous mornings, afternoons and evenings in servitude.

Under all this motherhood, we are still fabulous!

I practise self-care every day. This can be as small as finishing a cup of hot tea, actually having that shower (a shower really can be life-changing, can't it?), buying yourself a small bunch of flowers, or picking up the phone to rant to your best mate about how irritating your husband and kids are. Or this self-care can be as 'big' as treating yourself to a facial, going to the cinema ALONE, buying that dress you've had your eye on, or meeting up with your bestie for some wine ranting about how irritating your husband and kids are.

Becoming a mother made me realise how much I have changed; not just the landscape of my heart, but my body, my vagina, my mindset, my finances, my work, my confidence, my social life, my sex life, my home, my fashion and beauty regime, my independence – which of course can make you question your identity – and we all struggle to hold on to all this as much as we can.

Feeling good is important. If you are feeling good then chances are you're feeling happy. If you're happy, chances are your kids are happy. It all starts with you. Your energy will bounce onto your kids.

But how can you feel good and be happy when you're feeling and looking like utter shite and have a running to-do list bouncing around your every thought?

These are my very simple, easy and cost-effective self-care and beauty hacks that you can start immediately:

- **Drink 1.5 litres of water a day.** Or more! Your body needs water all day, especially if you are running around after kids. I usually have a water bottle by my side or strategically placed in the kitchen (where I know my kids can't reach it and swig from it) throughout the day. Drink water as soon as you wake up. I always remind myself to hydrate before I caffeinate.
- **Get outside.** Go for a walk within nature. Ten minutes of walking a day does wonders to your mental health.
- **Sleep well.** Leave your phone in another room. Try not to scroll when you go to bed or as soon as you wake up.
- **Eat cucumber.** Cucumbers are high in beneficial nutrients including vitamins C and K, magnesium and potassium. They promote hydration, can reduce blood sugar levels, help with regular bowel movements and are a great healthy snack.
- **Take your vitamins.** I highly recommend taking magnesium and a multivitamin, as well as vitamin D and evening primrose oil.

- **Menopause.** If you are experiencing any peri-menopausal symptoms such as anxiety, mood swings, brain fog, hot flushes and irregular periods, I highly suggest you speak to your GP or, even better, find a menopause clinic near you. As this book went to print I was experiencing hot flushes and brain fog – how I've managed to write it is beyond me.
- **Keep two dessert spoons in the fridge.** When you wake up, put these cold and crisp spoons over your eyes (the convex way) for five minutes to feel more awake, look less puffy and feel more rejuvenated.
- **Make your own facial scrub.** Use sugar and olive oil to remove dead skin and give yourself a fresh-faced glow for the cost of nothing!
- **Brush your teeth with bicarbonate of soda.** This is a much more effective way to get brighter teeth, but please consult your dentist first or have a check-up if you haven't had one recently. Step by step instructions:
1. In a small cup, mix ¼ to ½ teaspoon of bicarbonate of soda with enough water to form a paste.
2. Dip a toothbrush into the paste, and gently scrub your teeth using circular motions. Be sure not to brush hard or you might hurt your teeth and gums.
3. After two minutes, brush your teeth again with your regular toothpaste and don't forget to floss (dental floss, not the dance move that went viral). You'll see a difference sooner than using teeth whitening toothpaste alone.
- **Pick up a sheet face mask.** They are £3ish and really hydrate your skin. It's like a mini facial.
- **Use a dry shampoo.** If you don't have time to shower but have greasy hair (we've all been there), use dry

shampoo on your roots and have clean, full, sexy hair within minutes.

- **Tidy your bedroom.** Even change the sheets. Getting into a clean bed after a tiresome day is such a luxury. Buying new sheets is even better!
- **Listen to music.** Whether it's in the car, in the kitchen or on your headphones, crank it up and dance around like no one is watching (because they're not). Even better if you can work up a sweat and get your heart pumping.
- **Practise gratitude and think positively.** This will make you happy, which will show on your face and make you have an inner glow that will shine on through!

I found that being labelled a 'mother' came with some stigma and I have experienced feeling pushed aside, as if I am damaged goods, especially in my career. I was told I was 'done' and 'You'll never work again now that you're a mother.' I could have listened to this negativity, but I decided to call out the bullshit. This is how my online presence of 'Mama Still Got It' was born. I was determined to change the way people think of mothers, regardless if you're-a-stay-at-home mum or a working mum.

Because the truth is, you *have* still got it. In fact, you never lost it.

This mama still has it ...

It was November 2012 and my sister Bonnie was in her third trimester with her first child. We only lived a few doors away from each other and it was brilliant to live that close to her – my sister and I are extremely close. So when she called me one evening, utterly distressed and with her husband Steve still at work, both myself and Jesse were there to help her.

'Can I come over? I've done something ...' she said.

With Bonnie you never know what this could mean – it could be something normal, like, 'I've done a crossword puzzle' or it could be something like, 'I've locked myself out.'

Just to give you an idea of my sister, she once texted me this exact message: *Lou, what's that song that goes da da da da da da da daaaa da daaa da da daaa? You know the one?*

See what I mean?

Bonnie came over, heavily pregnant and genuinely upset. A pang of fear washed over me as I realised this could be something to worry about.

I gestured to her to sit down on the sofa and gave Jesse a look that he totally understood: 'Put the kettle on.'

Bonnie calmed down and took a deep breath. She was ready to talk.

'So, I was really horny.'

Suddenly, that pang of fear evaporated. I switched my cuppa to a glass of red and settled in for a good story.

'I was really horny. You know what it's like when you're pregnant ... I was really horny and Steve was at work.'

'OK. And?' I gave her an encouraging nod to continue as both Jesse and I reached for the popcorn.

'I've never done this before, but I started to watch some porn.'

Yup, this was going to be a good story and I wondered to myself if this was a story I could include in a wedding speech. (For the record, it was mentioned when Bonnie got married a year later.)

She continued, looking concerned. 'And then something flashed up on my screen saying I was breaking the law!'

Jesse, who is probably more accustomed to this sort of online activity, shrugged it off and said, 'Yeah, it happens sometimes. Ignore it. It's a scam.'

Bonnie looked at Jesse in bewilderment. 'No, no, I was told it was the FBI and I had to pay them £300 or they'd report me to the police.'

Oh gosh, I could see where this was going.

'What did you do?' I asked her, thinking the first thing she would have done was to call Steve for advice. Or perhaps realise we didn't have the FBI in the UK.

'I called 999.'

'And …?'

'I asked for the police.'

'What on earth did you say to them?'

'I told them I was pregnant, I was horny and I was sorry.'

'What did the police say?'

'They told me it isn't a crime.'

My sister – a professional woman who went to university and started up her own award-winning company – called 999 to report she was horny and watched porn while her husband was at work.

I mean, pregnancy does do strange things to us.

Fair play to the twenty-something-year-old policeman who had probably never heard this emergency call before. It is not, indeed, a crime for a pregnant woman with a sexual urge to watch porn, and hats off to him for handling it so professionally.

However, her laptop was blank. The hackers had done a very good job of making it seem like she had to pay the £300 to get her laptop working again. Steve saved the day by taking the laptop to a tech specialist on the high street. But he wasn't prepared for the porn to restart playing in the shop for all to hear.

For the record, Bonnie gave me full permission to write this story.

The naughty list

November is the month where parents all over the world start to pull out the 'I'll call Santa' card. It really is the best and most effective threat to children. It works like a charm. And now there are even apps that can actually call you, and where 'Santa Claus' flashes up on your phone screen. There are other apps too that make it look like Santa has spoken your child's name and made a video just for them. They work really well for 'normal' names like Olivia, Sam, Max, James, Harry, Sarah, Laura etc – these are said with perfect distinction. But when you have children's names such as Basil and Inca, they use a robotic Alexa-style voice that is trying its hardest to sound like Santa, but not quite achieving it …

'What's wrong with Santa's voice, Mummy?'

'He's had too many mince pies and one too many sherries, darling.'

But why do we wait until November to pull out the Santa card – why can't we do mid summer on the beach, when your kid decides to sprint into a cave that you can't physically fit into? Or on a regular day after school, when your child protests about going to the supermarket to pick up that evening's dinner? Is it that if it's over-used, it loses its value? Probably. It's like counting to three or five (whatever works for you) when your child needs some reasoning with, when doing something out of line.

For us we count to five – it gives a little more time for them to straighten themselves out, and the more numbers we count creates a deeper impact, as we count along with an ever-more-stern facial expression. Although there have been many times, with all my children, where the count goes something like this:

'1 …

'2 ……

'3 ....
'3 and a half ....
Yikes.
'4 ....
'4 and a half ....
Shit.
'4 and three quarters ....
Shit. Fuck.
'4 and seven sixteenths ....

PANIC STATIONS! What do I do when it reaches 5????? The kids always do wave their white flags and retreat to what I want them to do before I reach the dreaded number 5. I give them the look of, 'Good choice, my son' but inside I am rejoicing as I'm genuinely never really sure what I would have done when I reached five. Clearly I would have had to have done something dramatic – put them in their room or sent them to bed; or with my older son, I can always take away the Wi-Fi ... this always seems to work. (Until it doesn't, and I quickly give the Wi-Fi back to save the play fighting that quickly turns into an actual fight, which always finishes with my youngest son crying. Standard.)

BI (Before Internet)

My eldest son Basil and my middle child Sonny love hearing stories about 'the olden days', when I was a child in the eighties and growing up without any internet or mobile phones or social media. They cannot believe that I only had four TV channels to choose from and most of their programmes weren't for kids until a certain time. I remember Channel 5 launching and thinking, 'This is the future.' I show them pictures of TVs when they were much bulkier; cassette tapes and winding the tape back into place with a pencil in the hope that the marks and dents in the tape wouldn't ruin the music. It was a simpler time. We were outside more. We used our imaginations more – or were we more trouble?

As a child I was pretty silent (hard to believe – you can't shut me up now), but I loved to be slightly rebellious, as no one would think it was me. I did things that would make me very worried if my kids did them. I used to play 'Knock Down Ginger' (when you ring doorbells and run away) with a girl called Joanna, and throw stones at parked cars. One time the rock hit the windscreen and shattered the entire thing. I pranked my friends too. My friend Vicky and I had been dancing to 'Vogue' by Madonna and I knew at some point Vicky would be thirsty, and for whatever reason I poured a large amount of Fairy Liquid into her orange squash and watched her down the whole thing. To this day Vicky still cannot drink orange squash. Vicky, I am so sorry. But we were young and internetless.

And, when you think about it, it is wonderfully crazy how we managed to live perfectly functioning lives without the internet. I'm really pleased I've experienced writing letters to each other, and called a house phone where if they weren't in, you left a message.

In 1996, both my sister and I were dating men with the same name.

The land line would ring. Mum would inevitably answer it. 'Hello? Oh, hi, Lee. Yes, how are you? Yes, she's here – I'll just get her for you.'

My sister and I would be poised at the top of the stairs, wondering which Lee it was, ready to pounce on the telephone in my mum's room. (It was always for my sister, but I usually managed to pick up the receiver in the kitchen and listen to their entire conversation anyway.)

Growing up there weren't any screens, there were arguments about reading maps in the car, arrangement-making was very specific (no mobiles for last-minute changes) and kids weren't allowed in the pubs – kids were more seen and not heard. Pizza Express used to be a decent place for a quiet, intimate date night. Maybe we got it right back then? Entering Pizza Express these days is like entering a zoo – an ensemble of children's birthdays parties, loud kids with uneaten pizza (most of it on the floor), crayon shrapnel on every surface, and usually some screen-glued toddlers, all accompanied by parents drinking large glasses of red wine. And to be honest I actually do love it. It's a great place for kids and parents to hang out. Mentally exhausting, though.

School trips

November seems to be a time for school trips – we had three last year, in a month, which added a lot of extra school admin to the full parenting plate. Extra permission slips were left on the kitchen table every morning until it was the day of the trip and I found myself running to the teacher boarding the coach with the permission slip flapping away in my hand.

'Can you come on the trip too?' the teacher asked.

'I would, but I don't want to.' (An honest answer and obviously I don't say it.) 'I can't. I'm afraid I have to work.' The truth is, the last time I went on a school outing on a coach, with 30 kids (parent helpers looked after 10 each), to the seaside, I found myself wanting to smash the emergency glass with the small red hammer that is attached to the coach windows and run the fuck away. The *noise*. The constant *noise*. The feeling of over-heating, the travel-sick kids who vomit in a bag and want to show you, the ARE WE THERE YETs, the kid who accidently soils their trousers, the ongoing questions – and that's just on the coach. Once at the beach, I had to help ten kids (yes, TEN) get their swimming costumes on and make sure none of their school clothes got mixed up, and then get them dry and dressed again. AND get in the sea myself to make sure none of them drowned or went missing.

I AM NOT MENTALLY SUITED TO THIS.

After playing paranoid lifeguard-in-a-swimming-costume-that-shows-too-much-bosom (I could totally sense some kids staring too much), we headed back to the beach to eat our packed lunches.

I love to see what is inside other kids' packed lunches to check how 'normal' I am with my food choices – or how 'normal' the kids are with their eating habits. My kid didn't eat the grapes, the apple or banana that I packed for him, and I knew he wouldn't eat them because he refuses to eat fruit, but they weren't for him: they were actually for the other parents doing what I was doing, and comparing packed lunches.

Now here comes the hideous part.

We were not prepared for the attack of seagulls. Set the scene in your imagination: there were 30 kids on a beach eating bread and crisps (the odd child eating apple or sliced watermelon), when we noticed seagulls flying above our heads. Within seconds there were more seagulls than children. One by one, they swooped down and attacked the kids' lunches.

Understandably, the kids went crazy, screaming and throwing the food away from them, running in all directions.

FUUUUCCCCCCCCCKKKKKKK.

I was chasing kids down the beach holding my boobs in place as I ran so they didn't slap me in the face, although by that point I probably needed a good slap in the face due to mounting hysteria. I was comforted by the fact that there were at least other parents who were helping with the situation, until my parent partner ran after me to tell me that she had a huge phobia of birds. Any bird. And she couldn't handle this situation.

So now I had 20 kids to look after, and a grown woman to reassure.

Think *Saving Private Ryan* as a school beach trip.

By the time we arrived back at the school and were greeted by the parents waiting to collect their child and hear about the wonderful school trip to the beach, I was in a state of shock, with vomit (not mine) in my hair and clothes, my ears ringing, and I hadn't felt myself blink for a while.

I'm not even sure what the point of the trip was. Educational? No. Spiritual? Absolutely not.

When Jesse returned home from work he told me he'd had a stressful workout at the gym. Insert your own choice of curse words here: _____

Anti-bullying week

November is also a time to talk to kids about bullying, as the schools share awareness of it by letting your kids show up to school in odd socks.

I've had three WhatsApp messages, a text, a reminder text and a couple of emails about this day – and I have a reminder alarm set up on my phone.

The one day of the school year where we are allowed to send our kids into school wearing odd socks I was full of beans – I was to gain back a good seven minutes of the school run timing in not having to find matching socks.

Usually I find myself scavenging around to find a pair of matching black socks to ensure my boys look respectable at the school gates – and we do always find a rogue pair of black socks, and I congratulate myself with this small win first thing in the morning.

However, this day seemed to be the most stressful yet: my middle child, Sonny, is quite fashion conscious, and categorically did not like the fact he had to wear odd socks.

'Mummy, these aren't the same.'

'I know, it's OK – it's to show your support for anti-bullying week.'

'No, Mummy, I don't like it – they're not the same.'

'I know, but it really is OK – it's for anti-bullying week.'

And this was our conversation, on loop, for about ten minutes. I had actually *lost* time in the morning, trying to negotiate with my son to wear odd socks.

'Mummy, nobody else is going to do this.'

'Yes, they will. I promise they will.' I paused. 'I tell you what – I'll pack a pair of matching black socks in my bag just in case you want to change when we get to school.'

This negotiation was brilliantly executed, if I do say so myself, and I got back to my other school run chores. Until Sonny was at my heels wanting me to show him the pair of matching black socks in my bag.

FFS.

And then we had to negotiate which odd socks would be worn – black and grey or bright pink and yellow … It took some time to decide, but we ended up wearing the pink sock on the left foot and the black sock on the right foot.

I love that we encourage children to speak up about bullying, and not to take part in it or instigate it. To talk about it openly without feeling vulnerable. This is a day we never had at school when I was growing up.

But it's not just children who need anti-bullying week. There are people who bring others down on a day-to-day basis.

Whether it's on a WhatsApp chat, online, gossiping or as a direct message on Instagram, there is still a lot of toxic energy circulating. We need to work on shutting down conversations that are only there to harm others. Call it out. How can we tell our kids not to bully when we may do it ourselves?

From childhood through to adulthood I have experienced bullying. Whether it's from friends at school, ex-boyfriends, work colleagues or fashion industry folk, I really feel (as I'm sure we all do) that I've had my fair share of toxic energy thrown in my face. I'm not here to write 'woe is me', but if I could go back in time, there would be so many occasions where I would now have told certain people to fuck off. It's taken me a long time to gain confidence and to rise from this and learn how to defend myself – by becoming indifferent and learning to be happy in my own skin. Basically, I've learnt to love and respect myself. I highly recommend it. What people think or say about me (or anyone) is none of my business and what they're saying is usually a reflection of themselves. So crack on being your awesome self.

Becoming a mother has mentally made me a stronger person in this respect. Yes, my children drive me crazy sometimes and I think I can't cope with the noise, the meltdowns or the ongoing to-do lists; however, my children, or perhaps getting older, have actually given me a superpower I didn't have before. I'm sure there is a better phrase for this but all I can think to call this power is the 'I-have-risen-up-and-don't-care-what-people-think' power. And it's priceless.

Remembrance Sunday

Remembrance Sunday – a time to reflect on the many millions of men and women who have fought and served for our country, and a time to educate our children on the importance and respect for this day. A day where I talk to my kids about my grandfather – their great-grandfather – and about how he was a pilot for the RAF during the Second World War.

The boys' eyes lit up when I told them we were going to see lots of war planes later on that day, if they were good …

We had decided to go to that year's Remembrance Sunday service, and the church was packed with families and war veterans. Everyone was very quiet and respectful, and we stupidly hoped that our children would also fall in line with this.

We'd briefed the kids before we arrived: 'Guys, when we get to church there will be a two-minute silence to pay our respects to all those that have lost their lives during wars, so please try to be as quiet as mice.'

No answer from the boys, and I thought to myself that it would all be fine – it was only two minutes. What could go wrong?

Thirty seconds into the silence and I could see my middle child starting to fidget. He was looking around, and focused on the back of his older brother's head. I reached out and caught his hand just in time, before he grabbed his brother's attention – and hair.

I bent down to Sonny and mouthed the words with a stern look: 'Stop. It.'

He was still for about five seconds, but then started very slowly to floss. I watched him from the corner of my eye and gave him *the look*. The floss very quickly started to speed up and within seconds he was flossing so vigorously he looked like he was about to take off. He also managed to knock the pram, where Inca was sleeping soundly. She woke up and pierced the sound of silence with a deafening shriek, which was followed by Sonny crying too, from the injury to his hand.

The entire congregation looked around to find where the noise was coming from, and I was given *the look* by a good 75 people.

We were deliberately standing at the back of the church for a quick escape, but our plan was ruined due to crowds of people standing at the back of the church. 'Sorry, excuse me. Excuse me, sorry ...'

'SHHHHHHH!' I was told as I clambered to get out of the church with two crying children. Jesse pretended he wasn't with me and stayed in the church with Basil, who was equally as embarrassed to be seen with me.

As soon as we got outside, the two minutes' silence was over and magically my kids stopped making any noise.

Jesse meandered out of the church, gave me *the look* and casually threw in, 'Well, that was embarrassing.' I wanted to staple something to his head.

Weekends away – sans kids!

November is the month where, traditionally, after school drop-off on a Friday, Jesse and I will head to Gatwick airport and jet off somewhere for the weekend, leaving the kids in the safe hands of the grandparents.

I strongly recommend any sort of break with your partner, or going alone to have some quality 'me' time. Being away with your partner without the kids is like a therapy session. In all honesty, having some one-on-one time with your partner can be so necessary. It doesn't have to be abroad – it could be at your local pub or even just a walk, but having that time together to talk about something other than the kids is important.

There is still bickering along the way, mind, due to the initial getting-to-the-airport-on-time stress and after the usual Husbanned questions such as 'Is this yours?' (holding up a passport and waving it around in front of his face, gesturing to me to take it off him) …

'Open it and see,' I replied, my hands full of bags and coats.

We weren't even at the airport yet and I was already annoyed with him. Added to which I had a drag of guilt for leaving the kids. However, having champagne with breakfast in the BA lounge really did sort that out. And I couldn't wait to spend the weekend away with Jesse: just us to do whatever we wanted, whenever we wanted.

That novelty doesn't ever get old.

I took a nap during the usual 'witching hour'. I took a shower during the usual book-reading-with-kids time. I had a cocktail during the usual putting-kids-back-to-bed-when-they-get-up-over-and-over-again period.

It felt so wild and free to be rebelling against motherhood!!

Naturally, being away *sans* kids comes with its own trials and tribulations. It seems that when I am 'off duty' as a mother my mind goes to mush. I become completely vacuous and like a child myself. I am pretty much useless.

This became apparent when I left our passports on the plane when we landed in Florence and only realised when we were standing at passport control. PANIC. Thoughts of not getting home to the kids terrified me – and then full-on mum-survival mode engulfed me as I ran back down the many corridors and back onto the plane – which you're not actually allowed to do. I was stopped by a very angry-looking Italian man who didn't speak a word of English and I don't speak a word of Italian. After trying to convince him I wasn't a terrorist and dodging handcuffs, they let me back onto the plane and luckily both mine and Jesse's passports were in the back of the seat pocket where I had left them. HURRAH.

It would never have happened if I'd had the kids with me.

My mum was looking after the kids at our house to make it easier for her. Which it totally wasn't. She called me during the witching hour and I could hear the kids kicking off in the background: 'Louise! I can't work your oven! The icons are too small and I can't read them.'

Then: 'Louise! I can't find Inca's dummy!'

There is more: 'Louise! Is it true Basil and Sonny have chocolate by their bed when they go to sleep?'

My kids were totally messing with her.

I decided it may be a good idea to have a FaceTime with the kids.

First up was Basil, my eldest.

'Hi, darling,' I trilled at him.

Basil was watching TV and not looking at me.

'Helllloooo?' Still nothing.

'BASIL!'

'Oh, hi, Mum – here's Sonny,' and he passed the phone over to his younger brother.

'Hi, Sonny!'

Sonny's entire face filled the rectangular screen as he said: 'Mummy, watch.' But all I could see were his eyes and nose.

'Sonny, I can't —'

'Mummy, watch, Mummy, watch!'

I had no idea what he was doing but I was confident it was probably nothing.

'Mummy, canihaveasnack?'

FFS.

'Why don't you ask Grandma? She's there with you today, not me.'

He went to find my mum and handed the phone to my youngest, who seemed to only want to throw and bash my mum's phone on the kitchen table.

'Inca, darling … Inca???'

'Mummmmmmmmmmmyyyyyyyyyy!' She sounded very pleased with herself and I was reassured and happy that all my kids were ok.

Turned out the person I needed to worry about was my mum.

'Inca, no!' I heard Mum sounding like me when I discover Inca doing something she shouldn't, followed by a scuffling sound which I could only guess was Mum taking the phone out of Inca's grip.

Then, on screen, there appeared my mum, but one who had been replaced by a fractious and tense version of herself. And, like the kids, she too enjoys a FaceTime with her face too close to the screen.

'Mum, move back! I can't see you properly.'

She pulled the screen away from her face and I could see her hair in disarray and a smudge of ketchup on her white T-shirt. 'Louise! I shouldn't have worn white!'

'Borrow something of mine, Mum.'

'I can't leave the room, Louise! Something will happen! I have to go, Louise – your youngest is quite a handful!'

By this point I was feeling quite smug that I didn't have to deal with the kids that night. I glanced over to Jesse, who was lying on the bed watching football on the TV, another football match on his phone, and drinking a beer.

Quite literally living his best life.

Time for me to swoop in and ruin it for him. 'Babe, we need to get going for our dinner reservation.'

'We've got loads of time.'

'No, we don't, and we can't be late.'

'We have loads of time.'

'No, we don't!'

'Get off my back! I'm just chilling.'

This turned into an argument about who chills more at home (him, obvs) but Jesse has this amazing ability to remember each and every time I have apparently 'chilled' and likes to remind me, yet I can't remember the last time he chilled – but it's every sodding day.

We ended up going to the restaurant not speaking to each other and spending the meal avoiding eye contact.

But I've got to say the 'off duty' argument we had without the kids around was oddly satisfying. Arguing when we're on duty is very different. Firstly, we argue behind a closed door away from the kids, in an angry whisper. It will usually go something like this:

'This is rubbish! I'm going out – see you later!'

'Yeah, go on, fuck off, then – *but I need you back by 5.30p.m. to pick up Sonny from Beavers. But in the meantime* – FUCK OFF!'

Or: 'If you get in that car and drive off you can forget our date night later! *But if you do, can you take the pram out of the boot because I was thinking of walking to the nursery today, it's such a nice day?* But bugger off!'

We've had arguments that have fizzled into a laughing fit because of the kids. The number of times I have stormed out of a room and stepped on some Lego, which is just as bad as stepping on glass, and vice versa with Jesse, can actually (after the initial pain) put life back into perspective.

Dad loo break

Another reason to argue – the toilet issue.

'I'm going to the loo.' This is code from my husband for: 'I am taking a number two and I will be indisposed for the next 40 minutes or so. I will not be able to hear you or help you. I do not exist at all whilst on the loo.'

I'd like to take this moment to list the things I have achieved in the same amount of time the father of the children spends going to the loo:

- Given birth (no exaggeration – my labour with my second child took 40 minutes from waters breaking to placenta making an appearance).
- Hiking. I drove myself to some nearby woods and hiked.
- Made and ate a meal from scratch.
- Painted a room.
- Cleared out a wardrobe.
- Watched two episodes of *Friends*.
- Did two loads of laundry.
- Wrote chapters of this book.

Added to this, for us mothers, we are not alone when we go to the loo. The kids will find you. They will hunt you down, calling out your name countless times as you hope they may tire before you have to answer. Of course this doesn't work. As soon as the kids know you are on the loo, it's their cue to ask a million pointless questions whilst trying to use you as a human climbing frame, watch you pee, be disgusted by it, ask why you have hair there …

'Why don't you lock the door?' I hear you asking. From experience this makes the process even more stressful. I would

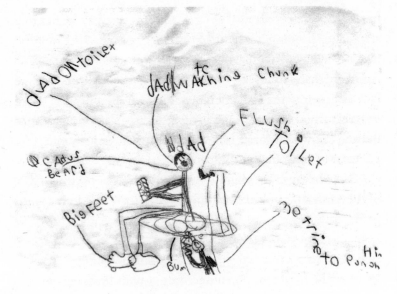

Jesse on the toilet, by Sonny.

rather be a climbing frame than re-hear the supersonic shrieks of my toddler as she simultaneously banged on the door with my perfume bottle.

My husband doesn't get this kind of attention on the loo. But when he does, my toddler kindly offers him a nappy and politely goes to get one. I'm jealous.

Siblings

Having more than one child can be useful when a new baby is born. When Inca was born, Basil was six and very willing and capable to help out with his little sister (on the other hand, Sonny, after three weeks of Inca being at home, asked when she was going back to the hospital).

Basil would fetch me nappies, wipes, nappy cream when I needed it, and would also offer me a glass of water when I was breastfeeding. It continued as far as Inca starting to take her first steps, and speaking her first words. This was when the helpfulness turned into mischievousness.

During bath times, Basil and Sonny were intrigued by the fact that their sister had different genital parts to them.

Basil turned to me one night, very matter-of-factly: 'Mummy, did you know that Inca's bottom goes all the way around?'

'Yes, Mummy. Inca's willy looks like a butt,' Sonny piped up.

'That's because Inca has a vagina and you have a penis.'

'PENIS!' The boys fell about laughing. 'Willy, penis, willy, penis, willy, penis!'

Inca was at that age where she would grab anything in her sight – and in the bath, the boys' willies were no exception. Quite early on, the boys realised they could use their willies as some sort of visual distraction when Inca was upset or when I needed some help with her and, to be perfectly honest, at home it worked (as a mother of three small children during Covid and home schooling, whatever worked to keep my youngest quiet was fine by me). Besides, it was all innocent fun and we were at home, in private.

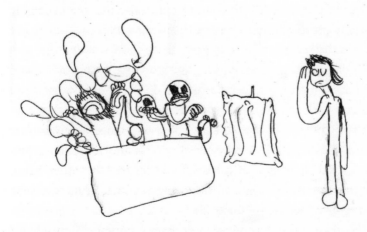

Chaos at bathtime, by Sonny.

When life started to open up again, we went to a pub when Inca was around 15 months old and had a lovely family lunch out (I say lovely – it was a stress, of course, and we probably should have stayed at home, but the idea of someone else cooking and clearing up was a huge luxury). Whilst we were at the pub, Inca started to kick off about something – perhaps it was the colour of the menu, or the air conditioning vent (she was six months old when lockdown hit us, so things we usually found normal were totally alien to her). She wasn't happy anyway, and myself and Jesse were pulling all sorts of entertainment out of the bag (literally), but nothing worked.

Just as the waiter came over with the kids' chicken nuggets, Basil wanted to get Inca's attention to help me and Jesse out, so he very seriously shouted: 'Inca! Inca! Do you want to look at my willy?'

'Yeah, mine too, Inca!' echoed Sonny.

The waiter side-eyed us and Jesse and I laughed it off – *Ha ha ha, nothing to see here. We are a normal family* – as if we had no idea what they were talking about … until Basil and Sonny started to take their pants down, at which point Jesse and I clamped down firmly on all the tomfoolery. But I've got to say the suggestion did stop Inca from having a total meltdown.

For the record – she didn't get to see their willies at the pub that day and from then on we put a stop to it. If Inca was going to have a meltdown then we would deal with it how we dealt with it with the boys: a lot of patience, gin and the threat of Father Christmas not coming …

It's incredible what kids will believe or think. The following is a story I absolutely love and one that continues to come up in family conversations. It was 1989 and we were eating at a Little Chef on a motorway break: my mum, my sister Bonnie, my little brother George and me.

We were on our way back from Bournemouth where we'd been visiting our paternal grandmother, who had her own line of stories she told us when we were kids holidaying there: 'Don't run on the carpet, dear, you'll crease it.'

'Did you know that jeans are out of fashion?'

'Don't do that, you'll break the TV.' (We could be blinking or breathing and she would say this.)

'You don't need a towel – run around instead.' (This applied to when we were out of the bath or sea. Mum once politely asked her to provide towels for us so she gave us a flannel to dry ourselves with.)

'In the war ...' (This was usually said before anything she said. Anything at all.)

'You'll never find a husband, dear, with a hole in your cardigan.'

'Nope, that word doesn't exist.' (Followed by slamming shut the Scrabble board during a heated game. She always insisted on using her dictionary 'from the war', which was as outdated as cave paintings.)

Back at the Little Chef – my mum needed the loo so she told Bonnie, who was eleven (I was nine, and George was five) to stay put at the table in the restaurant whilst she went to the ladies.

The three of us were waiting at the table, when little George piped up, innocently asking: 'Why do women take so long to go to the loo?'

The floodgates had been opened for Bonnie and me to play havoc with our little brother's mind.

Bonnie and I have always had the same energy, the same sense of humour and the same mind.

Bonnie and I exchanged looks – *'Let's mess with George'* – and we were off. 'Well ...' Bonnie leaned on the sticky Formica table top, accidently pressing her white Mickey Mouse jumper sleeve into the remnants of the tomato ketchup from our burger meal.

George's eyes met Bonnie's – he is intrigued to be let in on some female secrets.

'When women go to the loo ... they take a spoon with them ...'

George was so gripped by the story that he was all ears. He'd even stopped playing with his toy cars and hadn't touched his ice cream, which was melting in front of him. 'Why do they take a spoon?'

Bonnie and I glanced at each other: the sign for me to take over and continue this fabrication had been granted.

'You can't let Mum know you know but ... women with boobies take a spoon with them to the loo to help them ...' I continued.

'Help them do *what*?!?' George hadn't blinked for the last two minutes.

It's Bonnie's turn to continue the story. 'When Mum goes to the loo, she uses a spoon to make her boobies look better and higher. She uses the spoon to make them more pert.' Bonnie demonstrated this by licking the ice cream off her dessert spoon and then cupping her (non-existent) breasts, moving the spoon up and down to mimic trying to hold up a heavy breast.

It was genius. What a great story we had just come up with from nothing ...

George looked a little worried, but a look of understanding was also washing over his face as he listened. *It's the spoons.*

We continued: 'This is why there are always spoons on the table and Mum doesn't eat dessert. It's a pretend spoon for dessert, but really it's for her boobs ...'

When Mum came back to the table George could barely look her in the eye. Little did we know, but George carried this belief until he was a teenager.

I also believed, for a long time, that George's big toe on his right foot had actually been replaced with a baboon's toe at birth. (To be fair, his feet are very chimp-like.) I didn't question it at all – of course my brother's toe was from a baboon, even though it was identical to the human left toe.

I think I was about 13 when I realised the truth.

Poor George – my sister and I had a lot of fun with him growing up. But it was done in a such a way that he never knew we were teasing him, so therefore couldn't tell on us to Mum.

Bonnie and I liked to play schools – usually Bonnie was the teacher and I was the student. We turned our bedroom into a classroom and played 'times tables', which pleased my mum (none of this Times Tables Rock Stars rubbish, which is just another way to get your kids on the computer and to not be imaginative). Ask me any times table and I am immediately back playing schools with my sister.

One day, George wanted to play with us too. Of course we initially said no, telling him he was too young and a boy and we couldn't possibly play with him. George going crying to Mum made us rethink our playing strategy so we decided George *could* play with us ONLY if he played the head teacher. We told him it was a very special part to play in our game, that the head teacher was the best role you could play.

George was thrilled and took this part on with a heart full of joy and dedication. He would not let us down playing the head teacher.

We told him that the role of the head teacher would need its own office, so we set him up in the attic – aka the head teacher's office – and gave him a chair to sit on.

'You wait here in your office and wait for a naughty child to see you.' We backed out of the room, closing the door and running back downstairs to continue our game of schools – where no children were ever naughty.

George stayed in the attic, sitting on the chair waiting for a naughty child to tell off, for I don't know how long – when he finally emerged, Bonnie and I were already on to our next game of playing beauty parlours. This time he was allowed to play, and we dressed him up as a girl and called him Georgina.

Sorry, George, I'd never realised how much we must have messed with you – still, it's something we laugh about over dinner on the occasions when we all get together, like Mother's Day.

December

Advent Calendars

A small win for me is buying the advent calendars well in advance, and for refraining from eating them late one night when feeling premenstrual. (But it's always close.)

The choice of advent calendars is much more advanced than it was in my day. (There I go again, sounding like my mother.) When I was a kid I had to share my advent calendar with my brother and sister. We'd all race downstairs to see who would be the first person that day to open the flappy bit of cardboard to reveal a dodgy picture of Mary, Joseph, Jesus or a donkey, sans the chocolate. My sister's windows always seemed to be more fun than mine: she got angels and Mary, and I got hay in a stable with a random lamb. One Christmas, I opened up all the windows to make sure I got the best pictures. Inevitably, this led to me being told off and a Santa threat from my mum.

These days, they've evolved into branded ones for kids, like Peppa Pig and Thomas the Tank Engine, while beauty ones and even alcoholic ones are aimed at the grown-ups. I usually go for the £1 Dairy Milk advent calendar as it has chocolate and a Christmas question behind the little cardboard doors. It's a good all-rounder.

Last year, I excitedly placed the advent calendars on the breakfast table the night before, ready for the next morning – the first day of December! I was usually up before the boys due to my toddler waking up at 5 a.m. and was looking forward to seeing their reactions.

However ...

At 4 a.m. I was awoken by a sticky hand slapping me on the cheek. 'Mummy!'

'Wha–what's going on?'

I was startled to see my six-year-old, Sonny, with thick brown smears all over his mouth and hands – and now on my right cheek. My first reaction – and indeed every mother's reaction – was to smell it, to rule out that it could possibly be poo.

It wasn't poo. Small win. 'Is it Christmas yet?' Sonny's eyes were wide and alive with sugar. I looked at my phone next to me, and double grimaced – at the time, and at Jesse next to me, who was fast asleep.

'It's four o'clock in the morning!' I loudly whispered to show some authority, and to show that I was clearly cross at what was unfolding.

'Is it Christmas yet?' he asked again, his eyes ever widening with sugar-euphoric adrenaline.

I got a waft of chocolate from his breath and I immediately knew what had happened. I couldn't believe I could be so stupid as to leave out chocolate on the kitchen table.

'Did you open your advent calendar?' Rhetorical question, but I wanted to know if my child would tell the truth.

'No!'

Sure.

I rephrased it: 'Did you eat all the chocolate from your calendar?'

'YESSSSSSSSS!' Sonny looked so thrilled with himself for opening up all the windows I hadn't got the heart to really tell him off. I found myself wondering, as I crawled out of bed at 4 a.m. to clean up the chocolate, if he opened the windows in ascending order – a glimpse of education within this cluster-fuck of a situation might make it a bit more bearable. (It didn't.) I continued to clean up the advent calendar massacre with Sonny, who could have given the Duracell bunny a run for its money, as my husband, toddler and eldest son slept on.

I didn't manage to get back to sleep and noted as the alarm went off that I'd only had four hours' sleep.

Elf on the shelf

Next up – the Christmas elves. This was something that wasn't around when I was a child, and nor was it for Basil in the early years, but in 2016 there seemed to be this Christmas-elf epidemic – they were everywhere, and it soon became the norm to have these sodding elves in your house pretending to watch your kids and reporting their behaviour back to Santa.

I tried to stay away from this trend, telling the kids the elves didn't need to come to our house as they were already well behaved (sure). What I really meant was that I didn't need an extra chore to do for Christmas admin, because inevitably it would be me coming up with creative ways to place this sodding elf in a different position in a different place for 24 days. Don't we already have enough on our plates?

But, inevitably, I caved when the boys said all their friends had elves ... so we wrote to Santa to ask them to come.

The elves are borderline Chucky-looking, which if you think about it is really quite freaky. One night, I placed an elf directly above Basil's head, so that it was peering over him like a reading lamp. Basil couldn't sleep that night and, when he did finally drop off, he woke up with nightmares at 2 a.m.

The next night I left the elves in the living room and kitchen area only. One elf in particular was definitely watching me. So we got chatting. Suddenly, I was like Tom Hanks in *Cast Away* talking to Wilson the basketball. This elf listened to all the shite that I had to do in the weeks before Christmas – free therapy session! (Alas, one did end up in the bin after giving me evils when I mentioned I hadn't yet bought any raffle tickets for the school Christmas fair.)

I remember lying in bed late one night, about to drop off, when the panic hit me that I hadn't moved that sodding elf. So there I was, at midnight, manoeuvring an elf into a really creative position ready for my kids to find in the morning. And they have to be moved once or twice a day for TWENTY-FOUR FLIPPING DAYS!

Note to self: make sure you pack the elf away with all the other Christmas paraphernalia and back into the loft, and not stuffed arse over head in a kitchen-bits drawer.

Basil found a lone elf in the drawer one day in June, whilst looking for Sellotape, and I had to come up with some ridiculous excuse.

'Mummy, what's this?'

'Oh, you found one, well done! It's very tricky to find an elf this time of year!'

Please, please, believe this shite.

'But why is he here?'

'Well —' (Pause for making something up that sounds remotely true.) '... the elves are watching all year round and hiding in all sorts of places around the house. A bit like EETV.'

'Don't you mean CCTV, Mum?'

'No, this is "Elf Elf TV".'

Shut up, woman. I mean, what is coming out of my mouth? EETV?? But, bless him, my son believed it. That's the brilliance of kids – they look up to us so much they will literally believe anything.

Apart from, in my case, that green food is good for you.

Buying presents

Buying presents for Christmas starts off being really enjoyable. I usually start around mid October when I'm out buying Halloween costumes from the supermarket, and pick up some bits and bobs that I think my mum or mother-in-law would love. I put them in a 'safe place' and then can't find them when it's time to wrap up the presents, randomly finding them under my bed around March time. *Hurrah, I can use this for Mother's Day!*

Buying Christmas presents doesn't just mean buying for your immediate family, like it did in the good old days when you were single and fun-sponge-free. Now there are so many people to send a card to, donate money to or buy a gift for, I've put together a checklist for myself to refer to every year:

Christmas gift list
People I live with (including children and partner).
The family I used to live with (mother, sister, brother – my
 father is no longer with us).
My sister's partner, and my sister's two children.
My brother's partner, and my brother's child.
My mother-in-law.
My father-in-law.
My other mother-in-law.
My brother-in-law and his partner.
My other brother-in-law.
My closest mates' children (this is optional, but I usually
 do).
My son's teachers.
My other son's teachers.
My daughter's teachers.

My agents.

My milkman.

My postman.

My accountant.

My hairdresser.

I can see you questioning why I buy for my husband's side of the family, as well as my own. My husband seems to play 'Secret Santa' with himself, by himself, every year, in that he finds out what 'we' have bought the family the same time as they do. In fact, Christmas and husbands is a whole new level of stress with more, even longer 'to do' lists.

To be honest, I wish I had Jesse's laidback attitude to getting everything done for the Christmas break.

But if I did, we wouldn't have Christmas.

If I really think about it, I don't think Jesse has any input towards Christmas Day apart from the cooking. He does like to cook and is very good at it, and he does eventually buy gifts, going out alone on Christmas Eve on a day trip by himself, whilst I stay at home with the children, decorating the house and making sure all the presents are wrapped, the stocking fillers are at the ready and very WELL HIDDEN, the table is all set up for Christmas Day, the food is in the fridge, the turkey is prepped, the spare room set up for my sister and her family, the carrots and biscuits are ready by the fireplace, the kids are bathed, fed and in their Christmas plaid onesies that I bought back in October, and I'm hosting the odd glass of wine with neighbours as they knock on our door throughout the day. Jesse arrives home four hours after the shops have closed with a couple of bulging bags and a roll of Christmas paper and expects a medal for his contribution towards Christmas.

Statistically, married couples with children argue 85 per cent more in December than any other month. And Santa is a man???? Yeah, right – you know it's Mrs Claus doing all the work behind the scenes.

Generally, my husband's contribution to Christmas goes something like this:

'When does the school close for Christmas?'

How Sonny sees me – looking after the whole family.

He has asked this on a Tuesday at 11.30 a.m., two days before Christmas Day, with the kids at home on the sofa watching TV. 'It's closed, dear,' I inform him. Did he even realise the kids were at home? Or did he think it was the weekend? Or realise that it was Christmas at all?

And then:

'What do you want for Christmas?'

It's midday on Christmas Eve, and I've packed the kids' clothes for a sleep-over at Grandma's house. I've also packed all the wrapped presents that I went shopping for, as well as all the stocking paraphernalia; sent out Christmas cards to all our family and friends; have bought cute outfits ready for Christmas Day; have the trifle pudding wrapped up in foil ready for transit; and have even left a Christmas card and money for our postman and milkman.

What do I want for Christmas?? WHERE DO I START???

School in December

There is so much to organise, buy, decorate, make, shop, cook, write, wrap and build – and that's just at home. The added Christmas school admin juggle becomes a full-time job as the WhatsApp messages and reminders come flooding in daily: what days to wear certain jumpers, socks, scarves; the Christmas parties; the cupcakes for the endless cake sales after school; the costume you need to make for the nativity play; the tickets that need to be bought (and sold) for the nativity play; the help for decoration-making for the Christmas fete; the help needed on the stalls for the Christmas fete; the gifts for the raffle at the Christmas fete; the need to buy (and sell) the raffle tickets; the random £1 that we need to bring in on what seems like every other day for Christmas jumper day, Christmas party day, the Christmas fete … I sometimes have visions of all mothers at the school gate having ammunition belts full of £1 coins that are at the ready to be thrown into the teachers' money tins at any given time. And who even has actual cash anymore anyway?

Hats off to the class reps who collect and organise all the contributions towards the teachers' gifts – but how do you know how much to contribute? There is no manual on this! No one wants to over-give and look like you're sucking up to the teacher (I've seen this happen) and no one wants to under-give and look like they're ungrateful for the wonderful job the teachers are doing. No one talks about how much they have contributed in the WhatsApp chats! AND there are three teachers in each class to think about! Is there an agreement of what teacher works the hardest, and that one gets the lion's share?

Nativity plays

I actually really enjoy going to the school Christmas play – I get so excited to see my children on stage in the makeshift costumes that took me all night to sew, cursing under my breath at 11 p.m. as I have to google if Jesus did indeed have a pet dog called Spot, and questioning why I didn't just order an outfit on Amazon.

All this torment evaporates when I see my child walk onto the stage with said outfit on (and, yes, Jesus was there with his dog), and sing with their class.

In my twenties I would queue up for nightclubs looking fabulous in my high heels and false lashes. Now it's all about queuing up for the school nativity in trainers, and I'll be lucky if I've applied some mascara. Mothers have been known to queue up to get the best seat in the house an hour before the show starts to make sure they too are in the spotlight, so that their children can find them in the audience. It feels like a competitive sport of who can get to the hall first and get the best seat. (It reminds me of putting your towel down on a sun lounger around a pool to 'bags' it.) But we all know that if we get there too late, we'll be the one at the back and spend most of the performance hoping your child will spot you as they scan the room trying to find you.

And when he saw me – our eyes locked, and just to see his reaction meant all was well in the world. We did our special and secret hand gesture to each other ('I love you') and I felt myself starting to well up. (Definitely peri-menopausal.) He spent most of the time picking his nose, mouthing the songs and not actually singing them, and generally not paying attention to the brilliantly over-enthusiastic music teacher, who was conducting the performance while simultaneously mouthing all the words to the songs, reminding them to smile (with her huge smile), and giving the odd frowny side-look to children who were misbehaving. It was a multi-tasking job that even the conductors at the BBC Proms wouldn't have the skills for.

I was watching Sonny on stage not singing and being a beat or two behind with the hand gestures that have been choreographed with the song, when he obviously suddenly had this urge for me to … yes, you've guessed it … watch him. My eyes were locked on him the entire time and yet he was checking to see if I was watching him, checking to see if I would look away, which I won't, and I was making a huge point of watching him ALL THE TIME so that my eyes were starting to sting and dry out.

The song finished and the teacher instructed the children to sit down. She then welcomed to the stage the chosen, budding child actors playing Jesus and Mary – who were actually pretty good, making me wonder if my kids would ever get to play the part of Jesus or Mary. And it was then – just when it was all quiet and the children on stage were delivering their lines as they'd rehearsed – that Sonny decided this was his moment to get my attention.

He started to look around for me – his eyeline bobbing around the heads of the other children sitting in front of him. His eyes met mine and even though we were (still) very much looking at each other, he piped up loudly, whispering:

'Mummy ...'

(Waves at me.)

'Mummy ...'

(More waving.)

'Mummy! Mummy!'

I wave back and put my right index finger to my lips, signalling him to *ssssh*.

'SSSSSHHHHHH!' reiterated the teacher. It was so loud, she might as well have just spoken it.

Thankfully, Sonny's attention was back on Mary and Jesus, and he was getting ready to stand up again and sing. Although this time he sung whilst holding his willy, squeezing it every now and then. *Oh no, he needs a wee.*

I prayed (and I was in a church) that he didn't wet himself. He hadn't in years but there is always some kind of regression with kids when you least expect it.

The squeezing of the willy continued throughout the whole song of 'Little Donkey' and I tried to gesture to him to 'Leave yourself alone!' But Sonny was simply day-dreaming, mouthing words, staring into space ... and fondling himself.

A mother next to me touched my arm and pulled me in to whisper something into my ear: 'Fancy a glass of wine after this?'

I love her.

Luckily Sonny didn't wet himself, but he did find a huge bogie that he ate whilst singing 'Silent Night'.

School Christmas fair

The school Christmas fair is around the same time as the nativity play. It involves lots of organisation from the brilliant PTA team (hats off to you, as ever) and is something that I love the idea of getting involved in – then regret offering my help shortly afterwards.

In the school my children attended before we moved out of London, there was a genuine alpha female in the PTA who insisted on taking on most of the responsibility then passive-aggressively threw it back in our faces for not being more 'hands on', and *then* bit your head off if you tried to help or offer advice. It was HER fair, and it was going to be done HER way. (It was very much Amanda from *Motherland*.) She scrapped the mulled wine and Prosecco table, which the year before had taken most of the income for the Christmas fair (if anyone needs to drink over Christmas, it's mothers), so that when most mothers arrived they were totally perplexed at the idea of having a Christmas fair without the essentials.

I watched as some mothers circulated the hall, scanning the room. 'What do you mean there isn't any booze? That's the only reason I came!'

Well, that and seeing the caretaker of the school, Mr Bins (this no joke) dress up as Santa and tell all the kids to be good for the sake of their mother during this month of mentalness.

I volunteered to help with some other mothers who I felt were on the same wavelength as me.

I had offered to be in charge of the popcorn machine. All kids and adults love popcorn, and I actually had a machine, given to me ten years before as a Christmas gift from Jesse.

If you have ever gone to the cinema with me you will know I will happily demolish a large box of popcorn. I even had it at my wedding, for crying out loud, and ordered my favourite cheese-flavoured popcorn from America when I was pregnant for £60 for two bags. Gotta love those pregnancy hormones and childhood memories … I think it's because I wasn't allowed it when I was a child. My mum's diatribe against it, at the cinema popcorn kiosk, back in the late eighties, always went something like this: 'How much? For popcorn? It's corn that's popped! That's absurd! I could run to Sainsbury's and get some for a third of the price. I could farm my own corn for a cheaper price! Well, I'm in the wrong business – I need to make popcorn for a living! No, I'm not paying that. Louise, you'll have to do without.'

Inevitably this was always in front of the cool kids at my primary school who saw the entire display of humiliation whilst holding their own large box of popcorn. Basically, you don't need to be Freud to figure out my subsequent obsession with popcorn.

Anyway, I hadn't used the popcorn machine for a good seven years but thought it was a good time to dust it off and put it to use. The smell of fresh popcorn circulated around the hall inviting a queue of kids (and adults) to my stall. I felt slightly smug when 'Amanda' saw my stall was busier than hers – I was truly embracing my role at the Christmas fair.

Weirdly, however, I started to feel very sick. Awfully sick to a point where I was close to throwing up. This wasn't like me. My mind wandered as I tried to track my last period. And there it was – I realised I was late. *Am I pregnant????* I made a dash to the loo to have a word with myself, leaving a line of popcorn-hungry children waiting (including my own). 'I'll be right back, guys.'

Didn't turn off the popcorn machine.

Whoops.

When I came back, there had been a slight disaster as the machine had overheated and had started spitting out burnt popcorn kernels. The school hall was engulfed in smoke and an exodus of children and parents had started to leave the hall. Mr Bins aka Father Christmas came running out of his makeshift Santa's Grotto, scattering children along the way, to make sure all emergency exits were open. In the resulting chaos, his fake beard got pulled down to his chin, exposing the school care-taker as Father Christmas as he came out of character.

It was fair to say 'Amanda' was, and I quote, 'alarmingly disappointed' with me.

I did a pregnancy test later on that day and there it was … posi-tive! Third baby was on the way. OMG!!!!!! *This explains why I need to pee every given moment …*

Jesse and I kept the news to ourselves (I was only about seven weeks along) and tried to think of excuses I could say to my family as to why I wouldn't be drinking over Christmas. Something I knew wasn't going to be easy!

Christmas cards

One year I thought it would be a lot easier to use an app to send all my Christmas cards – you can copy and paste to send the same message, and send the cards via the app – no need for stamps or go to a post office. It's Christmas-proof for mums.

Or was it?

Our Christmas card was a photo of all five of us in a Santa's Grotto, wearing Christmas jumpers in shades of red and green, all smiling away apart from Inca, my youngest, who was crying, terrified of the Santa. I actually felt like I was bossing it until I realised there was a typo in the message. But it was too late to change it. What was meant to read: 'Hope we can see you next year!' was actually: 'Hope we can't see you next year!'

Really pleased my husband's 104-year-old grandmother received this card, as well as all the family members that we hadn't seen for over two years thanks to Covid. I'll stick to the old-school pen and paper from now on.

Writing to Santa

Writing to Santa is an insightful experience, as it allows you to see how good your children's 'best' handwriting is, how good they think they've been all year, and to see what they actually want for Christmas. This can backfire, of course.

One year Sonny asked for a PS5 – a gaming computer console that not only was out of stock around the world, but also cost around £500. This was definitely not happening.

'I'm not sure Santa can get that for you, my love.'

'Why not? You said I've been a very good boy this year.'

'Yes, you have, but —'

'Then he can get it for me. He's Santa – he can get anything.'

'Yes, but this is a little bit expensive.'

'Mummy, Santa makes the presents, he doesn't buy them, so it's OK.'

Shit.

I mean, how do you get out of this one without undoing all you have told your kid in the first place? This was only going to end badly and either make me look like a liar or make Santa look like a twat.

Luckily, Sonny's letter read as follows:

'Dear Santa,
I have been a very good boy but my big brother hasn't so I
want his presents too. This can be our secret.'

Perfect! I knew I could use this as leverage if he asked why there
wasn't a PS5 from Santa: 'You didn't make it clear, darling – you
must make it clear what you want.'

But what about next year? Will Sonny remember these Santa-
gift-asking instructions?

Do you believe?

The first year Basil understood the whole 'Father Christmas'
tradition we thought it would be nice to visit Santa at a grotto
at our local garden centre. Jesse and I were overly enthusiastic
about the whole experience, sporting matching Santa hats and
fixed smiley faces that looked like we'd swallowed a hanger.

We briefed Basil that he'd be expected to sit on the lap of
an old man he'd never met before who'd be wearing a very
dodgy red and white suit (it *is* a weird outfit if you really think
about it) and that he was to tell him he'd been a good boy, at
which point the old man would decide if he was naughty or
nice.

We kept back the bit that when Basil was asleep, he'd break
into the house through the chimney and watch him sleeping,
then leave him a present that we'd know nothing about.

When you really think about it, the whole tradition sounds
rather odd. Let's unparent again all the lessons we've taught our
children – don't speak to strangers, don't sit on strangers' laps
and definitely call the police if someone breaks into your home.
Maybe children know this already and that's why they scream
the roof down when placed on Santa's lap. We have so many

photos of the kids when they're younger, screaming their heads off, sitting on Santa's lap. (It does make the perfect Christmas card, I may add.)

Last year, when my eldest son was nine, he said he didn't believe in Santa anymore.

'Do you want to tell him that to his face?' I asked him.

'What – you mean go to the North Pole?' he grunted in reply.

'Yes, exactly. We're off to the North Pole because Santa heard that you didn't believe in him anymore and he wants a word.'

And we did exactly that – we went to the Arctic Circle to meet Santa.

Parenting can feel like an oxymoron sometimes: we encourage our children to tell the truth and yet we lie to them on a daily basis – probably more than we realise:

'If you watch too much TV your eyes will go square.'

'Eating the crusts of your bread will make your hair curly.'

'Your homework is really good.'

'If you don't wipe your bottom, mushrooms will grow there.'

'When the ice cream van plays its music, it means they have run out of ice cream.'

'Santa, the tooth fairy and the Easter bunny are all real.'

So we went to Lapland to meet Santa and to convince our clever-clogs nine-year-old that his intelligent theory of Santa being a story instead of being real was in fact not true.

Annoyingly, and without wanting to, we met two Santas in Lapland. With the first one, Basil told him what he wanted for Christmas – something to do with PlayStation and a VR headset or something, which I googled when he was talking to Santa and thought, '*ABSOLUTELY NOT! It's £350 and for 12-year-olds*' – but naturally Santa said, 'Well, if you've been a good boy this year ...'

'I have! I really have, haven't I, Mummy?' Basil looked to me for confirmation to tell Santa that he'd been a good boy – and I couldn't lie in front of Santa and when Basil's eyes were so bright with excitement.

'Yes, he has – very good indeed,' I replied. *We'll just ignore the time this year you threw the remote control at the TV, which shattered the screen and it cost us £1500 to fix it.*

'Well, then I'm sure you'll get it,' said a smug Santa.

FUCK OFF, SANTA! Thanks for royally stitching me up! What happens if I don't get this sodding present my kid has asked for? Who's going to be there to explain to him on Christmas morning why Santa gave him Lego instead of an Oculus 3000 or whatever it is?

Just add 'therapist' to the long and never ending 'mum' job description.

The following day we stumbled across another Santa – I have to say the best Santa I've ever seen – and Basil went to go and talk to him. This time I stayed extra close.

'Hello again, Santa – can you remember which children are good and which children are bad?' he asked.

'Yes, of course I can,' replied Santa, smiling through his REAL grey beard. 'I can remember everything!'

'Then can you tell me what I asked for yesterday when I saw you?'

SHIT.

Cue me silently mouthing the words as clearly as possible in the hope that Santa might magically know that I was saying: 'Oculus 3000.' I doubted he'd ever heard of it and I was pretty sure I was mouthing it incorrectly.

Of course, this Santa had no idea what Basil had asked for the day before, but he did very cleverly answer with, 'The elves write everything down for me so you don't have anything to worry about. I know what you asked for.' Phew, Santa saved that situation! I felt relieved for a moment, which was quickly followed by cursing when I realise that now I had to actually buy the damn present.

That trip did make Basil believe again – but I fear he's close to figuring it all out. We want our younger children to believe for as long as he has – but older siblings have that urge to shatter younger siblings' dreams. Not looking forward to this.

One of my earliest memories is at nursery school at Christmas time. I was dressed as a fairy with gold tinsel around my head as a halo, a bright pink leotard and a skirt with more tinsel sewn around the bottom of it. Santa had come to the nursery that day and I felt that I had been so lucky to sit on his lap. I had really felt a connection with him, and I could tell I was his favourite. It was a memory I'll never forget. Fifteen years later, when I was nineteen and having Christmas lunch with my dad, he mentioned this day when I was the fairy – and it was then I realised Santa had been my dad all along. Looking back at the photos it's so obvious, but I had no idea! The same year I remember getting one of the greatest gifts I ever received: it was the 'A la Carte Kitchen' by Bluebird. In the TV commercial the little girl made breakfast for her dad and she used real baked beans. When I got my kitchen my mum told me I wasn't allowed to use baked beans (and quite right too – I was a threen-ager) but I remember how disappointed I felt at not being able to cook. False advertising right there! (Maybe this was the seed that flowered into my campaign in 2019 'Honesty in maternity advertising', calling out brands who used models with fake bumps to state this, as a disclaimer, on their websites – or use REAL pregnant models of all shapes and sizes. They say everything stems from childhood …)

And if you're wondering if my son did receive an Oculus 3000 gift from Santa – no, he didn't. He got it from me and his dad. There was no way Santa was taking the credit for making my son that happy. This was mine to take. And it was fabulous!

It's behind you!

Pantomimes are perfect for kids. They're their mothership. They are allowed to *not* sit still … they can shout, point, shuffle around, stand up, throw things … and no one bats an eyelid, apart from the dame of the panto who is always wearing eyelashes so long that she could take off in them. It's a sanctuary everywhere for parents to not feel embarrassed or need to leave a theatre.

But there is, of course, always one thing that can make it all go horribly wrong. (Standard – there's always something, right?)

The dame asks for a child volunteer to come up on stage and a sea of little arms shoot up into the air followed by their bodies, followed by standing on the chairs – which is when parents remember they have to parent, and ask their children to sit down on their bottoms. The children do try and sit on their bottoms, but all the while straining to make their raised arm look even longer, using their other hand to prop it up from under the armpit and flapping their hand like a fish out of water for attention, eyes wide and little voices saying over and over, 'Me, me, me, me – pick me! Pick me! Pick me!' I know you know exactly what I mean, and it's great that all the children have such confidence to want to get up on stage.

But when this 'pick me' enthusiasm was conducted the first time we went to a pantomime, I got an uppercut from my middle child which resulted in a small nose bleed that stained my new white blouse from Whistles that I had been looking forward to wearing for Christmas Day. Sonny cried, which made Inca cry – I was mortified, and off we went to the loo to sort ourselves out. In fact, we all had a little cry in the loo together. I think I actually just needed to have a good cry to get out all the pent-up stress over the Christmas break.

I highly recommend crying and/or screaming into a pillow in stressful times. I once watched an episode of *Everyone Loves Raymond* when I was in my twenties. In the episode, Raymond's wife had some alone time and she spent the time crying on the sofa. At the time I didn't get it. Now I get it. Sometimes having a good cry resets everything.

As I wrote this, I asked Jesse if he had ever cried due to being overwhelmed as a parent.

'No.'

Naturally.

Christmas parties

One Christmas I decided to have a few friends and their small children over – we all met at nursery and I thought it would be nice to get to know everyone a bit better. We hosted a party and I mentioned that Santa would be coming too.

Santa was my brother George, whose physique is the complete opposite of Santa's: George is 6'5" and very slender, and at the time was 31 years old and childless. He arrived with a hangover but was very enthusiastic about playing the role of Santa to ten toddlers – perhaps he was still a little drunk, but he very much enjoyed dressing up in the £15 Amazon Santa outfit that, quite frankly, was awful. I think the red coat was more of a pink and the synthetic grey beard looked more like wire wool. Nevertheless, I was really happy that my brother stepped up to the challenge – he had even written a poem and had practised his deepest, poshest voice, channelling Stephen Fry.

Before Santa aka semi-sober George started his performance of a lifetime, a dad of one of the children came over and pulled me aside. 'This is the first time Rufus has ever seen Santa in real life. I really hope you don't shatter his perception of the real Santa. This is a big deal.'

Riiiigggghhhhhtttttttt. No pressure then, mate. I glanced over to the slimmest Santa I'd ever seen, who was swigging back a bottle of Becks. I quickly concluded that the dad was right, so I stuffed a pillow down my brother's Santa outfit and added a pair of my glasses. Out he went to the children.

It was a huge success and I love the photo taken from that day – it's in the book, so take a look.

Christmas Eve

The prep for Christmas Eve is a military operation. Roger that. This is when parents play the role of a very special person (if the children actually fall asleep at a decent hour and stop creeping out of bed to see if Santa has arrived). It's very cute to see the kids place carrots and reindeer food (porridge and glitter) by the fireplace, along with a glass of sherry and cookies for Santa. The stockings are in place and we're ready to go!

I find myself double, sometimes triple checking that the kids are actually asleep and not pretending before I start Mission Santa Has Landed. Luckily, my kids do a really rubbish impression of themselves pretending to be asleep: they never normally lie like sleeping angels on their backs. My eldest son falls asleep while playing with a toy most nights, ending up looking like a taxidermy animal catching a frisbee, and my middle child is always catching flies.

The best way to see if your child is asleep is simply by saying these two words: 'Don't smile.'

I say this to my eldest son Basil, and watch the corners of his mouth upturn into a huge smile. 'Mummy, how did you know?'

'Mummies know everything.'

Cue my son asking a MILLION questions when it's already late and I've got work to do.

I eat chunks out of the carrots, leaving a few with bite marks to show that the reindeer have actually come down the chimney. After I've decorated the fireplace hearth with demolished bits of the carrots, I move on to the cookies and sherry, again leaving just a few crumbs for some added effect. I could put the cookies back in the packet, but every year I eat them – then question why I give myself a sugar rush before bedtime with a full-on day to come the next day. Sometimes I even write a letter from Santa to say how much he loved the cookies. I mean, it's a real operation!

I also like to take it that little bit further with snowy footprints around the fireplace heading towards the Christmas tree, which Jesse finds ridiculous.

'It's not even snowing outside!'

'Yeah, I know, but it is in the North Pole!'

'Our floor looks like we're in an episode of *Bake Off*.'

'Just shut up and help me.'

Which leads to standard marital Christmas arguments over who has done what over the Christmas period, and who is more stressed.

'Babe, the flour is stressing me out. It's unnecessary.'

'Unnecessary? UNNECESSARY?!' I know he knows he's opened my beast box. 'LET ME TELL YOU WHAT IS UNNECESSARY!'

I stand up to make my performance even more dramatic.

Deep breath.

'Writing cards to 3-year-olds pretending Inca wrote them, decorating a Christmas wreath with cotton wool and holly leaves for the school, dressing up as an elf for the school fair, spending 20 minutes trying to find the beginning of the Sellotape, going food shopping with ALL the kids whilst you're

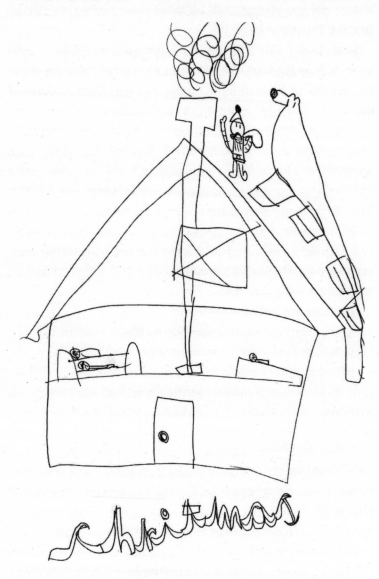

Santa coming down the chimney, by Sonny.

at home "gardening", writing letters to Santa that he'll never see, decorating the table with small bits of rosemary from the garden that no one will notice ... DO I NEED TO GO ON? IF I WANT SNOW FROM THE NORTH POLE IN OUR LIVING ROOM, I WILL HAVE IT!'

Jesse looks like he's been caught in a tornado – eyes wide, hair blown back. Wisely, he just nods, as I am foaming at the mouth and breathing heavily, ready to pounce again if needed.

Christmas Day

The big day arrives and I am already exhausted.

'Santa' finished her chores around 1 a.m. The kids excitedly woke up at 5 a.m., after an interval of my husband snoring and the youngest waking up wanting to be in our bed around 3 a.m.

The kids jumped onto our bed, one of them managing to accidently slap me in the face with their stocking on the way. How come Dad never gets slapped in bed? I did my best surprised reaction to their gifts – that I already know they have. Jesse was still asleep and had absolutely no idea what is in their stockings – I wondered if I could slap *him* awake.

'Mummy, what's a decade?' asked Basil.

'A decade? It's ten years. Why?'

'Why do you keep calling Daddy a decade?'

A small smile appeared on my lips as I remembered calling Jesse a dickhead yesterday and now this morning, in what I thought was under my breath.

This is the one day a year they all wait for. The kids were at the height of excitement, and I questioned if putting chocolate coins in the stocking had been a good idea. Of course it wasn't.

They were high on sugar at 5 a.m. and I knew I'd find a half-melted chocolate coin in my bed sheets at some point. And I was sure I'd eat it when I did.

The idea of hosting the family – cooking, clearing up and preparing myself for the disappointment on the kids' faces due to not getting the gifts they asked for – exasperated me. Maybe this is why mothers traditionally indulge in a Bucks Fizz on the morning of Christmas Day? Makes perfect sense.

However, the house was looking great, everything had been perfectly organised, the presents were wrapped, the fridge was full and the table was ready for the feast.

We usually host 17 people on Christmas Day, from both my side of the family and Jesse's. When they arrived, it was full steam ahead.

'Jesse, the place looks amazing, and it smells so good too!' gushed my mum to my husband.

'Thanks! Yes, it's been quite busy here, getting it all ready in time.'

I wanted to kill him. Was he really taking the credit for all my Christmas graft? We locked eyes and he gave me a smile and I gave him the look of death whilst holding up a carving knife – I was in the kitchen, poised over some carrots.

He knew. 'Actually, kudos to Louise – she did all of this.'

The knife and my stress levels lowered. But he continued: 'I would have helped, but I was so busy with work.'

The knife was replaced by an electric carving knife, and I pulled the trigger.

Oh *gosh* the anger was about to erupt … 'I too have a job! And a very busy one – and I'm writing a book! If it wasn't for me, there wouldn't be Christmas!' I must have looked crazy as I shouted this over the sound of the electric knife.

Mum came bounding over and handed me a glass of Prosecco as she took the weapon out of my grip.

Is it even Christmas Day without a marital spat and a possible meltdown?

The Christmas lunch maths always baffles me.

Time it takes to go to the supermarket to get all the food shopping done with three kids: 60 minutes

Time it takes to get all the shopping out of the car and into the fridge and cupboards: 15 minutes (much longer if Jesse does this, as the food will stay on the kitchen counter tops for a few days if I don't put it away).

Time it takes to prep all the food including the turkey: 8 hours

Time to eat the meal: 10 minutes!!

And let's not forget the added narration from the kids saying they don't like it and pushing their food around their plate and asking, 'WHEN CAN WE OPEN PRESENTS?!'

Call us mad but we open our presents after lunch. It's a tradition that we had when we were kids, and it can also be used as bait to get the kids to EAT UP.

When I was a child waiting for Christmas Day to arrive and seeing the Christmas tree get more and more surrounded with brightly coloured wrapped boxes I would, I admit, always make a small tear in the presents that were addressed to me and have a peep in. It wasn't a good move, as it made opening the presents on Christmas Day such an anti-climax. Mum figured this out so one year she thought she was being really smart in not labelling any presents – however, not only did I tear all the presents open, but Mum didn't have a clue what present was for whom. My brother George received a curling iron. He had a skin-head at the time.

I know my kids are the same, so I wrap ALL the presents the night before. I pour a glass of red and watch a Christmas romcom like *The Holiday* with Jude Law (he's so fit in it) and

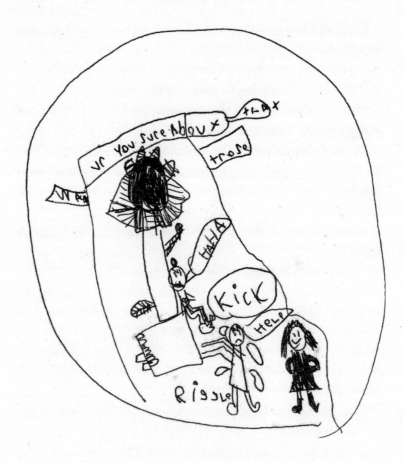

Shopping in Waitrose, by Sonny.

Cameron Diaz, and make an evening of it. Again, this is disrupted way too many times from the kids getting out of bed and trying to catch me out, so out comes the Santa card yet again.

The only time kids don't lie is when they're opening presents: their instant reaction is what they really think and they can't hide it. My sister Bonnie was pure gold at this (in a bad way). She could never hide her true feelings of utter disgust with gifts she was given – admittedly, she was a hormonal teenager. I remember she'd actually stomp up the stairs in a rage followed by my mum saying she was ungrateful. I actually *did* learn how to control my emotions and handled it really well when I was gifted a box of noodles from my mum, followed by a potato peeler that had already been used – and I didn't ever cook. (This is still an ongoing joke within my family at Christmas.)

Presents now come with an added stress once opened: the majority of toys are screwed into the box so well that trying to get the toy out of the packaging is like trying to break into Fort Knox. And who *has* that teeny tiny screwdriver that undoes the screws – that get destroyed if you use a larger, 'normal' screwdriver? Inevitably, the tool box makes an uninvited appearance on Christmas Day and is left in the corner of the room until March, when I realise that no one else is going to put it back apart from me.

I have a theory about gifts for kids – why not just wrap up a huge cardboard box and be done with it? That's the gift – my kids have more fun and use way more imagination by playing in the box that the gift came in, and not the gift itself.

Hiding pregnancy

It was Christmas Day 2018 and I was ten weeks pregnant with Inca. And feeling as rough as a bag of spanners. Really rough – low energy, constantly feeling sick, I looked awful and the whole Christmas spirit and theme made me feel sick. I even let my kids decorate the Christmas tree because I didn't have the energy to do it, and for once I didn't care if it looked like crap. We ended up with a Christmas tree that had a cluster of twenty-odd baubles all within the same few branches of a seven-foot tree that we'd had to circumcise because Jesse decided to get the biggest tree – which didn't actually fit in our house.

It's an ongoing tradition that Jesse always buys the tree too big, so that we have to cut it down to size *and* it takes up half of the living room space.

It's also a tradition for him to allow the kids to be wrapped in the plastic netting that the Christmas tree arrives in; a tradition that he started when obviously I was either pregnant or breast-feeding and couldn't come with them to supervise. Last Christmas I went with them to choose the tree and gasped as I saw both my children climb into the netting machine. Jesse was looking proud and I was petrified. This is the difference between mums and dads. (Well, it is in our house.)

As usual that year, we had loads of family over. Cooking made me feel sick – the smell of the turkey was disgusting and all I wanted to do was throw up, curl up in a ball and sleep.

I could feel the weight of my sister's and Mum's stare on me the entire day – checking to see if I was drinking my wine. They knew … we are all so close, and I knew they knew but I put up a strong fight to steer them off the pregnancy scent.

'You're pregnant, aren't you?' Bonnie my sister is extremely witchy and very in tune with her intuition.

'Nooooah …!??!' I said, unconvincingly.

'Hmmmmmm. You're sure you don't have anything you want to tell us?'

By this point my mum's ears had pricked up. I was pretty sure they had both talked about the possibility of me being pregnant for weeks, but still I persevered to make them believe I wasn't.

The reason for my secrecy? When I was pregnant with Sonny I told my sister my news PRIVATELY who then told my mum, and then my mum told her friend who blurted it out to me in a café one day, not knowing that my mum didn't know that I knew that she knew. I was heartbroken that my news wasn't news … Mum tried to make out that my pregnancy news was brand-new information to her, but her acting skills are awful and I saw straight through her reaction: 'What was that? What did I miss? Hmmm? Oh, really? Oh, Louise, I did not know this. How great. Ahem. No, I didn't know …' and so on and so forth. I made a vow to myself there and then to not divulge a pregnancy until after my three-month scan the next time.

I was so keen to throw my sister and Mum off the pregnancy scent I drank a glass of champagne in front of them, gagging all the time and hating every moment of it – but it worked. They gave up interrogating me and I had the greatest pleasure in announcing my pregnancy a few weeks later …

'WHAT? Don't lie to me, Louise – look me in the face and tell me the truth. Are you? Are you, really? Oh my gosh [sobbing starts]. Oh my gosh, Louise, this is fantastic! I am so proud of you …'

This time I *knew* she hadn't known.

Boxing Day

If your partner is into football you'll know that Boxing Day is a day when the best games all year are being played. Why? Why, why, *why* have a game on this particular day?

We also have wider family to see on Boxing Day. This is when we travel to Croydon to see Jesse's family on his dad's side. His dad, Geoff, is anti-football and he cannot understand why football is on over Boxing Day either. And to be fair to Jesse, he did listen to me and didn't go to the latest game on Boxing Day. It was so nice to have him around to lock himself away in his dad's office watching the game instead.

Boxing Day is a day of arguing over what we're watching on the TV too. The kids aren't really used to watching real TV, so when we all sit down and decide to watch a classic movie that is on the actual telly, and not Netflix, the kids are perplexed.

'Do we have to watch this? It's boring.'

'It's a classic!'

'Yeah, in the olden days.'

And then:

Trying to chill and watch a programme we can all agree on, by Sonny.

'Mum, skip the commercials.'

'I can't, it's normal TV.'

And so forth.

Usually this will ignite general sibling bickering about whose turn it is to hold the remote etc to a point where you can't hear or see what's happening on TV so I give up and head to the fridge.

From the other room I can hear the kids bickering: 'You can't. You can't! YOU CAN'T!'

I open the fridge door, staring into it as if looking for answers. I don't get any answers – just a load of leftover food from the day before.

Like a pack of meerkats, the sound of the fridge door opening stops the kids in their tracks. 'Canihaveasnack?'

No man's land week

Christmas is over and there is that week in between Christmas and New Year's Day when you have absolutely no idea what the day is. You're in this limbo of no man's land – the Christmas build-up is over. A sigh of relief? Or a pang of the Christmas blues? How is it all over? All that hard work and all I got was a pair of socks that have 'Pass me' on the bottom of the left foot and 'Prosecco' on the right. In what world would I be putting my feet up and being fed Prosecco? I mean, it's a bit sadistic to give this to a mother, no?

You'd think this would be the time to chill a bit more, at home with the kids, all occupied with their new presents, but no.

'Mummy, are we having any more presents?' asks Sonny.

'No, that's everything, my love. And you've had quite a lot!'

'Can I have some money for Roblox?'

What is it with kids' computer games? It's like another language. I have absolutely no idea what my sons are talking about when they explain Roblox or Fortnite, V-Bucks and whatnots. In all honesty, I just let them get on with it in this period and give them extra screen time so I can scan eBay and see what rejected Christmas gifts I can pick up at a bargain price.

And I ponder if we should go out and celebrate New Year's Eve – difficult conundrum when you're a parent with young children. Still, we persevere and tell ourselves it will be fun to have some friends over and stay up later with the kids – totally blocking out how tired they were when they stayed up for New Year's last year, when you promised yourself you wouldn't ever have a hangover that bad ever again …

New Year's Eve

This particular New Year's Eve party included the cornflake box game. If you don't what that is, let me explain. An empty cereal box is placed on the floor surrounded by all the participants of the game, and one by one we take it in turns to pick up said cereal box with our teeth (knees aren't allowed to touch the ground). If you can't reach the box, you do a shot of Jäger. (Wow, look how cool and grown-up we are.) Sounds easy, right? And at first it is … the cereal box is at full height and even Jesse, who is as flexible as a plank of wood, can get involved in the game. However, the game continues by tearing off a couple of centimetres or so all round the box, each round. When the box is at the height of 1cm and your hands are behind your back, this gets tricky …

Imagine six responsible parents all bending and flexing in ways we hadn't done for years – even our yoga classes don't push us this far and yet it was fascinating how competitive one got in the early hours of the morning whilst listening to 'Yacht Rock – easy listening for the over 40s' playlist on Spotify.

This was the moment when my favourite pair of jeans (you know they're good when you wear them on New Year's Eve) gave way with a RIP sound – both ripped, and rest in peace.

At the time, Night Louise thought it was hilarious. Yes, I think of myself as two people most of the time. 'Morning Louise' is sensible, responsible, thoughtful and hardworking. Then there is 'Night Louise', who basically couldn't give a hoot but is *so much fun*. I think she's the twenties version of myself and it's nice to revisit her every now and then. Night Louise doesn't worry about how she'll feel the next day or how she'll manage three kids with a lack of sleep and major dehydration, much to Morning Louise's annoyance. It's almost like I am another child to myself … (like I really need that extra responsibility).

Anyway, Night Louise decided to show off the rip by bending over, hands on the floor, bum in the air, shaking my (ample) backside around chanting: '*I like big butts and I cannot lie, you other brothers can't deny* …' All this in front of the new parents who haven't been introduced to Night Louise yet.

(Morning Louise was mortified. And very quiet on the group WhatsApp chat the next day.)

We had two couples over from our primary school. Our kids were in reception together and we had yet to experience a night out with them. We had met them at the school gates and, as we know, the chat at the school gates is always very pleasant and normal … apart from the one time when a mother asked me if I had a lighter. *Mate, we're in the school playground, for crying out loud.*

Jesse and I didn't know what to expect from our new parent friends and their kids over New Year's Eve. When kids know they are allowed to stay up later than usual – WOW, this is like them being told they have won the key to a sweet shop, in Legoland, with Father Christmas as the store owner. They go feral – but it's OK because for one night only we don't give a shit about getting them into bed on time. It's almost like parents and kids are both having a night off from each other, and we're all lapping it up.

At around 9 p.m. the kids decided to put on a show for the adults. They'd been practising their show for the last hour upstairs, leading to much debauched behaviour from the parents downstairs. We were into our third bottle of wine and banter had started to flow. These guys were definitely mates for life. We got each other.

This is one of the many highlights of being a parent that no one really talks about – the friends you meet along the way. To this day, I have met the most incredible women from the school gates that I know will be in my life forever. My mum, who is in her mid seventies, is still having lunch and dinners with the mums she met when I was at school. It's really special.

High on sugar and clearly fighting their obviously overtired demeanour, the kids proceeded to demonstrate their acting abilities for the parents. It was total shit and it was taking way too long. After 20 agonising minutes of nobody knowing what they were doing apart from dressing up half as Elsa from *Frozen* and half as something that looked like a dominatrix, throwing in a few on-stage arguments about who was standing on what part of the carpet coupled with 'No, that's not what you're saying', cue all parents applauding with much enthusiasm whilst hollering 'Well done!' and 'Bravo!', camouflaging the yells from the kids of, 'It's not finished yet!'

The kids were tired and fractious. Sonny had just told his brother Basil that he was 'A big stupid dumb-dumb with a dumb face and a big butt and your butt stinks and you smell like a butt' (thanks to the Lego movie for this), so Jesse came up with a genius parenting hack that he learnt from some mates, and which I highly recommend any parent to try. (Oh my gosh, maybe this book *is* a manual?)

Get YouTube up on the TV and play last year's New Year's Eve celebration around 10 p.m. and pretend it's this year's celebration. UTTER GENIUS! Then send them off to bed. They think they've experienced midnight and have watched the celebrations and yet ... *mwwwoooooohahahhahhahaha*. I can guarantee the kids will all be asleep by 10.30 p.m. latest, thus leaving you all to enjoy the evening and the real celebration!

January

HAPPY NEW YEAR!

A new year is here! All the couples share a kiss with their partner, and now it's *our* time to party. Night Louise is in full party flow and loving it. Look at us! We've got it all … we are parents and can still have parties, stay up late and be really cool. We'll be absolutely fine tomorrow …

It's very likely that, once again, you did not have a lie in and you're immediately regretting that extra glass of champagne at 3 a.m., not to mention the shot of Jäger and participating in the cornflake game that ripped your favourite pair of jeans in the crotch area. It all seemed so cool and funny only a mere four hours ago and, as ever, Night Louise found it all hilarious and wasn't really thinking how Morning Louise would feel.

There is a theory that the later kids go to bed, the later they wake up. I can confirm this is utter crap. The sad fact is, it works for anyone over the age of ten, but small kids are a different kind of breed.

The kids were up at 7 a.m. on 1 January and came bounding, unapologetically, into our bedroom asking me (not my husband) for snacks.

It's almost like kids know you were up late the night before: they come as close as they possibly can to your head, leaning on the mattress, and speak at full volume directly into your eardrum, so close you can hear them breathing when they aren't even talking.

It started …

'Mummy, watch.'

'Mummy. Mummy, watch.'

'Mummy *watch*.'

I was finding it very hard to peel open an eye to look at my kid doing something not worth watching and yet I truly tried my hardest to sound interested in the absolute nothing that my kid was doing. With one eye open I watched my child flare his nostrils whilst humming at the same time, his face so close to mine I could feel his nostril-flaring movement touch my cheek. 'That's great, darling. Why don't you show Daddy, too?'

'Daddy's asleep, Mummy.'

Yes. He. Is.

Look at him sleeping soundly, blissfully unaware of this nose flaring phenomenon. Part of me was cursing him and part of me was admiring him – how did he manage to block this all out, and how did the children know not to wake him but me instead?

I closed my eyes in the hope of falling back to sleep, but was once again disturbed by my kid, who had started forcing my eyelid open. He literally pulled back my eyelid for attention.

This made Basil laugh so loudly it sent shock waves through my body and triggered my headache, that I had been expecting.

'Do you want my phone?' A desperate attempt to get the kids away from me so I could get some more sleep – even five minutes – anything, please!

'OK, thanks, Mummy.'

I thought my plan had worked until the heavy breathing in my ear doesn't go away. As I peeled a mascara-smudged eye open again to see what was going on, I realised I was being photographed.

'Mummy, what are those lines on your head?'

'What lines?' I asked, through gritted teeth.

'These ones.' I opened my only working eye and saw he had zoomed into *the* most unflattering shot of me EVER: it appeared that my frown lines had been tattooed on my face that morning.

I grunted and closed my eyes. 'Why don't you show Sonny.' Anything to get him away from my side. Sonny, I could hear, was in the living room watching Jelly on YouTube – possibly the most irritating person to watch but the kids love him.

My plan worked and Basil left my side, taking my phone with him, laughing at the photos he had taken of me moments earlier.

'Sonny, look at Mummy, ha ha!'

'She looks dead with lines on her head, ha ha ha!'

Thanks, guys.

I had an extra 27 minutes of golden sleep until the inevitable happened. My boys had an argument about something to do with Roblox or changing 'skins' … I wasn't really sure, but my youngest was in tears and it sounded like the situation needed to be defused, so I decided to step out of bed into a new year with a new-me-positive-outlook attitude.

Hydrate then caffeinate.

Morning Louise was in full swing until I felt the absolute agony incurred by attempting to do the splits hours before. My legs felt like I'd been hit by a bus; I was hurting in places I didn't even know I had muscles. I waddled to the kitchen rubbing my back, hunched forward, resembling a heavily pregnant version of myself, trying to work out where my phone would be. Naturally both boys had no idea where it was and ignored me anyway, their eyes gripped by an overstimulating, loud, and utterly ambiguous Netflix show. The volume of the TV made me groan.

I finally found my phone lodged in the sofa cushions, and straight away saw I had lots of Instagram notifications – which was odd as I had taken some time off Instagram over Christmas and New Year's. Maybe I had been tagged in something.

My phone didn't actually recognise my face to unlock my phone (I wasn't surprised) so I used my password. As I did, it dawned on me that Basil knew my password (in case of emergencies) …

And there it was, in all its horrific glory – the photo of me my son took 27 minutes ago lying in bed, looking dead.

It's had over 2,000 likes and 189 comments.

Awesome.

'Hahaha!'

'Have you been hacked?'

'Stunner'

'Is this really you?'

'You should hide your phone'

'Sign up to my health programme – 50% off today'

'Good night last night?'

'You sure you're a model hahaha'

'Wow'

It continued …

I decided to delete the photo and changed the password on my phone, but just for you guys I have included this photo in the book … were you one of the ones who commented?

New Year's resolutions

Dry January

So, it's 1 January – a new year. I can do this. This is *the year* that I do all the things I want to do – I am a different person, I can feel it. I will go to the gym more often, and I will do better with the kids' homework, and I will definitely be healthier and perhaps I'll even do Dry January.

Ahh, Dry January. A dry gin? A dry white wine? A dry Martini? Nope, *nope*, we are going full-on no alcohol for the whole month of January. Who cares if January is the most depressing month of the year – alcohol isn't going to help that, is it? Alcohol is a depressant so I should definitely stay away … yes, good plan. Let's forget about the tax bill looming at the end of the month too … I can do this! I am a new person and this is my year!

Just to be clear, I say the same speech to myself every first day of January.

At this time of the year, all around us magazines are bombarding us with weight-loss recipes, gyms are offering us discounts, and vegan green juices are everywhere. So it should be easy to try and be the best version of myself.

To be completely honest, Jesse and I actually enjoy Dry January. We usually do it every year and stick to it. The first three or four days I find tricky (whereas Jesse shows zero signs of suffering from the challenge), as I try to break the routine of pouring a glass of wine as I cook supper. By the third week into January I genuinely feel great: I feel more focused, have more patience with the kids, my skin is clearer and mornings seem easier.

Who needs alcohol? Every January, Jesse and I actually convince ourselves we won't need alcohol ever again. Maybe we should only drink when there's a party we've been invited to? Maybe we should only drink from Thursday to Sunday …? Maybe we should go to the pub now? It's Wednesday at noon. We never stick to it – as soon as February hits, we are all over that hit!

On the evening of 3 January 2021, however, the then prime minister, Boris Johnson, announced school closure from 4

January until 8 March. Parents all over the nation watched the news report with bated breath, in disgusted disbelief and with peak levels of anxiety for some. Was it just me who counted how many days in total this was so I could set it on my day countdown app? (For the record, it was 63 days.)

So this particular January was a tough one to say the least. It was cold, Covid was back, schools were closed, the kids were at home all day, every day; I had a lost my laptop to home schooling, only to find Wotsits crisp dust in my keyboard and an open tab on YouTube for 'girls bums'.

This was the tipping point for me. I knew it was time to cancel Dry January. Boris had quite confidently said we had to work with our 'support bubbles'. I realised my support bubbles were in the form of a large bottle with an orange label that went by the name of 'Prosecco'.

Fresh air and exercise
This has got to be in the top three of all new year resolutions, right? But try telling that to your kids.

'I'm not going!' shouted my eldest. 'I'm not going on another stupid walk!'

Bribery with snacks and an extra ten minutes on the iPad, and we were all set. We went on many walks in the January of 2021, which with an 18-month-old toddler was actually more stressful than tranquil. In fact, I doubt 'toddler' and 'tranquil' are ever used in the same sentence.

We'd be halfway through a walk and Inca would decide she'd had enough and would sit on the ground and refuse to move. She didn't want to be carried, she didn't want to walk, she didn't want us looking at her ... we just had to stand still, negotiating with her why we needed to walk. In the meantime, through the screaming 'Noooooooo' from Inca, from afar I could always hear:

'Mummy, watch ...!'

'Mummy! Mummy, watch!'

'Mummy, Mummy, Mummy, *watch*.'

Every time I replied to Sonny and Basil, who would be about 50 yards away, my voice raised in volume, it would still be swamped by Inca's even louder 'Noooooooooo!'

The self-care walks I had been hoping for turned into self-dare – to even *dare* to take a toddler out ...

Do more hands-on activities with the kids

The idea of baking and painting with kids is a delight, isn't it? In the Instagram world of painting and baking we'd all be neat and tidy and spend hours of quality family time together moulding the creative brains of our offspring. We're all smiling, whisking the cake batter and singing songs from *The Sound of Music* whilst painting a masterpiece that ends up in the local paper with the title 'The Toddler at The Tate' ...

In reality, as soon as the words: 'Shall we paint?' or 'Who wants to bake a cake?' leave your lips, you immediately regret asking it. We've already argued about what chair to sit on, what plate to use, what spoon to use, who will open the oven door, not to eat too much cake batter, argued over how to tie a bow in the apron, caught the kids with their licked fingers in the sugar bowl too many times – and this is only 30 seconds in ... Clouds of self-raising flour particles end up in places you never expected, butter gets splatted on your iPhone, there is screaming from the kids about who is going to lick the spoon ...

WHY DID I THINK THIS WAS A GOOD IDEA? Not only have my stress levels gone up a few notches, but the place is a mess, my kids (and I) are both on a sugar rush, the kids are crying and I am reaching for a glass of wine and it's only noon. The only silver lining is that the flour is working as a form of

dry shampoo, and the butter as a form of anti-aging moistur-
iser, which bodes well considering how much this whole process
has aged me.

Soft play

January is a dull month, let's face it. The weather, for one thing,
is awful and, as we know, bad weather with kids means finding
activities do to indoors – but at the same time trying to avoid
iPads and screens in general.

One January afternoon we headed out to soft play. I have a
huge love/hate relationship with soft play. If the play area is
small and quiet you're on to a winner: you can happily watch
your child navigate the stuffed multi-coloured shapes, climb the
steps of the slide and watch them repeatedly run around and
around whilst you finish your takeaway (just in case) flat white
and manage a scroll through Instagram. Naturally, every minute
or so, you'll hear the calls from your child showing you how
high they can jump on the bouncy castle:

'Mummy, watch …!'

'Mummy! Mummy, watch!'

'Mummy, Mummy, Mummy, *watch*.'

They jump.

'Wow, darling, that's fantastic – shall we try and do it
again?'

[Adds Zara jumper to cart.]

'Mummy, watch! Watch! Watch …'

'Excellent!'

[New jumper purchased.]

Yes, this is when I like soft play. I can sit, watch, shop and
think my child is the cleverest little darling ever to wave, jump
and hop. What a good mother I am …

Then there is the other, darker, side to soft play. When there are too many children all on a sugar rush and destroying everything and everyone in their paths. Kids climbing the wrong way up the slide, pushing each other, finding squashed good-ness-knows-what in the corners (have you ever thought how they *clean* a soft-play area?), mothers climbing up the ladder to save their screaming toddler from other feral children, and natu-rally the air conditioning is on the warmest setting. Cue sweaty upper lip and forehead as you leopard-crawl through a plastic tunnel with rainbow unicorns looking too happy on it. It's barely wide enough to let you in it and you realise your attire is not soft-play-ready: you reach your crying child at the other side of the soft-play obstacle course with your bum crack on display, and your iPhone, which was in the back pocket of your low-rise jeans, has now fallen out and you see an unknown toddler running away with it. You have a massive sweat-on BUT you have reached your child who needed you so much ... only for them to tell you they have a bogey as they hand you said bogey.

'Mummy! Watch, Mummy, watch!' is echoing throughout the entire soft-play centre, millions of children saying the same thing over and over. It's a 'Mummy, watch!' hell. I see mothers sitting at the tables outside the soft play area all looking at their children, nodding and smiling (or grimacing) ... it's universal. And I feel like I'm part of a hood. A motherhood.

Funny that ...

Of course, before you've gone in, you've briefed your kids before they enter the primary coloured kingdom of viruses to be kind to the other children. To share. To play nicely. This usually lasts a good sip of weak coffee before a child comes out crying and you pray that it's not your child crying. And then you pray it's not your child who has provoked the crying. Generally, if your child is the bully that day, it's because they're tired or hungry – but if it's a child that doesn't belong to you, that child is clearly trouble, an outcast, there's obviously something wrong with them and your children should stay away from them *at all costs.*

When Sonny was two years old he was in the 20 per cent of children who do *not* experience the terrible twos. He was an angel. (Hence why we decided to have a third child. We assumed we had nailed parenting, it was so easy with Sonny. *What brilliant parents we are.* How very, very stupid we were. Well played, karma, well played.)

One day, I took my little cherub to a nice soft-play day where there was only us and another mother and her son.

I tried to start a conversation because it felt odd not to. We were both submerged in a neon coloured plastic ball pit within close proximity of each other, so I thought I'd start a conversation … but she didn't want to talk. And that's fine. I didn't know what sort of morning she'd had, I didn't know what was on her mind and sometimes you just don't want to talk. To amuse myself, I decided to place two balls under Sonny's top so he looked like he had a pair of boobs. (Great boobs, I may add, as I admired them from afar – my breasts now resemble testicles rather than pert breasts.) I took a photo and sent it to Jesse thinking it was hilarious. Jesse replied saying I needed to take them out and that it was inappropriate (prude) – so I took them out, but not before the other mother saw me giving my two-year-old son boobs. (Photo is in the book – check it out.)

Sonny, at this point, wanted to put the boobs back and in the middle of playing around with the balls/boobs he accidentally fell on the other little boy. I helped the other boy up and was talking softly to him to make sure he was OK when the mother swooped in and starting saying how dangerous my son was. She took her son away from the ball pit and continued to deliberately stay away from us during her entire soft-play experience.

I just wanted to take this opportunity to say to that lady: I hope your day got better … please chill out!

Getting your child to actually leave a soft play area is another challenge – one that is both mental and physical. There have been plenty of times where I've spent a good 20 minutes just trying to locate my child, get their attention and make it clear it's time to go. Usually this is ignored as they spring into another quarter of the enclosed soft-play confinement, and you know it's time to go in. Shoes off, revealing the last remnants of a pedicure that is a good 6 months out of date, cursing yourself under your breath for not wearing socks, you enter the soft-play arena.

I can do this, you say to yourself. *I can crawl through this massive, spider-web-looking rope sculpture* (I am an arachnophobe and my imagination can sometimes be my worst enemy when it comes to anything at all relating to spiders). *I am a grown woman who has given birth three times. I can do this.*

Children race past you, screaming with glee directly into your eardrums as they pass.

Then I hear mine: 'Mummy! Watch! Mummy, watch!'

I'm lying on my stomach, slightly out of breath, exhausted from climbing up the ladders and through the massive spider web to find my son about to demonstrate something. I'm pretty sure he thinks I am there to play with him and he's so happy with the idea that I play along for a while. As I am continuing to watch him, he asks me to watch him as he attempts a cartwheel, which to be fair isn't that bad, but I'm done – I need a wee – and it's time to go.

I start by softening him up: 'Wow, that's brilliant – let me see it again!' *Thank goodness I'm wearing a pad today,* I think to myself.

He shows me again.

'That's great – let's go home and show Daddy.'

'Noooo, I don't want to!'

The negotiations start – I know I'm in the danger zone of a small meltdown and I want to try and keep this exit strategy as simple and seamless as possible.

I want it to look like I know the art of parenting.

'Extra snack on the way home? Wi-Fi? Roblox? V-Bucks?'

He's listening and the deal is done. He agrees to vacate the soft play quietly and off we go.

Please listen to my advice in this next sentence: Do not, I repeat, DO NOT attempt soft play when you are hungover. There is something about the noise, lights, plastic, smell and kids that DO NOT go well with a hangover.

Screen babysitters

On occasion, giving kids an iPad on a wet-weather day or if you're hungover or if you need to get home and have to use it as a bribe to leave a situation is absolutely fine.

Naturally there are some people who object to the use of technology and these people are usually those who do not have children.

My brother George was a classic example of this. We went for lunch when Basil was a toddler and boy, oh, boy, was he hard work … He was at that age where toddlers decide to spend your precious lunch dates with your friends and family doing anything but sit down and eat.

I usually spend pub lunches walking around after my toddler who is happily checking out everyone, walking past tables of people actually enjoying their food and having a conversation. Sitting down and eating in peace – a small and normal thing – is so missed as a parent – and, in turn, listening to someone you want to hang out with talk and to hear their response.

Jesse and I usually take it in turns – one eats while the other walks behind the toddler making sure they don't fall over, grab a random handbag, walk into the kitchen, put their hand down the toilet, take a sausage off a stranger's plate, fall down the stairs, run outside heading for the road, take another toddler's scooter … all of which usually happens within ten minutes of our arrival.

Sometimes an iPad playing *Little Baby Bum* or *Mr Bean* to keep the kids still so you can eat your Sunday roast lunch is a godsend.

My brother, George, however, who was childless at the time, frowned, tutted and outright banished the iPad when we all went for lunch one day.

'George, I really want to catch up with you – and we only have an hour.'

'Weezie [my childhood nickname], we don't need this.' He made a hand gesture towards the iPad as if he was batting away a fly. 'Put it away … we can all talk together without this technology.'

I stared at him blankly, knowing this was never going to happen. In fact, it took me back to the time when I was pregnant with my first and frowned upon a couple doing exactly the same thing – introducing the iPad to a toddler as the food arrived. 'We'll never do that,' I had whispered to Jesse.

OK, SURE.

'I'll put away the iPad on the condition that you look after Basil when my food arrives.'

'Yeah, course.' *Oh dear, George, you're in for a rough ride.*

Our food all arrived at the same time and I asked George to put Basil in his highchair instead of being on George's lap. George stepped up to the challenge with a spring in his step – until Basil refused to put his legs into the highchair leg holes and instead pulled his legs up to his chest in protest at being made to sit down. This continued a few times, and I noticed a slight glow starting to appear on George's brow. My brother was experiencing his first toddler sweat-on.

Basil at this point was also feeling uncomfortable – being lifted under his armpits, his shins were banging against the wooden highchair's bars, and he started to whimper.

'Just let him sit next to you – he's not a fan of the highchair unless something holds his attention.' (Sly remark, obvs.)

George snuggled Basil next to him, a satisfied look on both their faces. George did mean well and I really loved him for trying, but mother knows best and in T minus 4 seconds I knew that Basil would slide off the leather booth chair and disappear under the table. Once this happened, and as I or George would try to pick up Basil from the floor, the clever sod would somehow make himself feel twice as heavy and turn his arms into fluid, allowing his arms to somehow flow through our grip under his armpits, resulting in a triumphant toddler back on the floor.

Sure enough it was happening, and I watched George try to eat his lunch and look after Basil, who was doing all of the annoyances mentioned above.

George spent 15 minutes walking around with Basil, watching his food get cold, and another 10 minutes in the bathroom watching Basil turn on the taps and manage to splash water on George's crotch area. I honestly think looking after a hungry and tired toddler is the best form of contraception.

George finally admitted defeat: 'Give him the iPad.'

I used to feel really guilty about screen time but at the end of the day, if the kids are happy then I am happy. And when it's January being happy has to be a priority. There are more mental health issues in January than any other month in the year, so in all honesty, do whatever works for you.

February

(A nyone else need to spell out 'February' in your mind before you type it out? Or sing the alphabet to figure out what letter comes after J? Good, glad it's not just me. Anyhoo ...)

Half-term – again

Feb – ru – ary is here and oh, look at that, it's half-term. Again.

I'm still getting over the stress of Christmas and yet here we are again, with kids off school for a week. Whether you take time off work (if you work) or not, you still have to find activities for your children to do that don't consist of hours on the iPad or cost a fortune. Which, let's face it, is nigh-on impossible these days when even just a simple outing to the cinema will put you back £40.

And it's not just the expense of said cinema trip. There is the stress of my toddler not sitting still at all but instead wanting to ride the escalator up and down and up and down and up and down outside in the foyer, whilst my boys keep running out of the cinema to see if I am still there. We all leave the film with anxiety and stress levels at an all-time high, and I wonder why I just didn't make my own popcorn at home and throw on Netflix.

What I've learnt is, generally, when your children are small, what you imagine will be a lovely day out with them actually

A trip to the cinema. Sonny helping himself to pick and mix, Basil ordering popcorn and me running after Inca. By Basil.

won't be plain sailing, rainbows and butterflies, but more like a car crash, and can't wait to get home from your museum day out in London and wonder why you thought your kids would be interested in the toys that you played with in the eighties. (It was great nostalgia for me, but what on earth was I thinking?)

Car stress

Driving anywhere in the car over half-term is stressful. There are more cars on the road, natch, and each and every one will be filled with kids bickering about whose hand is resting more on the arm rest.

Added to this, I usually have my three-year-old unbuckling her seat harness and casually moving from seat to seat, ignoring my pleas and bribery to SIT DOWN. One time, we pulled over so I could strap Inca back into her seat. Inevitably she turned her body into a plank. As I struggled to put her back in her car seat, I was deafened by her overtired shrieks, which were accompanied by a kicking slap that knocked my glasses off my face.

I looked over at Jesse who was ignoring the entire performance and looking at his phone.

LIVID.

'Jesse, a little help here would be great. Perhaps engage in what is happening instead of being on your phone.'

Jesse could barely hear me over the ridiculous amount of noise my little one was making, so I repeated myself even louder and with more passive aggression than before.

I was greeted with a fast and furious flying cocktail sausage that hit me perfectly on my right boob.

'Did you just throw a cocktail sausage at me?'

'Yes, I did.'

'Are you kidding me? What the *heck*?' (I make a point of saying 'heck' around the kids.)

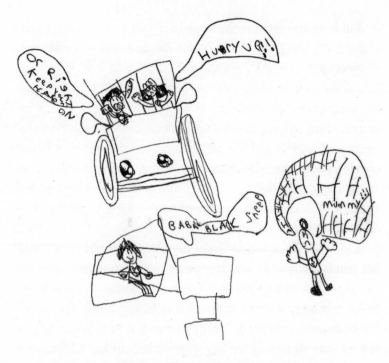

In the car. Jesse telling me to 'keep my hair on' as I tell him to 'hurry up' and Inca singing baa baa black sheep. By Basil.

'I was paying the congestion charge and ULEZ. Last time we got fined, remember?'

Valid point. But no need to throw a sausage.

Wee breaks

'Does anyone need a wee before we get in the car?'

A unanimous 'no' from all three kids.

I think we know where this is going.

Of course it's all bollocks, and they all need a wee about five minutes in, when we're on a dual carriageway.

'Why didn't you go when I asked you to go?'

'I didn't need to go then.'

Sure.

Next time you are driving, make a note of how many cars you'll see pulled over with a mum helping the kids to wee. For boys: making sure they stay on target and pee outside the car and not inside it, or on their shoes; and for girls, you'll see the mum holding the girl like a football, bum-first in a half-squat, trying to dodge the pee that is spraying in all directions.

Being in the car and trying to dodge the usual backing track of 'Are we there yet?', 'I'm bored,', 'Canihaveasnack?' and 'I'm still bored,' can all be avoided by playing the game called 'I Spy'. All my three kids are instantly interested in playing this game and I'm thrilled that I've managed to keep the kids occupied and happy whilst I can't be hands on.

We let Inca (she's two) go first. There is some gibberish for the opening phrase, which goes something like this: 'Eeeeeeye sppeeeeeeyyy sumFING ginnig wif …' She pauses and we all wait for her to speak. 'Sumfing ten and four.'

Moving on to Sonny, who has newly learnt phonics at school: 'I spy my lie somefing beginning wif CH.'

'CH??' I ask.

'Yes, Mummy, CH – it's a diagraph.'

And I am so impressed that we are playing I Spy with diagraphs (something I didn't learn at school in the eighties), I excitedly fully commit to the game:

'Church?'

'No.'

'Chair?'

'No.'

'Chin?'

'No.'

'Chimney.'

'No.'

We're looking inside and outside the car, and I genuinely think my son must be a genius.

'I give up, darling. What is it?'

'It's "tree", Mummy.'

'Tree starts with a "T", darling.'

'No, it starts with a CH … CH – UR – EE. Tree!'

FFS – sodding phonics!

Danger naps

And then there is the inevitable 'danger nap' in the car on the way home. It's 4.45 p.m. and your toddler, five-year-old and nine-year-old all pass out in the car. As much as I'm enjoying the peace and quiet and can listen to LBC feeling like an adult with-out any 'Canihaveasnack' interruptions, I am fully aware of the second wind they're all recharging themselves for, and how it will definitely affect my evening ahead. I was planning on watching the latest season of *The Crown* on Netflix at 9 p.m. but I'm pretty sure it'll be around then that I'll hear a chorus of, 'Mummy, watch.'

Potty training

It's called 'training' for a reason. This very messy and extremely challenging chapter in parenting can be difficult, frustrating and can end in an injury (you, not them), especially if your child is not ready but you *want* them to be ready. If this is you (it was me first time around), you will spend the majority of your time changing clothes (yours and theirs) and mopping up the floor in almost every situation. You may even get a nice surprise when you least expect it and step in their poo, feeling it squidge through your bare toes. Such joy.

Early on in my eldest son's potty training, we went to a vintage car museum. It probably wasn't the best idea to let Basil sit in a classic convertible Mustang – he used it as a potty and urinated all over the leather seats. I was mortified and left the museum as quickly as possible. It was the quickest £35 I've ever spent. And the most expensive toilet experience I've ever paid for.

'Please tell Mummy when you need a wee,' I told my youngest child, who was voluntarily taking off her nappy all the time.

Note to self: this does not mean they are ready for the potty; it means they are taking off their nappy because they have figured out how to do it and they deliberately want you to you walk in their poo and wee.

'OK, Mummy.'

Easy, I thought to myself. *They just have to tell me when they need a wee and I'll take them to the loo.*

'Mummy, I need a wee.'

'Ahh, excellent, of course —'

And I saw my toddler fully clothed, standing up, legs apart, staring down at the warm puddle between her feet.

'I did it!' She looked so proud. I bought one of those seats that sits inside the larger 'adult' loo seat, but she HATED IT and instead only wanted to use the loo like the rest of us did in the house.

I agreed to her trying that out, and left her alone as she had barked at me to: 'Mummy, get out! My bagina is private!' (I mean, fair play to her for her independence and knowledge of what body parts are private.)

I walked out of the bathroom door, leaving her to it. *Easy*, I thought to myself.

'MUMMY!!!!!! MUMMY!!!!!! MUMMMMYYYYYYYYYYYYYY!'

She'd fallen down the loo. Her body had folded in half, feet up in the air, her forehead touching her shins and her knuckles were white as she gripped with all her might to the toilet seat, trying to wriggle out of it.

I helped her out, and she said to me, very matter-of-factly: 'Mummy, did you know my nappy is also a toilet?'

I never thought seeing a wee and poo in a potty would make me so happy. It's brought me such joy over the years that I have been known to pick up the potty and take a selfie with said wee and poo, ignoring the stench, and send it to Jesse – who was probably in a very important business meeting. But, hands down, there is nothing more important than this!

The last time I did this, when I didn't get a response from Jesse, I sent the image to various WhatsApp groups including my family, Jesse's family and two different mum WhatsApp chats. I also shared it on an Instagram story because I neeeeeeeeded to celebrate the moment.

Naturally, no one appreciated it as much as I did. A tumbleweed moment on WhatsApp, and a few replies from my followers on Instagram: 'This is unnecessary. Unfollowing.'

Pancake Day

Shrove Tuesday also makes an appearance in February, and the school mum WhatsApp chats are out in full force, either reminding you it's Pancake Day or that the school is having a cake sale after school for Pancake Day and yet – Pancake Day arrives and I have forgotten about it, only to be reminded by my kids that they want pancakes for supper. I rummage through my cupboards and find some plain flour that is just about still in date, and manage to make some pancake mixture.

'Who wants to make pancakes?' I asked, way too enthusiastically, one year. We all knew it was going to end badly, yet still I ploughed on with my pancake decision because if I didn't, the mum guilt would creep in and I'd convince myself that not making pancakes would somehow affect my kids' childhood memories, and I would be to blame.

The batter was prepped as quickly as I could do it (whilst googling how to make pancakes), and the questions came flooding in from my six-year-old Sonny who, without realising it, was standing on my foot.

'Mummy, what's that?'

'That's the weighing scales.'

'Why?'

'So I know how much flour to put in.'

'Why?'

'So I can make a good pancake.'

'Why?'

'Why what?'

'Mummy, what's that?'

In frustration I pulled back the foot that he was standing on – he didn't notice – as more questions bombarded my tired brain. I questioned myself why I hadn't just bought ready-made pancakes from the local shop and WhatsApped Jesse to pick some up on his way home as a back-up.

'Mummy, can we flip them?'

'Yes, sure!' As soon as the words left my mouth I regretted my decision and wondered if he'd heard my answer – his clapping and jumping up and down on the spot confirmed that yes, indeed, he had heard me grant him the opportunity to throw hot food in the air.

I tried to help him get a good grip on the pan's handle, but he dismissed me. I took this dismissal as a chance to scroll through Instagram and look at posts of families tossing pancakes in the air in slo-mo, showcasing the perfect pancakes and families rejoicing. I peered around my phone and caught a glimpse of my son trying to toss batter in a high-sided and weighty wok – still, he persevered.

'Mummy, Mummy, watch!'

'Mummy!'

'Mummy, Mummy, watch ...'

'Mummy, Mummy, Mummy ...'

'I'm watching, darling.'

And I am watching ... and for a moment I forget about not wanting to make pancakes and that it's a total waste of time (what is Shrove Tuesday, anyway?) and watch my six-year-old try to flip too much batter from a wok into a pancake which probably goes against all laws of physics, and I love it. One day he won't ask me to make pancakes with him anymore and instead grunt at the idea of it – so I tell myself to savour this moment, and to enjoy how cute my son is.

Sonny and I ended up eating slightly burnt, slightly raw, cow-pat-looking pancakes, and then my eldest son walked into the kitchen after an evening at Cubs and was immediately keen to make his own batch of pancakes.

I turned to Jesse: 'Did you get my message?' I gestured to the pancake mix massacre. 'About picking up pancakes.' I silently mouthed this part – like the pancake police are out on patrol and ticketing anyone who didn't make pancakes from scratch.

'No —?' replied Jesse, even though my message to him on WhatsApp had two blue ticks next to it.

Perfect.

So we went through the whole pancake process again with my nine-year-old, who was even more eager to flip the pancake into the air but realised quite quickly that it wasn't really working that well. He ceased his attempts and instead helped himself to his younger brother's pancake, which went down like a lead balloon.

Valentine's Day

A day of the year where you are forced into telling the person you're with that you love them, and possibly may want to get naked with them later that day.

But what if your partner promised you a lie-in and then didn't set their alarm for the school run? Or you did get your lie-in but when you entered the kitchen the kids were all still in their PJs and slurping cereal that they had got themselves, resulting in a huge mess explosion. This was not a good set-up for possible sexy time later. And with three kids, a full-time job and a messy house, I don't particularly feel that sexy, ever.

For a moment I wondered if I would cancel my appointment to have a bikini wax. (But I *need* to go; either that, or I'll have to find the garden shears from the shed.)

Last year, I produced a card that I'd spent a good 30 minutes out of my extremely busy day choosing from the best (and most expensive) card shop on my local high street: shuffling through the shelves, picking up cards one at a time, opening them, reading the insert, wiping away a tear, putting it back and repeating this over and over until finally I found THE ONE: a picture on the front that means something to us, and is funny and thoughtful and I know he'll understand the meaning behind it. I really think about what to write inside the card, making sure Jesse feels my love.

'Dear Jesse,

Thank you for choosing me to spend your life with. I cannot wait to grow old with you and make many beautiful memories with you and our children. I appreciate you every day and am so thankful to have you in my life. I love you.

Louise x'

I handed it to him on a silver platter with a 'Love' coupon that had no expiration date.

Then it was my turn to receive my card.

It was clear from the envelope, which had wet saliva around the seal, that it had only just been written. On the front of the envelope it read, 'To my marginally better half'. It was also oddly dusty.

Once I opened it, I knew it had been bought thanks to a last-minute dash to the local petrol station – and was a card that had been left there for years because of this.

On the front of the card it read, *'You are a good choice for my first wife.'*

I opened it up and Jesse has written a message in a blue crayon: 'I LOVE YOU MEGA WIFE. Thanks for putting up with me.' Thanks, babe. I'm so pleased you took the time and effort to really indulge in this day and make it special. (Eye roll.) My first Valentine's Day with Jesse wasn't what I had in mind: he took me to see his football team, Crystal Palace, at Selhurst Park. This is HIS TEAM – Jesse's a very dedicated fan to the point where he has kept all the tickets from every game he's been to since he was a kid; I believe the first one is from 1986. Jesse even proposed to me when his team were promoted to the Premier League. He tells me he would have proposed regardless, but I do think his endorphins were at such an all-time high that he just went for it. (Whilst on the subject, as a surprise to Jesse on our wedding day, I hired the Crystal Palace cheerleaders and performed a dance routine with them in front of all our guests. It was an amazing moment and one I know he'll never forget.)

Our first Valentine's Day was romantic – we won the game (he'll know who played and who scored). Whenever Crystal Palace scores all the fans sing the song 'Glad All Over' by The Dave Clark Five. Jesse sang the lyrics 'so glad you're mine' to me, and it's a moment I'll always cherish.

Thirteen years, a marriage and three children later, however, I am writing this as I listen to Jesse trying to put our toddler back to sleep at 10.49 p.m. She is currently complaining about the temperature of her milk.

'Daddy, it's too hot.'

'It's not, darling, it's just the way you like it – it's been in the microwave for 37 seconds precisely.'

'IT'S TOO HOT, DADDY!' and I hear the bottle being thrown across the floor.

Jesse sighs, goes downstairs and presumably adds cold milk to Inca's bottle.

'It's too cold, Daddy.'

'This is what you asked for, darling.'

'I DON'T LIKE IT!'

Jesse whispers under his breath, 'For fuck's sake.'

He exits her bedroom and waits for a couple of seconds, out of the view of our toddler. He does nothing to the milk. He then re-enters her room.

'Here you are – is this better now?'

'Yes!'

Coping with a toddler is a game of patience and strategy.

Jesse definitely has more patience than I do with the children – but I wonder if this is because I do more than he does on a daily basis? Probably.

*   *   *

My Valentine's Day wants and needs have definitely changed since becoming a parent. Before kids I would want roses (yellow ones, apparently), dinner and a meaningful card. Now all I want is a lie-in and a meaningful card. Actually, what would be even more romantic would be to follow through on the lie-in. It's all very well physically getting up with the kids and venturing into the living room but here is the catch, dear husband: you need to stay awake and actually *watch* the children. It does baffle me how, and I mean HOW, Jesse manages to be that relaxed, that 'off duty', to think it's OK to fall asleep again whilst I am also asleep upstairs.

Once during a 'lie-in' I heard such commotion in the kitchen I was forced to (very angrily) throw off the bed covers, bang open the bedroom door (almost taking it off its hinges), and heavily stamp my way into the kitchen. There I found both my sons fighting over a cardboard box in front of my sleeping husband.

Livid.

How could he sleep through such chaos? I was actually jealous! I would love to be able to sleep so soundly and be that relaxed to actually drop off whilst parenting.

'JESSE!!!!!!!!!!!!!!!!'

He woke up. 'Oh, hi, what time is it?'

I gave him *the look* that I have perfected over the years. No need for words – he knew what *the look* meant.

I dragged myself back to bed, too angry and adrenalin-ed up to fall back to sleep. But I realised I could still have some quality time to myself: I thought I'd look at Instagram or the Mail Online – going straight to the showbiz section, obvs.

I possibly got about a good four minutes, and then I heard the kids coming for the bedroom door. I listened, eyes wide open, praying they wouldn't come for me. If they did, I decided to quickly stash my phone under my pillow and do my best impression of being fast asleep in the hope they might leave me alone.

No such hope.

It's almost like my kids don't understand that Mummy sleeps. To them I am always awake. Mummy does not sleep – and even if she is asleep, she is still to be interrupted at all times. I also sometimes wonder if the kids would bother me for a snack at my own funeral – harsh but true, right? There I'd be, lying in an open casket, hands on my chest, and my kids would come along asking for something. And the truth is, I would probably come back to life and sort them out.

To be fair Jesse is a romantic and very thoughtful man – I am lucky to have him, and even luckier that I can mock him in this book (his 'right of reply' is at the back of this book so you get to hear his point of view on all this).

Jesse is also a great cook – he really does take pride in doing it, and when he offers to cook dinner for us I am very grateful. However, when he cooks, I know I should settle in for the night and probably have a snack before dinner is ready.

When Jesse cooks a meal that really shouldn't take longer than, say, 35 minutes to cook, it takes him two to three hours. And, of course, he'll use EVERY pot and pan available in the kitchen; even the utensils that we never use and are tucked away in the drawer that we never open will come out and make a special appearance: zesting a lime with a grater that I haven't seen since 2013; cutting the veg so carefully and painfully s l o w l y it's like he's actually asleep – did you see the Pixar movie *Ratatouille* when the main character Linguini is cooking whilst asleep? … Exactly like that. Once he even took a shower in the middle of chopping up the veg. Did you hear me? *He took a shower in the middle of chopping spring onions.* And don't forget Twitter scrolling too, and rifling through every herb jar we have to see what one may work, taking into account that every herb jar will be examined, smelt, and put back in the cupboard. (We have about 25 jars of herbs. Just saying.)

Yes, when Jesse cooks, we usually end up eating around 10 p.m. – which is why I prefer to cook. We'll eat at a reasonable time – albeit not as tasty a meal, but sleep is more important than perfectly chopped spring onions and herbs.

Married sex

How often do married couples with kids have sex? I've noticed the more kids we have, the less sex we have. We're just too damn tired. Throw in those pesky hormonal changes that give my husband whiplash, a dash of peri-menopause, and it's almost impossible for your sex life *not* to be affected. Now that our eldest is ten he doesn't really go to bed until 9 or 10 p.m. He'll come out of his room every now and then to ask some rhetorical question, mention he is hungry, ask for water, tell a joke (he wants to be a comedian), want to do his homework and, my all-time favourite: 'Mum, can I tell you something? Can I tell you something? Can I tell you something?'

Yes, just tell me! You don't need to ask to tell me – just tell me!

In a slight mixing of events, I used to hide having sex from my mum when I was younger, and now I'm hiding it from my kids … Foreplay is very different now, too. Before kids it was very much a sexual thing: a prolonged snogging session, a hand in the right place, and so forth. Now I get turned on by Jesse hanging up the laundry without being asked, or washing the kids' hair without wanting a medal or acknowledgments of him doing all the chores I do on a daily basis. Listen up, dads! If you want to get laid more, do more selfless good deeds around the house and with the kids, and tell us mums we're doing a great job and that you think we are amazing. To me THIS is the best foreplay. And please, *please* don't think that a cuddle at night means we want sex. We may just actually want a hug after the shit-storm of a day we've had. According to an online survey (my Instagram stories asking my followers), the average married couple with small children have sex once every three months.

To all the women out there who have lost their libido after having kids – IT'S NORMAL!

The truth is, I think there should be more conversations on sex after kids – not just between women, but between partners. Let's all open up and be honest and see if this takes the pressure off. We had sex for the first time after I'd given birth vaginally, when Basil was four weeks old. It was Jesse's birthday and being knee-deep in becoming a mother for the first time, I'd forgotten to get him a present. So, sex was his gift. And I gotta say he was very grateful. However, looking back, I didn't do it for me – I did it for him. My vagina felt different and I was still in pain from the birth, but a part of me wanted to feel like my usual self. Jesse had a great time and he was very understanding and caring and, bless him, said my vagina felt exactly the same.

To me, if felt like a sausage had been thrown into a cave. (Sorry.)

Luckily, vaginas and libidos bounce back and sex, although it can seem like another chore to tick off, can actually be amazing and just what you need. For those who need to hear it, here are some great benefits of having sex:

- Lower blood pressure
- Better immune system
- Better heart health, possibly including lower risk for heart disease
- Improved self-esteem

- Decreased depression and anxiety
- Increased libido
- Immediate, natural pain relief
- Better sleep (er, hullo!)
- Increased intimacy and closeness to sexual partner
- Overall stress reduction, both physiologically and emotional

Or … we can always just masturbate?

Don't try this at home

I have a different relationship with my vagina now. And this is totally my fault (I probably need therapy to help get over it). What I am about to tell you is my most embarrassing moment EVER – so please don't tell anyone, and I highly recommend you do not try this at home …

I had JUST given birth to my first child, Basil – he was lying on my chest in the birthing pool in my living room. Euphoria. A moment I'll never forget. We were still attached by the umbilical cord, but for some reason I thought this was a good time to have a feel of my vagina to see how it was after pushing a 9lb baby out.

Well, it wasn't pleasant – not going to sugar-coat it. She wasn't what I remembered, but why would she be? I'd just pushed something that felt like the size of a football out of her.

Two days later I decided to have another go – I wanted to see my new vagina and get to know her. Nervously, I had a feel but I couldn't quite visualise her, so I had the brilliant idea of taking a selfie of my battered and bruised vagina. A vag-ie, if you will. That way I could zoom in on her and really check her out.

As I studied the photo – a look of shock, no doubt, on my face – I heard Basil cry. He needed a feed.

Long story short, I ended up sitting on my phone whilst feeding and somehow, SOMEHOW, I managed to upload my vag-ie to Facebook.

ABSOLUTELY MORTIFIED.

I don't know if it was the wrong time to post (it was 10 a.m. on a Wednesday in May) or because it was so awful, but nobody liked it or commented on it. And it was up there for a good 2 minutes.

This still haunts me, by the way … I am so embarrassed, and if anyone saw it I apologise unreservedly. Thank you for being discreet, or perhaps you thought I took a photo of a bacon kebab …

So, to recap, please do not make the same mistake I made – I'll take this one for the team. And ten years on from this vag-ie and two more kids later, I can safely say I will not be taking any more photos of my vagina. Lesson learnt.

March

Mother's Day

March is the month where we celebrate my favourite event of the year – Mother's Day. It's a day that should be celebrated more than just once a year, so let's try and lap it up as much as we can when it happens. It's all about us!

Mother's Day for me and my family always used to be an excuse to have a boozy lunch with my mum, sister Bonnie and brother George before we were parents ourselves and didn't quite appreciate how difficult parenting can be. Now that I'm a mother I know this day is IMPORTANT and us mothers really want to use it as a day off. Because we *never* have a day off. And we need a day of rest; a day where we can have a lie-in without any small people interrupting or asking for a snack. A day of not having to wipe bottoms. Perhaps a day where we can go to the loo alone and apply make-up without a toddler grabbing our face cream and wiping it all over the mirror, or putting mascara all over their face and ruining the mascara wand by doing so. Drinking (and finishing) a cup of tea that is still warm, having a Zoom call without a little hand poking the screen face and leaving residues of God-knows-what on it. Eating a meal without someone on my lap taking the food out of my mouth, sitting down and watching the TV without having to negotiate why they have to go to bed ... the list really is endless.

We *deserve* this one day. And we're not asking for much. Just general basic stuff. Stuff that my husband gets to do almost every day. Stuff that *I* used to do every day. And when we do get to do these very basic things we start to feel like ourselves again. It's the little things …

It was Mother's Day. I woke up to a cup of tea handed to me by Jesse, which was a novelty. (A novel-tea, if you will.) I eased back down under the duvet rotating my shoulders one at a time like a sexy tango dancer (if only), cradling my cuppa and taking in every moment of this luxury.

Jesse then produced a beautiful bunch of flowers for me.

Wow, he really is pulling out all the stops! He does *understand how important this day is!*

I settled down to my book, which had been patiently sitting on my bedside table for the past four months, ready to be picked up. *Today is the day!*

Jesse came into the bedroom again and passed the bed, from where I was looking at him longingly. He glanced at me with a loving look, and then showed me what he had behind his back.

A loo roll.

He was heading directly towards the ensuite bathroom. And, just like that, my lie-in was over.

My love turned to loathing – and he knew it too, as he said, 'Don't worry, it will be a turbo poo,' knowing full well that even a 'turbo poo' is still longer than I have ever spent on that loo.

Off he went, and with the closing of the bathroom door, I heard the pitter-patter of tiny feet running straight towards my bedroom.

Three children army-rolled onto my bed, crashing into me, spilling my tea so that it went all over my white bed sheets, talking at me at a pace that made my head spin. My toddler was obsessed with my breasts at the time so I felt like I was getting manhandled, whilst my eldest son slyly took my phone to watch YouTube shorts. My middle child decided to hide under my bed covers but emerged saying, 'Uggghhh, Mum, that's disgusting,' when he spied my overgrown bush.

A day at the spa would have been a good idea.

I tried to make light of the situation and mentally pressed the 'reset' button (a button that has been pressed so many times I often think at some point there may be a malfunction) and got all the kids in bed with me under the covers. I put *Tom and Jerry* on the TV.

There is something about watching old cartoons with my kids that makes me really happy – I guess it's the fusion of my childhood and my kids' childhood. There is magic in this.

Jesse's turbo poo, as predicted, went on a lot longer than it should have done – within this time we managed to watch a whole *Tom and Jerry* episode plus all the faff beforehand, so a good 20 minutes of what should have been my lie-in and time to myself. He finally came out of the bathroom and saw me and the kids all snuggled up together. And it was cute – it really was … (for now – I knew I was on borrowed time). And then, just when I thought Jesse would also shuffle into bed with us, he announced that he was off to the tip.

The 'tip', as any mum knows, is code for a good two hours out of the house, where your partner does actually go to the tip – but the one furthest away from the house, so said partner can also grab some lunch and do some clothes shopping.

Jesse does at least bring back stuff for the kids, which is a very good tactic for redemption when I mention his leisurely 'holiday tip' trips.

But he reassured me: 'That tip is closed today so I'll go to the local one.'

Eureka!

Perfect, I thought, as the front door slammed. He'd be back in about 30 minutes, tops. Then I could get some quality time to myself and really enjoy Mother's Day. Perhaps I *would* go and get that wax that I really needed, according to my son – or maybe I'd go to the gym ... or perhaps ...

My phone bleeped.

It was Jesse. 'Do you want a croissant and coffee?'

Ahh, how lovely.

'Yes, please, thanks. See you shortly.'

'Cool. The local shop is closed so I'm off to the other one.'

FFS.

The 'other one' meant the coffee shop that was five miles away, so he'd be at least another 25 minutes getting the pissing croissant and coffee that, to be honest, I didn't really want.

The frustration started as I wondered how this Sunday morning was any different from the all the others. How was I still the one holding the fort with the kids? This was meant to be a day of rest for me!

Some 20 minutes passed and I got another message from Jesse: 'I've booked us the pub for lunch.'

Oh, how nice! I smiled to myself, erasing all the cursing I had done in my head towards my husband.

At the pub, I tried my hardest to make fun conversation and be creative with the kids and stay off iPads, which backfired on me as I was roped into being the model of a self-portrait that my eldest wanted to draw and where I wasn't allowed to move a muscle. Not an inch. This meant not moving my head to talk to Jesse or the waiter and I was certainly not permitted to take a sip of a well-deserved glass of wine. This carried on for a good 15 minutes as I tried to engage and encourage Basil with his artistic eye, until I realised I was basically being held hostage at my own Mother's Day lunch. I told Basil his time was up just as he finished his 'masterpiece.'

I took a look and saw that he had drawn me as a rhino.

It wasn't what I was expecting at all. I had even graced Basil with my best profile modelling poses, for crying out loud!

'Do you think my spirit animal is a rhino, Basil?' I sounded half-encouraging and half-concerned.

'Yes, because you have a really nice horn and you charge around the house.'

OK, I was intrigued. 'Where are my horns?' Did he think I was the devil as well as a rhino?

Me getting angry with Jesse, by Sonny.

'There, Mummy.' He pointed to a pair of earrings I was wearing that have a horn-shaped stone hanging from them. I wear them almost every day and I love them. I had no idea my son had picked up so much on them – and let his imagination turn me into a rhino.

Before I was a mother, celebrating Mother's Day was very easy: I'd go to Mum's and hang out all day. Once we went to a restaurant in East Sheen (where I grew up) for lunch, and ended up staying there through to dinner too. It was one of the best Mother's Days I can remember, and Mum absolutely loved that all her children were there under one roof drinking wine with her. I used to live in New York, my sister was in Sydney and George was basically 'Where's Wally?' – no one ever knew where he was – but this one day we were all together, and it was pure magic. We still talk about it fondly.

Mother's Day is now shared between me, my mum and my mother-in-law. One year my mother-in-law arrived at ours for a Mother's Day lunch. I handed her a card and a gift and told her how much I appreciated her, and wished her a 'Happy Mother-in-law's Day'. I was waiting for this to be reciprocated but – nothing. An hour later and Jesse raised his glass and made a toast to mothers, which obviously triggered her memory that I too was a mother: 'Oh my gosh, of course, you're a mother too … I forgot! Happy Mother's Day.'

Forgot? Really? REALLY? I had one child feeding from my nipple and another child wanting me to help him cut up his food that he wouldn't eat and would probably push across the table in disgust.

But, sure, it's easy to forget.

My day was made when my toddler said he needed to go to the loo.

Going to a public loo with a toddler

Changing your toddler's nappy in the loo of a pub or restaurant is quite possibly one of the most stressful tasks we can do as parents – particularly when you also need the loo.

Just as you have finished changing a nappy – after you have brilliantly juggled the equipment needed around your squirming toddler, all the while ignoring the thought that perhaps the baby changing table hasn't been wiped down for the last six months, and your child is back on their feet with a clean and dry bottom – you notice the loo next to you. This is the signal for your bladder to open its gates and demonstrate how weak your pelvic floor is. So you take this opportunity, in a nice, large-sized cubicle, to take a quick wee.

The one time I did this I realised, within 10 seconds, that trying to wee with my mischievous toddler there was an error. For starters, she wanted to watch me peeing, pulling at my knickers that were wrapped around my knees, and peeking into the bowl when I was in full stream. Luckily, I caught her little hands before they went too deeply into the toilet bowl, restraining her from grabbing my pubic hair.

'Why don't you go and wash your hands?'

Inca noticed the smaller and lower-than-usual sink and was enticed by it immediately. I was thankful to be left alone to pee in peace until, of course, the sink became the next obstacle to conquer. Inca had managed to turn the tap on at full flow: placing her hand underneath not only drenched her clothes but mine too. This turned into a mini meltdown as she realised she was neither dry nor comfortable. I advised coming over for a cuddle and we hugged it out whilst I was still on the loo with a cheeky number two on the way. (I hadn't been expecting that, and it was somewhat inconvenient timing.)

Once again I thought I was being helpful and distracting her by telling her to dry herself with the hand dryer.

Some of these machines are like a fast and furious leaf blower in your toddler's face: their cheeks ripple and change shape due to the force of the recycled air that is coming out of the dryer, and the loud noise scares the shit out of them. I forgot this …

Once again I was trying to defuse a meltdown situation, stationary on the loo, clutching my knickers like a security blanket. 'It's OK, darling. Come here, it's OK.' I beckoned Inca over to me with open arms, and felt my knickers falling to the floor.

We hugged it out as she sat on my lap and I could see that she was distracted by the loo roll. 'Do you want to help Mummy with the loo roll?' I sounded way too happy and positive considering what the last 25 seconds had put me through but Inca nodded and I let her be in charge of getting Mummy her loo roll.

Cue the Andrex puppy skills of unrolling the paper.

Who knew toddlers could unravel loo roll so quickly? There wasn't any left for me. I was fishing around on the floor with my hands, bent over, trying to find a few squares that weren't submerged in the water on the floor thanks to the previous sink episode.

For crying out loud, what else?

Well, I'll tell you what else … whilst I was bending over trying to gather some clean loo roll together, Inca spotted my most hated household item ever: the toilet brush.

Is it just me, or will the toilet brush one day be in museums in a glass case within an exhibition called 'The Disgusting Years'? In this day and age of technology, why are we expected to use a large brush with random bits of poo on it, that is kept in a vase next to the loo, there for anyone to pick up? And when I say anyone, I mean toddlers who, as we know, will touch anything ALL THE TIME.

So, as I was crouching over, my attention diverted momentarily in the Great Dry Loo Roll Treasure Hunt, I was abruptly
bought back to Planet Toddler with a hit on the head by the vile
PUBLIC-toilet loo brush.

This was quickly followed by Inca tugging on the emergency
red string.

*THAT IS IT! I AM OVER THIS SHIT! (AND POSSIBLY
COVERED IN IT.)*

'Go and stand by the door and STOP touching everything!'

Inca skulked over to the door and I took a moment to
compose myself as I noticed a button near the emergency string
that said 'Reset'. I nodded at this button with agreement.

I will reset. Whilst nodding at the reset button, Inca had
tugged many times on the red emergency cord and I realised it
was now definitely time to reset. However, I forgot to actually
press it and was hailed by a very polite voice from the other side
of the toilet door: 'Is everything OK in there?'

'Yes, thank you,' I replied, sounding chirper than I thought I
would.

'Mummy did a poo!' shouted Inca.

I didn't even care by this point. All decorum and dignity had
been lost in the last minute. I had been defeated by a toddler in
the loo.

And, just when I thought it couldn't get any worse, Inca
started to unlock the door; the door that was too far away from
me to reach across and stop her.

It was happening – the door was halfway open …

'Inca – please do not open that door. Darling, do not open
that door! Inca! Stop now before Mummy gets cross!'

She didn't give a fuck. The door was flung open and exposed
a wet, dishevelled version of myself to another mother, who
was waiting in line with her small baby to change a nappy.

I could tell by the look on her face that she was a first-time mum; and I didn't have the heart to tell her she had this all to come. Who was I to spoil the surprise? Also, I was pretty sure she'd think her child would never do something like this.

'What took you so long?' asked Jesse, who was comfortably sitting back in his chair at the table, his eyes on his iPhone. He looked up and saw how utterly exasperated I looked, carrying Inca on my hip, who was smiling like she had won the battle. And she had. She very much had.

Anyway, back to my relaxing Mother's Day.

I decided to take matters into my own hands and try to own the day; take back control of MY day.

When we were home, I asked Jesse if he had done the certain things around the house that he had promised to do with the kids, to make sure I could enjoy my day. I was met with the response: 'I haven't got around to it yet.'

How many times have you asked if someone has done something, and they've automatically replied with the very common expression: 'I haven't got around to it yet.'

Loads, right? It's a sentence used by too many, too often, and on a daily basis – whether it's my husband, my kids, the man at the post office, the lady I'm eavesdropping on the bus … and even myself. Apparently we're all stopping ourselves from getting stuff done – because we haven't got *around to it* yet.

A / round / tuit.

It could be as simple as reading a magazine, applying for that new job, joining the gym, getting your hair done, or going on a date night with your other half … we're all waiting for *something* that will make us pull our finger out.

But wouldn't it be nice for people to actually act on something, for once?

So, I've decided to have a little fun with this familiar declaration that I hear too frequently.

Drum roll …

As it's March, and it's Mother's Day, I present you with your very own round 'Tuit' to help you concentrate the mind: that 'someday' is TODAY.

Instructions:

1. Cut around the dotted line.
2. Keep it nearby (on a fridge door, a mirror or in your bag, for example).
3. Smugly hand your round Tuit to anyone the next time they use the excuse, 'I haven't got around to it yet.'
4. Skip away whistling.
5. Watch them get shit done.
6. This is your very own 'round Tuit' – look after it, as they are hard to come by. But now all those things that need to be done will surely be accomplished!

World Book Day

Ah, World Book Day – the time of year when children pretend to love books, dress up as their favourite literary characters for one day, then go back to their tablets and video games straight afterwards.

It's a joy to behold as they trudge into school in ill-fitting costumes, dressed as that wizard or princess, desperately trying to remember the book they're supposed to be representing. And let's not forget the mandatory book token, which inevitably ends up crumpled and forgotten in a school bag somewhere.

And let's be real, sometimes the execution doesn't live up to the vision. The parent spends hours crafting, and yet the crown concocted with printer paper and glitter still looks as basic as you like, and the wand still looks suspiciously like a twig, and you're left wondering why you didn't just go down the Amazon route. Then there's the awkward moment when they bump into someone else dressed as the same character. It's a real-life game of 'Who Wore it Better?'

Add a pre-teen to the equation, who absolutely despises dressing up, and it's a whole new drama. Basil would rather eat broccoli for dessert than dress up as a character from a book. I have tried everything from bribery with snacks to threats of taking away screen time, but nothing will convince him. He wore his normal clothes this year and told his teacher that he couldn't dress up because his book character was 'invisible' – actually pretty clever.

Yes, World Book Day is a wonderful opportunity for children to show off their literary knowledge – or lack thereof. However, as dull as reading books about Biff, Chip and Kipper is, the best books do have the power to transport you to incredible worlds. I also wonder if you have now been transported to a place of anxiety just by reading about World Book Day. Apologies if this is the case.

April

Easter eggs

For me, the Easter holidays always feel like the longest time off school. It's two and a half weeks off, plus it's basically Christmas again if you plan on hosting Easter Sunday, which we do. Cue fast and furious dashes to the supermarket, and don't forget to buy your Easter eggs in time.

Easter 2021 and I thought it would be safe to buy Easter eggs and all the Easter bunny paraphernalia on Easter Saturday.

I was horribly wrong.

NOT. ONE. SODDING. EASTER. EGG. Not even an Easter basket. Nothing. Seriously, not one.

I went to Waitrose, ASDA, Sainsbury's, LIDL – I even went to the sodding garden store, the local newsagent ... NOTHING. Not even a Cadbury's Creme Egg.

Panic set in as I tried to figure out what I was going to tell the kids about why the Easter bunny hadn't come this year.

I've never really understood how Easter is a celebration of Jesus resurrecting from the grave, yet we celebrate with a bunny and chocolate eggs. Rabbits don't lay eggs. And the kids don't question it (probably because it involves a sugar rush).

I thought about dressing as a bunny and explaining inflation, obesity and tooth decay, instead giving them carrots and explaining how cool they are because they help you see in the dark and we could all train to be ninjas or burglars.

I played this out in my head – and saw it all going horribly wrong. (Apart from which, the only bunny outfit I own is from a Playboy party in LA back in 2004. Ahhh, the memories. That was a very different Easter.)

But you see how mums negotiate almost anything to make any justifications sound like they're as much fun as they can possibly be.

I remember my mum doing this when I was a child. I had no idea of her struggles as a single mother to three children under the age of six as she never, ever showed us her worries. She was like a swan: full of beauty and poise on the surface, gracefully gliding through rough waters, whilst under the surface she was furiously paddling away.

I didn't realise we grew up with very little money as she never made it an issue. When other friends of ours were away on Easter holidays, Mum would drive around in the car and ask us, the small children, to direct her where to go. No sat nav. No phones. No seatbelts! And we'd just get lost ... Mum would make it fun, making it a huge adventure. And we loved it! Whilst driving, Mum would hum a music note and the four of us (brother, Mum, sister and me) would have to harmonise, so we'd end up driving to God knows where in four-part harmony. We'd pull up at traffic lights with the windows down, sounding like a bad barbershop quartet, and I remember getting odd looks from the cars next to us. Mum would fall about with laugher ... and, as we know, laughter is the best medicine.

Mum always sings in the car – not just sings but harmonises, and now I find that I do this too, even when my kids tell me to stop because I am ruining the song. (Thanks, guys.) In the seventies, Mum was a singer and even made it to number six on *Top Of The Pops*. We found her on YouTube singing with her partner, Philip (they were actually in love) looking really stoned

– AND, my gosh, I can see my eldest son Basil in her. If you YouTube 'Two Sleepy People' by Philip and Vanessa you'll find her.

Little did we know at the time, but all the driving around and singing was her form of self-care: getting out of the house, with a change of scenery and the kids all contained was a release for her.

We all have our own ways of ensuring self-care: perhaps it's a walk, finishing a cuppa, masturbation … For Mum, it was driving into the abyss, harmonising and laughing.

Easter egg hunt

It's funny how kids believe in the Easter bunny – an overgrown rabbit that can apparently talk (great work, Miriam Margolyes – the voice of Cadbury's Easter bunny in the now-classic eighties advert) and produce chocolate eggs for a living, and has enough time to deliver eggs to the gardens of millions of kids – but they won't believe that brushing their teeth will keep them from rotting, or that eating your greens is good for you.

So this particular Easter, when I had nothing to produce for the children apart from carrots and a Playboy bunny costume, I decided to call in outside help.

My sister, Bonnie, saved the day – she was joining us for Easter Sunday and is one of those organised people who thinks ahead and had bought Easter eggs weeks prior. So, thanks to her, all the kids had an Easter egg, and the Easter bunny had come, too!

Bonnie even arrived with a selection of cute pastel-coloured Easter egg baskets with flowers and little chicks on them. Easter had been saved … what on earth could go wrong?

I enthusiastically turned to my toddler: 'Shall we go on an Easter egg hunt?'

'YESSS, Mummy!'

'OK, what basket shall we use? This one?' I held up a pink Easter basket with yellow and green flowers and white ribbons.

'NOT THAT BASKET!' She was disgusted with me.

'How about this one?' I held up a brown wicker basket that was slightly bigger.

'NOT THAT BASKET!!!' I mean, how dare I try and give her a basket to find chocolate eggs in our garden that a rabbit has left us?

I offered one more basket and then questioned why I had even given her the option to choose one. (It usually worked with what clothes to wear in the morning or what cup/plate to use, but it was failing miserably with the Easter egg hunt basket.)

The basket ordeal was starting to grate on me and I found myself fighting off the urge to say: 'FUCK IT, THEN! I DON'T CARE!' But instead I contained my impatience, my frustration and sanity and waited for my toddler to let me know which basket would meet her needs to find all the sugar in the garden that would keep her up past her bedtime and potentially damage her teeth. (I mean, what are we *doing*??)

She ran out of the room and came back moments later, managing to bump into every wall in sight.

She had found a basket.

It was the laundry basket.

A massive laundry basket that was too big for her to carry, too holey for the eggs to stay in, and is a disaster in the making.

Yet I appeased her with an over-the-top, enthusiastic: 'Yes! Well done – OK, off you go!'

I turned and reached for my lukewarm coffee that was just about still drinkable and smiled to myself, knowing she'd have some fun in the garden finding the eggs that my husband had hidden earlier.

I had a good 27 seconds to myself before: 'MUMMY!!! Mummy, come here! Mummy, help meeeeeeeee!'

Still clutching my coffee and exhaling a sigh that only mentally and physically exhausted mothers will appreciate, I walked outside to help my toddler fill her oversized, gappy basket that was completely useless for the egg hunting task.

'Mummy, where are the eggs?'

'The Easter bunny has hidden them – you have to find them ...'

'Mummy, YOU FIND THEM!'

After a quick and gentle explanation from me about why she couldn't speak to Mummy like that, and a slap in the face from her, I agreed to help her find the eggs. *It won't take long, and then this ordeal can be over – and we can move on to something else that is as equally unproductive.*

I started to hunt for the eggs with my toddler by my side, creeping around. (I'm not sure why we decided to be quiet – clearly the Easter bunny had already hopped away, but it added to the excitement, I suppose.)

We were looking ...

Nothing.

Still looking ...

Zip.

Where the fuck are the eggs?

My toddler could sense I was perplexed.

I leant into the garden door and hollered to the boys who were playing upstairs: 'Boys ... boys? BOYS!'

'Yeah?'

'Did you take all the eggs from the garden?'

'No, there weren't any.'

I was *enraged*.

My husband had one job. ONE!

We couldn't put the eggs out now either, because then the kids would know it was us and not the Easter bunny.

'Jesse —?'

He was on the toilet.

I angrily whispered through the door, hoping my three kids wouldn't hear us. 'Why didn't you hide the eggs?!'

I could hear talkSPORT coming out of his phone and wondered how long he had been in there. I'd asked him to hide the eggs in the garden about 35 minutes ago, and he'd been MIA ever since.

He opened the door and I was slapped in the face by a rush of potent turd stench. I also noticed the empty loo roll standing to attention on the window sill. Oh, the indignity! (*Thomas the Tank Engine* reference – if you know, you know ...)

He looked up from his phone. 'I did!' He clearly understood what I was going to ask just by looking at my expression. 'You told me to hide them, so I did!'

He paused and I tried to form sentences in my brain, let them marinate a moment and travel out of my mouth. My brain was having a slight malfunction ...

Jesse continued: 'I wanted to make them really *look* for the eggs. What's the point of making it easy for them?'

'She's *two*!'

His phone pinged and he looked down at a WhatsApp thread called FYP (Five Year Plan) – it's a Crystal Palace football chat that pings more than a microwave meal factory.

He'd moved on from our chat but I was so intrigued/infuriated that I kept at him: 'Show me where they are.'

What had started out as an Easter egg hunt for our three children had now turned into an Easter egg investigation for myself. Off we went into the garden to find those sodding eggs. The kids may have given up and moved on to something else, but not me. I was in this now and I suddenly felt as demanding and irrational as my toddler.

'They're around here somewhere.' Jesse pointed to a mound of earth where we planned to plant tomatoes. He prodded his finger in the earth and it cascaded down like a brown avalanche. 'It's in the saaaand!' he said, pointing at a pile of earth with a comical look on his face, mimicking the kid in the AA advert when he loses his dad's keys on the beach.

I stuck my hand in, rummaged around and finally found a single egg. Eureka.

'Don't you think this is a bit difficult and messy for them to find, babe? I thought perhaps leave a trail for them in the garden, making it easy to find? Like a normal Easter bunny? Like a normal person?'

You know that scene in *A League of Their Own* when Tom Hanks plays the coach and he's trying with all his might not to get angry at one of this team players and really has to hold his tongue, which makes his body shake?

Yeah, that was me.

What I've learnt as a parent is to try and make activities like finding eggs in your garden with sugar-hunting kids as simple, stress-free and mess-free as possible. This will reduce the chance of a meltdown by either you or your toddler considerably. Whereas my husband's ability to hide Easter eggs had caused a meltdown for my toddler, for me, and confirmed for my eldest two sons that they were correct and that the Easter bunny did not exist.

OVER IT!

I asked Jesse to dig out all the eggs and make it easier on us all, but naturally he couldn't find them.

It's been two years. There are still rotten eggs somewhere in the garden that we cannot find, but I have all faith that my kids will find them someday and eat them regardless of finding them in soil, mouldy or muddy – if they see a sparkly wrapper and sense it's sugar, they will eat it.

It's a bit like cooking them a meal that they've enjoyed over and over again for years that one day they decide they don't like, and refuse point-blank to eat it. But find a sweet down the back of the sofa covered in fluff and stuck to a piece of Lego and this, THIS, they allow into their mouths.

Bubble wands

After the Easter egg hunt disaster, I decided to get out some bubbles.

Kids love bubbles. You can't go wrong with them. Or so you think …

It started out beautifully. I blew some bubbles, and the roles were reversed as *I* was the one saying: 'Darling, watch … watch … darling, WATCH!'

The toddler looked up and was immediately interested in the spherical floating soap that was dancing before her eyes. She playfully and joyfully tried to pop all the bubbles and laughed when they burst on her nose. It left a slightly foamy residue – and it didn't bother her. Hurrah! This was a beautiful moment between mother and daughter and all was well in the world of parenting.

Maybe parenting isn't so hard, after all?

'More, Mummy. More!'

The bubble police were on duty and I was very much standing to attention. We got carried away with how big we could make the bubbles, which excited my daughter immensely.

And then the wind changed. Both the bubbles and the toddler's behaviour took a turn for the worse, and I was very quickly fired from my bubble-blowing duties, to be succeeded by my toddler.

She was delighted to hold the bubbles bottle in her hand, and dip in the circular wand ready to blow and make her own.

Watching toddles blow bubbles (or candles, for that matter) is always good entertainment – because they're not actually blowing. As hard as they try to blow, they are just blowing a raspberry through their teeth and it doesn't quite do the job: bubbles are not born from the wand, and candles are never blown out.

But she tries: 'Mummy, watch … watch! Watch!'

'Mummy …'

'Mummy!'

'Mummy, watch, watch, watch!'

Thbbftttt. (She blows.)

Thbbtfft. 'Mummy, watch!' *Thbbtfft.*

It continued, and I let it because I found it super cute. In the meantime, however, as she was focusing on her blowing attempt, she was also spilling the entire bottle of bubble solution onto the grass and all over her feet.

'Darling, hold it upright before it all spills.'

I reached out to help her but she moved away from me, pulling the bottle closer to her body, which inevitably spilled more bubble solution on herself.

'No, Mummy! I do it!'

'Yes, but just hold the bottle —'

'No, Mummy! MINES bubbles!'

'Yes, but hold it —'

'MINES BUBBLES!!'

'OK, fine.'

Reluctantly I backed off, knowing exactly where this was going. My internal clock started to count down from 10 to 0 knowing that in ten seconds I would be summoned to make more bubbles, but this time without any solution.

The toddler continued to spill the bubble solution and blow teeth raspberries in perfect unison, without any luck in actually producing one bubble.

She persevered a little longer then decided to put the soapy bubble wand in her mouth. Because this totally makes sense, right? *Can't blow a bubble – I will taste it and see what the problem is.*

And now we had a huge problem on our hands. Not only had my toddler eaten soap – which she was trying to take off her tongue by spitting into her little hands – but she had also managed to spill the entire bottle of would-be bubbles on her socks, which were now soaking.

This had turned into a positively ghastly situation.

And here it comes, in 3 … 2 … 1 –

'MUMMY! FIX IT! I WANT MORE BUBBLES!' she cried, pulling at her tongue and still spitting out the soap, which was now landing on me too.

I explained that all the bubbles were now on the ground and that they couldn't come back – and then immediately regretted telling the truth.

We all bend the truth to our children probably more than we realise on a daily basis, but for some reason, in this particular highly stressful moment, I decided to be as honest as a judge … *Perhaps it'll help her next time to keep the bubble bottle upright.*

Wrong.

Instead, it was all *my* fault because I took the bubbles away from her – I became the bad guy.

I tried to explain and reason with her, which is never the easiest of tasks to do with a toddler.

I lost. Pathetically.

Inca raced to find Daddy, who was pruning a bush that no one ever sees at the very bottom of the garden, listening to a podcast.

* * *

I tried this once – putting in my AirPods, going out to the garden and cracking on with hanging washing on the line – but just like trying to have some 'me time' on the loo, the kids all came to find me, and asked for a snack – *even though Jesse was in the kitchen standing by the snack cupboard.*

I wonder sometimes if the same thing happens in all households – like perhaps the dads have this parenting secret that mums don't know about ... and it goes a little something like this:

'Ask Mummy' or

'Go to Mummy' or

'Mummy will do it.'

And the kids are picking up on it. The number of questions I get asked by my children on an hourly basis is overwhelming. It's ironic, actually, as I couldn't wait for my kids to start talking – I never thought I'd wish for them to shut up.

I'll never forget a particular day when I had to pick up Basil from school earlier than usual, as the school was closing early for parent–teacher evening.

'Mummy, how to you spell "Sonny"?'

'Mummy, how to you spell "Nobody loves"?'

'Mummy, why do you drive like Mr Bean?'

'Mummy, is it true Daddy has grey hair because of you?'

'Mummy ...' (Repeat on a loop.)

Later on that day, when the kids were chilling in front of the TV watching a classic Easter movie (thank you, BBC, for always providing the goods), I snuck off to make myself a cuppa. I realised it was a good time to call my father-in-law to wish him a happy Easter.

Why is it when I am on the phone, the kids will hunt me down and ask too many questions?

'Why can't I skip the TV?'

I turned my iPhone to my chest to prevent my father-in-law hearing my answers.

'Because it's not YouTube.'

And back again to the phone call.

'Mummy, what are we having for supper?'

Once again the phone was turned towards my body to muffle this second conversation I was having.

'I don't know yet but shhh! I'm on the phone.' And I shooed the kids away.

And yet they didn't shoo, and the questions kept on coming ...

'Mummy, can I have some Robux?'

Now, the amount of money I have spent on Robux to keep them quiet over the last year is insane, and they always seem to know when to ask me – when I am occupied – but this time I put my foot down.

I muted my phone call and sternly said: 'I AM ON THE PHONE! TALK TO ME WHEN I AM OFF THE PHONE,' and gave a more animated shooing, hand-swat gesture.

They retreated and headed back into the living room. But it was too silent for too long, which made me super suspicious. The most dangerous sound for a mother to hear is the sound of silence. I stood up immediately and ran towards the kids in the living room, whilst doing my best to sound 'normal' on the phone to Geoff.

The kids were actually behaving themselves. Wow. They were using my iPad to play a game, which doesn't bother me, so I got back to my cuppa and convo.

Just as I took a sip of my (just warm) tea, I felt a tap on my shoulder. I knew it was one of my children doing their best to not talk to me when I was on the phone but still needing my attention. I turned to face them and was confronted with my iPad screen in my face, followed by a 'ping' sound. I saw a tick appear on the screen.

They'd done it this time – hats off to them for being so creative, but my gosh how dared they use my face, without asking, to download a game? Face ID is a great invention until your kids figure out how to manipulate it. Grrr. That phone call cost me £5.99 – but they did repay me by doing some house chores, so all was not lost.

House chores with children

During the house chores, I like to put on music. I always find listening to music in the kitchen makes all the boring jobs like emptying bins and clearing out the fridge that little bit more exciting. I like to listen to Beyoncé or some Kisstory and dance around like a lunatic, nostalgic for my younger years where I actually went to nightclubs to dance, not gyrating against my fridge, singing into a wooden spoon.

I genuinely think my neighbours think I am bonkers.

During lockdown, almost every evening, once the kids were asleep, I would have a disco all by myself in my kitchen. I bought disco lights from Amazon, plugged in my headphones, poured myself a glass of wine and danced the night away. It was actually great therapy and a huge release ... there were some embarrassing moments, of course, like when Jesse walked into the kitchen, turned on the light and totally ruined my night during a slut drop to the kitchen tiles with a side of pelvic floor mishap. One night I had my friend Sarah over (when it was allowed), and she too joined in on my fantasy nightclub. We TOTALLY embraced it. It was great – we were even eyeing up guys in the corner of the nightclub, aka a broom in the corner of the kitchen. Sounds bonkers because it was – but when given lemons, make a gin and tonic!

Back to doing chores with the kids. I asked Alexa to 'play

some music I may like'. Straight away some shite was played that sounded like robotic techno, something that I have never played but the kids did once ... so I ordered her to 'skip'. She played some music from Erykah Badu – good choice, Alexa! I felt a sense of calm as soon as I heard the opening riff of 'On & On', and cracked on with the never-ending laundry.

We were about 30 seconds into the song when Basil piped up: 'Alexa, play "Believer" by Imagine Dragons.'

'Um, Basil I was listening to that – you have to ask me before you change the music.'

But Basil was already dancing around to the song and opening kitchen cupboard doors looking for snacks. He was happy and the song wasn't too bad so I let it go.

But then Sonny joined in: 'Alexa ... fart. Fart!'

Right on cue she farted continuously, with all sorts of fart diversity. The boys were falling about laughing and pretending they are also farting in time with Alexa's flatulence.

Oh gosh, this was somewhere between fun and hell, and I knew there would be a tipping point, when I would realise what side of the spectrum I was standing on.

In walked my toddler.

I had a feeling I knew which side of the spectrum I was about to be on.

She removed her dummy and shouted out: 'Alella, Alella, Alella, Alella!'

ON LOOP.

Of course, Alexa isn't designed to understand toddler talk so she ignored her, which infuriated Inca to the point of not giving up, and she continued to shout even louder with her mouth as close as she could get to Alexa. And still it didn't work.

By this point I had been pushed over that tipping point, spiralling into that parenting oblivion where you have to just roll with it and stay calm. I was surrounded by the chorus of my boys hysterically laughing, blowing raspberries and squatting like they were pooing on the kitchen floor, with my furious toddler daughter shouting and stamping her foot in rage.

With 'ALELLA, ALELLA, ALELLA, ALELLA!' and Alexa sounding like she'd got a case of dysentery, it could only mean one thing – bath time.

Surely this will chill them out?

Why am I always so naive? I should know better by now – bath time can be a *torturous* event: the arguments to actually convince them they ARE having a bath and to GET IN the bath, followed by my eldest son being cross at me for having the audacity to clean his face – and don't get me started on washing hair ... Anyone listening from outside the bathroom door would think I was doing something unspeakable to my children, when all I am doing is softly massaging their heads and lathering up shampoo. I try to make it fun by making their hair stand up like a punk rocker. This always works a treat and for a moment there is calm. Then there are more arguments about getting them out of the bath, and by the time they are out, I am as wet as they are and mentally scarred by yet another bath time fulfilled.

Dare I mention it? DINNER TIME! We all know *that* is never easy!

May

It's May – one of my favourite months of the year. The month I had my last first kiss, the month I got engaged, married and became a mother. Also the weather takes a nice turn and we smell sweet summer in the air.

There is also another half-term in May (of course there is). Just to mention it, but did you know that out of the 365 days of the year, children are only in school for 195 days? This means that 53 per cent of the time the kids are off school. Working and mothering is indeed a juggle.

However, there is something about the May half-term that I absolutely love; especially if you're planning on going away for some sunshine, as this is the half-term to do it. It's cheaper, not as busy and not as hot – the perfect combination for a family holiday.

Travelling with family

The May half-term is also the time that Jesse and I get to celebrate our wedding anniversary. Jesse was very smart to make sure he proposed on the same day as our first date – and also get married on the same day (years later), as in his eyes it's a lot easier (and cheaper) to remember one anniversary date. Good husband hack!

For two years in a row, we decided to take my mother and my mother-in-law away with us to hang out with their grandchildren and also to babysit for us when we wanted to go out for the evening. Great plan, don't you think?

I've learnt, however, that including your mothers on a family holiday away doesn't mean you always have extra help, but you do have two extra children to look after instead. You realise this pretty much as soon as you meet them at the airport.

Flustered and flummoxed, both the grandmothers fumbled for all the printed-out emails and documents (that they didn't need) in their over-sized bucket bags, in which they couldn't find anything. Jesse and I stood watching them as we heard: 'Tut! Agh!' on repeat as they dug further and further into their bottomless Mary-Poppins bags, pulling out their boarding passes before we even walked to the check-in desk.

'Ah-ha! I knew I had it here!'

Jesse causally got his phone out and explained that all the boarding passes were already safely on his phone and there was no need for paperwork.

Both grandmothers took the phone in turn, adjusting it to their faces by moving it closer or further away, all the better to focus on it.

This took much longer than it needed to, but still we waited patiently.

'Well, blow me,' said my mother, who was clearly impressed by all this new technology. 'Are you sure this is all we need?'

'Yes, Mum.'

'Blow me.'

'Mum, um, you can't really say that anymore … it sounds a bit rude.'

Jesse put his phone in his back pocket, pressing his lips together trying not to laugh, and was delighted that one of the kids needed attention at that particular moment.

'Why does it sound rude?'

I looked at her in the hope that she might understand where I was coming from but we just ended up looking at each other, trying to read each other's minds for much longer than I wanted this to happen.

'Mummy, watch! Watch ...'

'Mummy, watch ...'

Oh, thank God.

I'd never turned to watch my kid so quicky – and this is another wonderful thing about kids: you can always use them as an excuse to get out of certain situations. Like using your kid's high temperature to get out of a night out, or reacting to your kid's attempt to do a cartwheel at an airport to get out of a conversation with your mum about blowing people.

'I need a cashpoint,' my mother-in-law said.

'Yes, so do I,' my mother concurred.

And, just like a scene from a *Carry On* movie, they tried to work out where a cashpoint would be. There was lots of squinting, pointing and turning, and discussions about locating the cashpoint and not much else, whilst we were still trying to get rid of the bags and handle the kids, who were trying to scoot off on their Trunkies.

'Why do you need cash? I asked.

'Because we're at an airport and we'll need cash, Louise, to pay for things! Goodness!'

Deep breath.

'You can use your bank cards. Or your phone —?'

I had installed my mum's bank card on Apple Pay the week before the holiday for this exact reason. Keeping life as easy as possible. Especially when travelling with children and grandparents.

'I'd rather cash – you know, just in case?'

'In case of what?'

'Well, I don't know … what if you lose your bag and you need cash for a taxi?'

'If you lose your bag surely the cash would be inside the bag?'

'Or what if you need cash on the plane or when you get to the other side and need a taxi?'

'The majority of places don't take cash anymore, Mum, and we've already hired a car from the airport for when we arrive.'

By now, my youngest son was using my leg as a climbing frame, bored with me trying to explain to my mum that there was no need to try and find a cashpoint. My mother-in-law had already walked off to find one, so I asked my eldest son to run after her to get her back.

As I said – it was like having two more children.

We arrived in Italy and headed to the hire car depot. I'd hired a car large enough to fit us all in. The boys briefly argued about where they would sit but agreed to them both sitting at the back, which made most sense so the grandmothers could sit in the middle with Inca who was being pleasantly normal – for now.

The boys excitedly scrambled into the back, then asked for a snack just as I was packing the boot with the suitcases.

Always a snack at the most inconvenient times.

The grandmothers manoeuvred into the car accompanied by a harmony of 'Ooohff' – over-exaggeratedly heavy sighs, and a couple of farts that they chose to ignore completely.

'THAT'S DISGUSTING!' The boys fell about in fits of laughter.

Jesse and I closed all the doors – them inside, us outside – and enjoyed the full 30 seconds of all children and grandparents being contained and quiet in one place. These few joyous seconds felt like a very quick mini festival as we walked from the side of the car to the front of the car, ready for our holiday and what was to come next.

In the car, I asked my boys if they had their seatbelts on. They did, and I congratulated them both. I then asked the same question of the grandmothers, who only then began fumbling around, trying to connect their seatbelts. My mother couldn't find the plug and my mother-in-law couldn't reach the seatbelt at all. Eyes front, Jesse and I listened to the commotion happening behind us. More tuts, heavy sighs and farts echoed around the car as my mum and mother-in-law raced each other to get their seatbelt on. The car was actually wobbling from side to side and I was pretty sure people walking past would be thinking that something more exciting than seatbelt planting was going on inside.

'That's not my seatbelt ... Oh no, hang on ... is this it? No, wait ... blow me, where is it?' (My mum was back on about people blowing her.)

'Mine isn't working,' said my mother-in-law, who was tugging too hard on the belt, making it stop suddenly in its tracks – so, yes, it was very much working.

A good three minutes passed and I decided it was time to step in to help. Jesse was finding the route to our rented accommodation on Google Maps, doing his very best to block out the palaver behind him.

Once I was involved, they were both plugged in within 30 seconds and both told me they didn't need my help.

For the record, for the entire ten-day holiday, the same conversations and commotion happened, with the seatbelt faff and Jesse and I always ending up plugging my mum and mother-in-law into the car.

Every time.

We arrived at our rental accommodation, which we had found on Airbnb. It was pouring down with rain but, regardless, we settled in – the kids happily playing on their iPads, overjoyed there was Wi-Fi at our rented house, and I opened a bottle of red wine to toast the arrival of our holiday.

Our bottoms had just touched down on the oversized cloud-shaped white leather sofa when mum opened a debate about politics.

Now, I have only one rule when my mother and mother-in-law get together, which I always remind my mum and Jesse of before any family occasion.

Do not talk about politics.

My mum and Jesse's mum have totally opposing views when it comes to politics, and are both at the age when they're very opinionated (a bit like a toddler), and neither of them will 'agree to disagree' (very much like a toddler).

My immediate thoughts: *For fuck's sake.*

WHY?

I can't even …

Give me more wine.

Jesse closed his eyes and kept them closed, as if he had suddenly fallen asleep. When he opened them again, he was looking directly at me and I knew exactly what he was thinking.

I needed to put a stop to it before it got even deeper. I would have done anything for one of my kids to suddenly appear and ask me to watch them do something, or ask me for a snack, but naturally they were happy and content with what they were doing and even when I called their names to 'come here' they ignored me.

Instead, I thought this would be a good time to tell everyone I'd been asked to write a book.

'A book?' echoed my mum.

'Yes – with HarperCollins! They've asked me to write one.'

'Well, what's it about?'

'Motherhood – but writing about it in a funny, uplifting way. That we're not alone and how to make the mundane moments of motherhood seem marvellous.'

There was a slight pause and Mum looked almost disgusted. 'Well, who's going to read that?'

'Umm, I guess mothers, people. People and mothers. Carers. Maybe mothers to be?'

I'm starting to doubt myself.

'And how much is it going to be?' More awkward questions.

'Around £15 I think. It would be a nice gift, or —'

'Fifteen quid for a book on motherhood? Louise, do you understand the cost of living crisis at the moment?'

'They've asked you to write a chapter too, Mum.'

Another pause, but this time her face lit up. 'Oh, yes, I think people would love to read that. What a good idea. When shall I start writing?'

And, just like that, the conversation went from politics to politics, when I realised I hadn't asked my mother-in-law to write a chapter.

You can never please all the family all the time.

Birth

I became a mother for the first time in May. To be exact, it was 21 May 2012 at 2.18 a.m., in my living room. They say you forget your labour and that's why you have another baby but I beg to differ. I can still remember every single thing about that labour.

Jesse was at my step-dad Alex's house with my brother George, watching the Champions League final. It was between Chelsea and Bayern Munich and it had got to a penalty shoot-out. Both Alex and George are avid Chelsea supporters whereas Jesse is a Crystal Palace fan but he watched and celebrated with the boys anyway.

I was at home, a week overdue, watching the game with my mate, Jessie girl. We call her 'Jessie girl' so's not to confuse the two Jesse/Jessies in my life. Actually, my brother's wife is also called Jessie – it does get confusing:

'Jesse and I are thinking of going out Friday night – are you around to babysit at all, please?'

My mum: 'Now, which Jesse are we talking about?' *Here we go* ... 'Jessie Pickmoad or Picknose or Ingham or Ingram, or whatever is it ... you know, the lovely girl you went to school with ...?'

Yes, I know the lovely girl I went to school with – Jessie Pickwoad née Ingham – with whom I don't have children so therefore wouldn't ask you to babysit because Jesse my husband could actually do this (besides which, Jesse would 'parent' and not 'babysit').

She continues: 'Or Jessie ... you know, Jessie George – or JB, we could call her, or even JG ...'

Again, this Jessie had just given birth and really wouldn't have been looking to go out with me.

You get the drift – and yes, this happens almost every time the name 'Jesse' is mentioned around my mum.

But I digress ... It was the Champions League final and I was watching the penalty shoot-out with Jessie girl. We were totally into it – weird how penalties and a final can really get you heated up. So much so, I felt a cramp that was definitely stronger than a Braxton Hicks.

'Ooh.' I touched my tummy and Jessie girl looked at me.

'You OK?' she asked.

'Yeah.' And I was. But I was also very aware that this may be the start of something.

Knowing you're possibly in labour for the first time can be daunting, so I thought it best to call Jesse.

In the meantime, Chelsea had won the game so when I called Jesse, Alex, my (Scottish) step-dad was SO overjoyed at their win that he answered Jesse's phone and sung to me: 'Lulu Lulu

Lulu kkhlhgfhaskfdbnvalkj' (something in Scottish that I couldn't comprehend at all).

'Can I speak to Jesse, please, Alex?'

'Lulu, I love you! I'm so happy – Jesse is staying with me – he'll see you later, bye.'

And the phone went dead.

OK ...

I messaged Jesse: 'Babe, I think I'm in labour.'

He's typing ... 'But we have plans tomorrow.'

LIVID.

'OK, I'll tell my uterus to rearrange.'

LIVID.

A part of me hoped that I'd go into full-blown labour there and then and he'd come home to a baby ... but as it happened, it was very, very early labour and I decided it was best to call it a night and get some sleep.

The next morning I definitely felt like something was going to happen so decided we should take it easy at home. Jesse mentioned again that he felt bad for cancelling our plans. (LIVID.)

'It's been in the diary for ages and they haven't met you yet. Are you sure you're in labour?'

'DO YOU WANT ME TO PUT A CORK UP MY VAGINA? THIS BABY IS COMING!'

Absolutely fuming. This was NOT the mood I wanted to enter motherhood in.

As we'd planned to have a home birth, it was just the two of us in our living room getting ready to meet our baby. My contractions were four minutes apart when Jesse thought it was a good idea to 'quickly' head to Sainsbury's to get some food to keep us going in case we were up all night.

It was a good idea – our local Sainsbury's was at the end of our road so he could walk there in three minutes. I knew he'd be 15 minutes tops, and I could handle being alone for that amount of time.

ONE HOUR LATER.

My contractions were now three minutes apart, my breathing was deeper and longer, and I was worried as to what had happened to Jesse. My imagination took over and I went down a rabbit hole of thinking of the worst scenarios possible, which made me panic.

Maybe he'd been kidnapped.

Maybe he'd fallen over and was hurt?

Maybe he didn't want to be a father and had run away?

Maybe I should call him?

His phone picks up.

'Yeeeeeellllow?' Homer Simpson answered my husband's phone.

'Jesse, where *are* you?'

'I'm at Sainsbury's – at the cheese counter. I can't decide what cheese to have.'

L I V I D.

'Babe! I'm having contractions – I am in labour – I need you here!'

'Yeah, but you'll thank me for the cheese later.'

For the record, Jesse had never gone to the cheese counter before – or spent that long in Sainsbury's.

I have a theory that some men go into WTF mode when their partners are in labour. Women are *ready* to have the baby after nine months of carrying it, not being able to eat or drink certain things, not being able to sleep on our fronts, looking like a whale, feeling like a beached whale, waddling when walking, not being able to see our vaginas. After nine months of this we are DONE. GET THIS BABY OUT OF ME! I WANT MY BODY BACK! It is nature's way of getting us prepared. But men ... one day they provided sperm and then poof a baby has arrived.

Jesse came home and we did actually end up eating a cheese sandwich. I never admitted how delicious it was nor how grateful I was for it.

We had chosen to have a water birth in the living room as we both thought it would be as easy as using the hose and filling up the paddling pool. Right?

Wrong.

I was at the height of my labour, on all fours, rocking backwards and forwards 'riding that wave' of contractions, making noises that I didn't think my vocal chords could produce, wondering where Jesse was. Had he gone back to that damn cheese counter?

'JESSE, I NEED YOU!'

He came running to my side and tried to help me, but at that point in my labour, whilst I wanted him there, I didn't want him touching me or talking to me. The poor guy was so confused – I'm pretty sure he got whiplash from my Jekyll and Hyde personality.

What I didn't realise at the time was that the hose connecter to our tap didn't work, so Jesse was frantically boiling the kettle, had four saucepans on the hobs, and the microwave on to fill up the birthing pool. I didn't realise how stressful it was for him, especially as I was begging to get into the pool – and these pools are LARGE.

The midwife arrived and she started doing some hypnobirthing exercises with me, staying calm – but she could see the chaos unravelling in the living room, with Jesse, and she did a great job with not letting on that the pool may not be an option.

Somehow, Jesse managed to fill the pool in time and I slid into it with a sigh of relief. As I continued to have contractions, Jesse thought it was a good moment to tell me I was making faces like 'Tim Nice but Dim' from *Harry Enfield and Friends* when I was pushing. Thanks, babe. Nice thought to have in the height of labour, although I think that was the ammunition I needed for that final push to get Basil out.

EUPHORIA!

The midwife checked the baby and, pretty much an hour after I had given birth, she went home and left us to it.

We had absolutely no idea what we were doing. I had been so fixated on giving birth, I hadn't read the books on the part when the baby arrives.

Looking back now, giving birth was the easy part.

When Sonny was born I ended up in hospital having placenta abruption, which meant I haemorrhaged after I gave birth and ended up in intensive care, wired up to machines. I couldn't move and asked Jesse to get me some water. FORTY-FIVE minutes later he still hadn't come back and I was so out of it I actually started to convince myself that I had hallucinated Jesse there next to me. Was I high on gas and air? Anyway, Jesse eventually re-emerged – WITHOUT the water. He had been on the loo. I literally gave birth quicker than his toilet break. He did however go home, make my favourite Jamie Oliver pasta meal and set up the iPad so I could watch *X Factor* in my hospital bed. And he slept next to me in a chair in the corner of the room. All was forgiven. Giving birth to Inca was beautiful. I loved giving birth to her. I was prepared and calm and had practised a lot of hypnotherapy due to my previous traumatic birth. I had also carefully selected my favourite chill-out songs so that I could listen to them at the height of my labour.

At precisely 3 a.m. on 3 August 2019, I asked Jesse to pass my phone so I could play my playlist.

'Have you heard the latest Arctic Monkeys' album yet? You'll love it! Shall I put it on?'

Er, this isn't a road trip or a house party, babe. And, no, while I am straddling a birthing ball, rolling my hips in a figure of eight, practising my breathing work, timing the length of my contractions and staying calm and opening my cervix, the last thing I want to do it listen to Alex Turner singing 'don't sit down cause I've moved your chair'.

Birthday parties

Is it just me, or are birthday parties a really stressful and massively expensive faff? My children's parties generally end up with the birthday child in tears, my husband completely oblivious to what I've organised, and my knickers all sweaty.

Seriously though, it's like birthday parties have become the new engagement party. I've just paid £250 for 10 kids to climb a tree with a fancy (not fancy at all) certificate at the end of it that says they climbed a tree. And that's not all. We need a cake – and not just any cake. It has to be a themed cake that has absolutely nothing to do with the trees they just climbed. Yes, of course – I have tried to make my own cake many times but gave up after the time when 20 party children looked at my not-so-fabulous cake and didn't eat any of it. It got a few prods but that was it. Not one slice. (To be fair I didn't eat it either. Turns out my Eton Mess cake really does look like and taste like a mess.)

One year, we hired a room at the local leisure centre. I walked through the car park carrying all the party paraphernalia, including the helium balloons flying high and proud behind me, making sure they didn't get knocked, scraped, or popped, and carefully manoeuvred them through the fire doors and into the hall I'd hired that, moments earlier, had been a party room for another child.

There is always a kid hanger-on having a meltdown outside the room refusing to accept the party is over, even though the staff are sweeping up tissue-paper remnants from the battered piñata and throwing away triangular sandwiches.

I eavesdropped as I passed, and took note of the very patient gentle-parenting approach that was in process. The parent was demonstrating the most amazing resilience, keeping their cool with the three-year-old, who was screaming in her face. 'Darling, there just weren't enough party bags to go around, but we can go and get something special from the shop now, if you like?'

Oh, I felt for that parent. That's a hard card to be dealt at a kids' party. The room we had hired contained a huge bouncy castle, the only problem being that I had invited too many kids to actually jump on the damn thing. My daughter ended up with a cold compress on her head from a head clash and I spent a good 30 minutes of the 90-minute party filling out a health and safety/first aid form basically confirming it was all my fault and how dare I even think about having a party with this many people. Cue mum guilt.

Musical Statues is always a good shout, isn't it? Kids love this game.

I rallied all the children together and strained my voice over the RIDICULOUS amount of kid noise echoing off the non-air-conditioned hall walls. 'Who wants to play Musical Statues?'

Eyes lit up, hands shot up in the air, there was a unison of jumping and 'YEEEAAAAAAAAHHHH! MEEEEEEE!' was repeated and repeated as we waited for the music to start.

No music.

Still no music.

I looked to Jesse whose ONE job was to be in charge of the music – he's great with technology and knew how to connect his phone to the Bluetooth speakers in the party hall with ease.

'Babe?'

'Yeah?' Jesse looked up from his phone, slightly perplexed at my over-animated stance. I was ready to dance to 'I Like To Move It' surrounded by 20 children – who were all still jumping around and yelling.

I could feel sweat starting to trickle down my back. Wearing a wool jumper had been a very bad idea. 'We need music?'

'Oh, right.' Jesse very calmly addressed the situation and after an agonising two minutes of waiting for music to play – any music at all (by this point I would have danced around to the car alarm going off outside just to break the uncomfortable stance I was still in as I would not break out of 'fun parent' character) – the music started.

'I like to move it, move it! I like to move it, move it!' started to blare out of the speakers, and for some reason I ended up dancing like a knob.

Is this how 'dancing like a mum' is born? Because we only ever dance at our kids' birthday parties, and don't ever snap out of it? I was very aware I was the ONLY adult in the room dancing with such forced enthusiasm that I was actually sweating. I looked to Jesse, who was nodding his head along to the music, when it suddenly dawned on me he might not realise HE was in charge of starting and stopping the music. The song was half-way through already, and the kids' Tigger jumping was starting to lose its momentum.

I gave him *the look*.

And he was back in the room.

Another rule with Musical Statues and having to call children out of the game – don't go for the obvious, youngest child who never stands still to be out first. Chances are they will cry and you'll have to defuse the situation with a small bag of Haribo.

In the eighties, at birthday parties, I'm pretty sure we didn't get a bag of sweets when we lost – or when we unwrapped a layer of Pass the Parcel. Back in my day, if you lost or didn't win that was that. It was a good lesson in life. Now, of course, everyone wins, just to keep the peace. And in the case of Pass the Parcel, this also means there is the extra responsibility of making sure to stop the music at just the right moment, ensuring that every child has a go at opening the parcel. One year I lost track of who had ripped off a layer, resulting in a circle of kids all shouting at me and a child bursting into tears because they had been accidentally left out. The politics!

Prosecco is usually offered up at parties now, too – this is mentioned in the WhatsApp party invite as a reason (or bribe) for the parents to stay at the party instead of the dreaded 'drop off'.

I do love a drop-off party (when I'm not hosting). Invite messages look a bit like this:

Saturday May 31st 2–4pm
The Leisure Centre
Drop off optional – but there will be Prosecco!
Any allergies?

I was once invited to a party at 9 a.m. on a Sunday and Prosecco was served to all the adults, probably to make us all stay – it did the trick. Not that I wanted a drink at 9 a.m., but I could see that the Prosecco-pouring mother wanted us all to stay in the church hall and this was her way of doing it. And I'm not surprised, as she had invited the entire class of 30 children – I'm sure with huge regret.

It feels like you're packing for a small holiday when getting everything ready for a party that's not being held in your home. The party paraphernalia includes everything from balloons, Bluetooth speakers, black bin bags, birthday cake, bubbles, more bubbles, maybe the bloody bubble machine, tablecloths, party bags (these have also taken time and effort to get ready), party hats, party cups, party paper plates, sandwiches that you've cut into triangles and taken off the crusts in the hope that said cheese or ham sandwiches will look remotely edible, snacks snacks snacks and more snacks (including fruit so you look sensible to the other parents, even though you know you'll be taking home 30 satsumas and even more bananas), plastic champagne flutes, Prosecco, a cool box, lighter, knife and of course, the cake – and your children. Let's go! The handbag seems the safest place to keep a knife to cut the cake – I will never want to recreate the incident when my nephew found a knife in the party bags bag and used it as a sword during Musical Statues. Parenting fail right there. So a handbag that is zipped up and out of sight and reach of anyone is the way forward now. However, forgetting to take the knife out of your bag days after the party has finished could end badly – I once left a carving knife wrapped in a kitchen towel in my everyday mum bag, that my kids had been tugging on etc when I picked them up from the school gates. Thank *goodness* it didn't fall out of my bag in the school playground!!

Note to self: ALWAYS PACK A LIGHTER when having a party in a venue. There was an epic fail one year when Jesse and I decided it was time to sing 'Happy Birthday' to Sonny and realised no one in the building, or passing on the street outside, or ANYONE in the area, had a lighter or matches. I did consider rubbing two sticks together and making a science experiment out of the situation, but then quickly scrapped this idea and ran to the local DIY shop for matches. When I got back to the birthday party the kids were all chanting: 'We want cake! We want cake! We want cake!' I did get a round of applause from the other parents and Jesse when I arrived back with the matches, making my stress dissolve somewhat. I guess we've all been there. Right?

Jesse managed to video the bringing of the cake to the birthday boy brilliantly and I gave him a glowing look of, 'Wow, we
did it – how is our son six already?' He looked back at me and
his eyes told me he loved me.

But our fleeting moment of joy was rudely interrupted by
the sound of Sonny crying. He was not the one who blew out
the candles: his mate did it instead. FFS. I consoled Sonny and
assured him that we could redo the lighting of the candles, and
redo the singing, just so he could blow them out and make his
wish. The mother of the candles-blowing child made sure
Sonny got an apology, but Sonny was still not happy and spent
the rest of his birthday party in a sulk.

This is why there must be Prosecco.

Once the drama of actually managing to light the candles
and sing 'Happy Birthday', making sure you all sing in the same
key and get the cake to the birthday child with all the candles
still lit is over, you are winning. You have nailed it. You can
breathe and relax, knowing your excellent birthday party organ-
isational skills have passed with flying colours.

Or can you?

The party bags. A wonderful 'favour' to encourage the kids
to get the hell out of the party so you can hear the thoughts in
your own head again, and before they have their major post-
sugar-rush meltdown. But please take this bit of advice as a
warning. Make sure all the party bags are the same colour,
shape, weight and handed to any child using the same hand
each time. If these children feel any sort of discrepancy, you
will be held responsible for their tantrum on exiting the party,
even though all the kids really care about are the party-sized
Haribo bags that are inevitably amongst the carefully thought-
out contents of organic playdoh, vegan snack and biodegradable
balloons.

* * *

After a birthday party I am mentally and physically exhausted and my ears are usually ringing. But you're home with a cuppa – and just when you think you can relax and finish your tea, there are about 15 presents to rip open at lighting speed … I try to keep track of who bought what, make a note of it and then WhatsApp the birthday party group with messages of thanks. Videoing my son opening his presents for a live reaction was a lovely idea – but only if the reaction was one I could send.

Birthday party with a blast!

This story still shocks me to the core and one that I shared on my Instagram live when it happened (you can catch it on my highlighted stories under the section 'BOMB'.)

It was my son's birthday weekend and we were planning a family BBQ at our flat in Clapham. We always love to host parties, and we'd had many over the years in the garden.

This particular morning, Jesse was digging around at the back of the garden as usual when there were other, more important chores to do; however, it *was* an area that needed some attention, and Jesse had risen to the challenge with gusto. Very cleverly, he called it 'Romance Corner', saying that he was building it for us to hang out in – when I would huff and puff about him disappearing into the garden, he would pull out the 'Romance Corner' card and remind me that he was doing it for us, which would make me leave him to it and be thankful that he was building me such a masterpiece. (It's no Taj Mahal but the thought was there – or was it so he could listen to a podcast and not have to deal with the kids?)

Anyway, he was outside having some lovely alone time and I was preparing for our BBQ later, when Jesse suddenly sprinted back into the house. I'd never seen him move so quickly.

'Was it a wasp?' I asked him, feeling thankful for the small creature forcing him back into the house. I visualised giving the wasp a little fist bump.

'No, it was a grenade.'

Ummmmmmm.

Jesse had been digging around in the garden when he noticed a hand grenade roll off his shovel and land quite heavily on the ground.

'Are you sure?' I asked, even though I knew he was sure. Jesse is a very easy-going, relaxed man and this was the first time I had seen any kind of panic in his eyes.

'I'm going back to have a look,' he replied.

UMMMMMMM!

'What's happening, Mummy?' Basil asked. He was obviously acutely aware of something happening – he too had noticed his dad looking more anxious than usual, and he started to ask too many questions that I was trying to answer at the same time as persuading Jesse not to go back to the war zone, without sounding too panicked around the kids.

'I don't think you should go back.'

'I'll be fine – keep the kids away and shut the doors.'

WTAF?

Jesse managed to get a photo of the grenade and started a WhatsApp chat with his mates, who all confirmed after 25 minutes of banter that it was indeed a grenade. In the meantime I was peeling potatoes, heart thumping in my chest, trying to pretend to the kids that all was good and well.

Jesse called 999.

'Police, fire or ambulance?'

'I think I may need all three.'

'What's the situation?'

'I found a grenade in my back garden.'

Silence.

'How do you know it's a grenade?'

'Because it looks just like a grenade.'

Silence. 'I don't have any other questions to ask you …'

'Right.'

'Someone is on the way to take a look.'

'Thank you.'

It was 10 a.m. on a Saturday morning; the kids were still in their PJs and slightly on edge, as we had mentioned the police were coming over. We made it sound as fun as possible whilst inside we were freaking out – but, of course, as a parent it's best not to show your true emotions in situations such as these.

From the time it took the kids to walk from the living room to their bedrooms to get dressed, the police arrived at the front door. I quickly threw on the first dress I could find – I ended up wearing one that was impossible to breastfeed in but as the baby was asleep I didn't think much of it … *The police will be gone soon.*

A policeman and policewoman were at the door, full of smiles and with 'top of the morning to ya' kind of personas, which was appreciated, for both myself and the kids. The professionals had arrived and we were in safe hands – they could tell us it wasn't a grenade and we could go back to BBQ prepping.

'So … I hear you found a grenade,' said the policeman.

'WHAT?????' shrieked Basil.

Fucking nice one, policeman.

'Well, we're not sure, darling – we're just being safe … to find out,' I reassured him, whilst giving the policeman a look of 'Play along, dipstick!'

'But, Mummy, what about my playhouse?'

Ah, you mean the playhouse that took my father-in-law a bloody week to build when I had just given birth and had to wait on him every day until the job was done and now no one ever goes in it? *I hope it does get blown up.*

'Darling, your playhouse is absolutely fine.'

'I love it so much.'

You never, ever go in it but, yeah, sure.

'Right, so where is this "grenade"?' I noticed how the policeman raised his eyebrows and rolled his eyes as he says 'grenade'. I sensed he doubted us and thought we were wasting his time on this glorious Saturday morning.

'Right at the back of the garden,' explained Jesse. 'I was digging and it rolled off my shovel.'

The policeman gave Jesse a knowing nod, like he knew exactly what Jesse's intentions were when 'gardening': man code for 'alone time'. The policewoman and I stayed silent, and I knew she was thinking what I was thinking as she scanned the room full of laundry, toys, cereal bowls and general mess.

The policeman advised us stay inside and we watched them walk to the back of the garden.

They didn't even reach the grenade before they had seen all they needed to see. The policeman turned a sharp 180 degrees on his heel towards the policewoman, who was directly behind him. He made a hand movement that reminded me of an airline steward demonstrating where the exits are on an aeroplane, followed by, 'EVACUATE!'

Fuuuuuuuuuuuuuck.

The policeman and woman talked into the walkie-talkies attached to their jackets, seemingly talking in code and making arrangements that I couldn't quite follow.

It had all just got a bit serious.

'You need to leave immediately, Mrs Boyce. This house is not secure.'

Right.

Basil by this point was scared. He clung to me as I fumbled around, flinging in whatever I could find into the nappy bag. My eldest son's imagination is as vivid as mine so I knew he was probably thinking the worst. Sonny, our middle child, was as cool as a cucumber (he gets that from his dad) and asked casually, 'Does this mean I don't go to school on Monday?'

'Ummm, I think school will be fine on Monday.'

Sonny looked disappointed.

We evacuated our home, abandoning the half-peeled potatoes in the sink. Once outside, we noticed that police vans had arrived, along with the bomb squad and a terrorist specialist unit. Our entire road had been closed off. The police were knocking on all the doors of the surrounding neighbours also asking them to evacuate. One guy left his house in his pants, and our elderly neighbour who for years had tried to hide the fact that he was gay evacuated with his boyfriend, taking this moment to 'come out'. (I mean, if you're going to come out, come out with a blast, right?)

To be honest we were shell-shocked. We had no idea what was going to happen. We had no idea how long we were going to be away from our home. I had no idea if we could host the BBQ later that day for Basil's birthday ... *Probably not.*

We headed to our local café and tried our best to settle in looking normal, while Basil told everyone in there that we had a bomb and we might die. The café emptied shortly after this – not surprising, really – and also not a bad thing, as the baby was due a feed and my dress had to be hauled up from my knee to my shoulder, showing the entire right-hand side of my body, and my padded lady knickers that said 'Kiss' on them.

I opened my family WhatsApp chat. 'Morning all – slight change of plans. Not sure we can have you over today ... we found a bomb in our garden and had to evacuate.'

Everyone was typing ...

Mum called instead, asking way too many questions, so I pretended my phone had bad reception and talked like a stuttering robot, followed by hanging up the phone ... We've all done this, right? Right??

After a few hours we got a call from the police. They informed us that the bomb had been successfully taken away and detonated. It had been live. The grenade had been LIVE.

It could have exploded.

Now, this next part is probably as unbelievable as having a live grenade roll off your shovel as you're gardening ...

We arrived home, settled the kids in and I got back to my potato peeling. Suddenly, Jesse called out to me: 'Oh my gosh, look at this, Louise!'

PANIC! What the fuck now? My mind went into turbo drive and I imagined the worst worst-case scenario as I ran from the kitchen to the bedroom.

'Look!' Jesse pointed at our bed.

I was looking for a horse's head or a massive spider. 'What? What is it?'

'The police made our bed!'

FFS.

'No, babe, that was me. I do it every day.' I walked back to the kitchen, dumbfounded, and peeled the potatoes slightly more vigorously than before.

Can we please just take a moment to digest this? Why would a member of the police, after finding a grenade in a family home and evacuating the entire street, take the time to make our bed?

On top of this, I've been making our bed every morning for the past FOREVER.

A week later and we were getting ready to celebrate my son's birthday (again) with his friends from school. I was filling up all the party bags, cutting sandwiches into triangles and making sure there was a good political balance between sugar and fruit for the party (just in case of any raised eyebrows from the parents), wrapping layer upon layer for Pass the Parcel and doing basically everything while Jesse was digging up Romance Corner, listening to a podcast.

Once again he came running in. 'There's another grenade!'

What the *actual*?

The police arrived AGAIN and we were told to evacuate AGAIN but this time we were all a bit more casual and relaxed about it. I continued to pack the party bags and cut the diagonal sandwiches and the kids asked the policemen if they could take a look in their police van, which they very kindly agreed to.

After my party prep, we evacuated with all the birthday-party paraphernalia and headed off to my son's soft-play birthday party with a bunch of parents. In the meantime, the road was blocked off again, and the neighbours were told to leave, again. Even the neighbours were fed up of the same news. We headed to this birthday party not knowing what would happen, nor when we could go home.

There were parents at the party we'd never met before and we started polite chit-chat about how nice it was to meet and we should arrange play dates etc etc. It was around this time that the second grenade scare hit me, and a wave of anxiety suddenly overwhelmed me as I tried to hold a conversation with a parent I'd never met.

'We should have a play date soon —?' said the mum.

'I don't think so ...' I shook my head and looked away. She must have thought I was the rudest person ever. It's not the usual answer you expect when you ask for a play date.

I continued: '... we have live bombs in our garden.'

Well, that killed the conversation and, for the record, we never did conclude that play date.

The police called Jesse as we were singing 'Happy Birthday' to my son and I was holding the birthday cake and trying to shield the candles from other kids attempting to blow them out.

They confirmed that it was another LIVE grenade in our garden – where we have had many parties and play dates, and where a week before the first grenade was found we had a tree surgeon digging out a tree trunk with a massive digger drill thing, directly above the spot where we apparently had a military training camp. It was a miracle he was still alive.

Turns out the bombs were buried sometime soon after the Second World War, in the hope that no one would find them.

The police advised us to call the Ministry of Defence for a bomb specialist to sweep the area for any other bombs.

Surely they'd know what to do?

Wrong.

Maybe it was the guy's first day on the job but this was our conversation, word for word, with the Ministry of Defence.

'Hello, the police said I should call you. We found two live grenades in our garden and there may be more. I'd really appreciate a specialist to come over and sweep the area just in case there are more of them.'

The Ministry of Defence answer: 'I'm not sure what to do. Maybe you should google it.'

'Did you just say *google* it?'

'Yeah.'

'You know, for the Military of Defence, I don't feel that defended right now.'

And that was the end of that.

I hung up and cracked on.

When I am in any difficult situation where I'm not really sure what to do, I always remind myself of some home truths: I made three people inside me. I have birthed three people. I can handle anything.

So I sold the flat.

June

Dad Week

June is, I think, the only month of the school year where there isn't a half-term or any break off school. A whole month of a good routine.

However, June is pretty much all about Jesse. He has dedicated part of this month to himself. Yes, you heard me correctly. It's his birthday and Father's Day on two consecutive weeks in a row, so Jesse laps this up and calls this period 'Dad Week'. He's claimed it as his national holiday to a point where the kids actually believe this is a real thing, like Christmas or Easter. They even make cards saying 'Happy Dad Week' and ask him, 'Are you enjoying your Dad Week?' One year, Basil even made a banner saying 'Happy Dad Week', and on the last day of this so-called national holiday, Jesse actually did a speech at the dinner table.

The man is either a psychopath or a genius.

There is more.

Jesse likes to tax the children when they have a sweet. If they are lucky enough to get a small party-size bag of Haribo at a birthday party, Jesse will actually, legitimately, hold his hand out to the children and say: 'Daddy tax'. And the kids have to give Jesse a sweet from their bag. Why? Because Jesse has a tooth sweeter than the boys do, and this is his way of having a small sugar injection. It has nothing to do with teaching the kids to

'Dad week' card, by Sonny.

share, learn about paying taxes or care about the state of their teeth.

Taking a leaf from his book, I tried 'Mummy tax' when they were eating a 99 ice-cream during the heat wave of July 2022, when temperatures hit 40 degrees for the first time ever …

'There isn't such a thing as "Mummy tax", Mum.' Eye roll.

How does Jesse do it?

Father's Day arrives first, on the third Sunday of June, and of course we do the cards and tea in bed and all the lovely cuddles. But I realised something recently that I think a lot of us can relate to: doesn't it sometimes feel like Father's Day is every day? The small things that we get on Mother's Day – finishing a coffee without a child needing you to find a teeny tiny piece of Lego, or going to the loo without any children asking for a snack whilst you're reaching for the loo roll – feel to me like the kind of luxury fathers get on a daily basis. (And sometimes twice a day, for 40 minutes a time. Yes, I've done the maths.)

In one year I figured out (with two other mothers by my side, to triple check the maths) Jesse, and men in general, spends ten days on the loo. TEN DAYS of pure peace and quiet, just on the loo! And for me and the other two mums? We figured out we spend 15 *hours* on the loo in a year.

Ten days vs 15 hours. There it is, ladies. Actual man vs woman loo stats.

Then, of course, Jesse has a football season ticket to Crystal Palace, which involves a pre- and post-match pint. Add to this the 90-minute game time, plus an hour of travel to the game and back – that's 6 hours of me being alone with the kids on a Saturday. Hmmm. When I think that this happens almost every Saturday when it's football season ... Then there are drinks after work, a quick gym session in his lunch break – the list goes on. And I also work, but it seems that I don't get these luxuries. OK, OK, I do sometimes have a photo shoot in Italy or Portugal which will take me away for three or four days but GENERALLY the ratio of hours for mum vs dad on the parenting front is 10:1.

When lockdown struck, I actually hoped this would be the time Jesse understood how parenting is RELENTLESS and so demanding of every ounce of your soul. I hoped he'd find a new respect for me and mothers everywhere. I'm not sure it worked, though. He still always managed to disappear for a poo

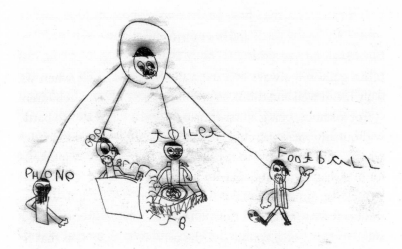

Jesse, by Sonny.

or have a Zoom call in the most inconvenient times, and once I even caught him having an afternoon nap when on a 'Zoom call' in our bedroom-turned-office.

So you see my point – Father's Day is every day. But despite all this, last Father's Day I wanted to give Jesse something really special; something that he'd remember.

So I gave him the kids all day while I took myself off for a coffee and pedicure.

'I'm babysitting?' Jesse asked.

'No, darling, you're parenting.'

And they had the best day ever. Some one-on-one father's time together. Jesse took them out on a really fun day and they all came back buzzing, which of course had my mum guilt creeping in and I had a pang of wishing I had been with them too.

Damn you, 'mum guilt'!

Mum guilt

Mum guilt will always bite us in the backside, even when we truly mean well and think we're doing the best for our children.

For instance, being a first-time parent is like going into battle without any weapons, and wearing a blindfold. We have no idea what's coming or how to deal with a lot of things and it takes a lot of sweat, blood and tears to figure it out.

A classic example was when I took Basil to A&E, followed by the Portland Hospital (a private children's hospital, spending a small fortune) only to find out the problem he had was that he was scared of the shark in *The Little Mermaid*.

Yup. That sodding shark swimming after Flounder in the shipwreck scene cost me good money, two days off work, a shit load of googling (which I highly recommend you never do), a visit from my mum to calm me down and a new love for whisky.

Basil had a night terror – a very real dream of sharks. If you've ever experienced a night terror with your child you'll know that it's actually awful and frightening. It didn't help that when it happened, Jesse was on a flight to America for work and I was six months pregnant with Sonny. I felt helpless, alone and scared. Basil was beside himself, so I took him to A&E with my iPad in the back of the car (watching *The Little Mermaid*, which didn't help).

When we arrived at A&E, unfortunately there were large shark and fish stickers on the walls of the children's waiting room and again Basil was terrified and screaming. To calm him down, I showed him more of *The Little Mermaid* …

He was still beside himself the next day, so I took him to the Portland Hospital, where the doctor examined him thoroughly. Then asked him very quietly, 'What's the matter?'

Basil finally said, 'I don't like the sharks.'

The doctor looked at me and handed me his invoice.

£445. *Awesome.*

I must admit, it made me realise how many sharks are used in children's books, movies, toys, clothes ... they are everywhere. He absolutely loves sharks now – just today he was wearing a shark T-shirt where the breast pocket opening was the shark's open mouth. Very cool. Still, the mum guilt was horrendous – and we haven't watched *The Little Mermaid* since. Simply because it cost me a fortune. For me, mum guilt is rife when I work abroad for a few days. It doesn't happen that often but, when it does, I make sure I have everything in place, making life easier for Jesse and definitely making myself feel better about leaving. I will have prepped the school clothes, Beavers and Cubs uniform, football kits, ballet leotard, swimming shorts and goggles; food will have been premade and frozen; and homework completed. Even a trained monkey could navigate our routine at home and yet when I am away, I am constantly wondering if everything is OK at home. Did Jesse set the alarm? Did he make a packed lunch for the boys for their Tuesday chess club? Will he get them to school on time? And the truth is – everything is ABSOLUTELY FINE at home and there is nothing to ever worry about. Even when I call Jesse to speak to everyone they aren't that interested in speaking to me and are happily ~~playing~~ fighting instead.

I asked Jesse if he ever experienced dad guilt when he goes away.

'Guilt? No. Why?'

Yes, why indeed? Why do us mums experience guilt more than dads do? I did another online poll (Instagram stories) and asked if dads feel the guilt. Only 20 per cent said that they do, compared to mothers at 92 per cent.

For the record – when Jesse goes away, he doesn't do any prep for me to help at home. Same for you? Thought so.

Bedtime

The longest day of the year is 21 June, and it's meant to be the first day of summer. That's right, parents – we are in the season of children going to bed later than usual due to Earth tilting towards the sun. Thanks, mother nature – I think I may tilt towards the rosé wine chilling in the fridge as I watch my kids stay up later than usual and argue in the garden over what section of the trampoline they're allowed to jump in.

Summer evenings *are* wonderful, and I truly believe that all the people who dance around naked for the summer solstice are actually parents who have completely lost it and have given up trying to put their children to bed when it still looks like 2 p.m. outside. Or they are rejoicing because they've found those suction blackout blinds that can make any bedroom dark. (You just pray they don't lose their suction and peel away from the window mid bed-time story, causing all sorts of chaos to your kids' melatonin.)

Usual chats around June at bedtime in our house go something like this …

Ahem.

'OK, bed time, guys.' I always make sure to sound chirpy the first time I announce this state of play, knowing full well I will definitely not be sounding chirpy in the minutes to follow.

'Ughhh, ughhhh, ughhhh.' (My eldest son channelling Kevin the teenager – a great character from *Harry Enfield and Friends*.)

'It's not bedtime yet!' my middle son agrees.

Luckily, my toddler is usually already asleep … for this and the blackout blinds, I am eternally grateful.

'It actually *is* bedtime, guys. Just because it's still light outside doesn't —'

'Ugh, ugh, ugh, can we have five more minutes?' Basil asks.

'Pleeeeeeeeeease,' pleads Sonny.

'Three minutes,' I negotiate, and the world is good again.

As ever, these three minutes actually turn into 20 minutes and now I really want them to go to bed.

'OK, time for bed.' This time I don't sound chirpy. I know what is coming. Again.

'Ughhhh, ughhhhhhh!'

'No! This time it really is bedtime – let's go and brush your teeth.'

'Mummy, it's still light outside so it's not bedtime.'

For the record, this conversation is like a broken record, to be repeated every evening during the summer months.

An overwhelming feeling of *Groundhog Day* sets in – how can they not remember the conversations we have to explain it, and the YouTube videos about the position of the sun during the summer months, and how this makes the days longer even though it's still light at bedtime?

A hack that works well when your children are old enough to tell the time is to turn the clocks forward in the kitchen so they can see for themselves that it is 9.30 p.m. when it's actually 8.30 p.m. (make sure all iPads and iPhone and their watches are away – they will check). Usually it works a charm. And it's particularly good at sleepovers too, when you have a bunch of feral children all wanting to stay up late. I once told Basil's sleepover mates it was midnight and showed them the kitchen clock, when in fact it was 9 p.m. They couldn't believe they were up so late and went out like lights! It really is genius, in fact.

And why is it that bedtime is when children want to talk? And I mean, reeeeeeallllly talk? All the questions I ask them at school pick-up are answered with a one-liner, but when it's time to brush teeth and go to bed they want to tell me all about their entire day at school with intricate detail followed by what they watched on YouTube, accompanied by a 'Can I show you?' and what their tummy looks like when they tense their muscles, what jokes they have made up that make no sense whatsoever but you laugh anyway, and as always and my ultimate pet peeve: 'Canihaveasnack? I'm hungry.'

They'll do anything to divert the idea of going to bed. Complaining that their toothpaste is 'too spicy' is a new one. I tried to explain to Sonny that now he was seven he could go up a toothpaste age – which changed the taste of his usual toothpaste. (And, actually, on this subject – I'm pretty sure when I was a kid we didn't have toothpaste that matched our age group. I have FOUR different toothpastes in our family bathroom. Flipping *four* for a family of five: 0–2 years, 3–6 years, 7–12 years and extra whitening for me and Jesse. And they're all about £4 each! I can imagine advertising executives sitting around a boardroom table laughing at us, the parenting consumers, because we got sucked into age-appropriate toothpaste! I mean, it is actually brilliant.) And the MESS! The toothpaste-smeared taps, light switches and towels, and the thrown toothbrushes onto the back of the sink instead of into the very obvious toothbrush holder that has an actual picture of a toothbrush on it.

Of course, the worst is when Basil spits out his used toothpaste into the sink at the same time Sonny is reaching for the tap, usually resulting in toothpaste spit splattered on Sonny's hand. Cue screams that startle me and wake up Inca. Grrrr.

When they are actually in bed, most children want a story and I really do enjoy reading to the kids. I get really into the characters and give them all accents (something I rather rate myself at) – usually American, Australian, South African and Mancunian. Sometimes I try to sound like Princess Diana – this one is my favourite one. It makes the bedtime story session a lot more fun.

Let's face it, it can be dull and frustrating sometimes, especially when your kids talk over you mid read over and over again.

Story time with my toddler usually goes something like this: 'What story shall we read tonight, Inca?'

'I don't like stories! I don't want a story!'

'You don't want one? OK, we don't have to —'

'I want this one.' She hands me *The Highway Rat* and very slowly gets into bed. I try to hurry up the task by helping her, at which she is disgusted: 'NO, MUMMY! I DO IT!'

'OK, darling, sorry. I was just trying to —'

'I DO IT!'

It's best to stay silent sometimes to avoid any shouting sessions at bedtime. I can tell I am already up against a bedtime battle tonight.

Inca is under the covers and I start. I open the book and read: 'The Highway Rat was a ba —'

'No, Mummy!'

She gets up.

FFS.

'Hold the book like *this*.'

She shows me how she wants me to hold the book, even though this is exactly what I am doing because she tells me *every night* to do the same thing and I am well trained for her book-holding style.

'Like this?' I don't change my hand position.

'Yes, Mummy.'

I continue with a medium sigh. 'The highway rat was a baddy, the highway rat was a bea-'

'Mummy, no, I do it.'

She snatches the book out of my hands and tries to read it herself, holding the book in the way she likes; it's very cute watching her 'read' using animated inflections and playing out the characters, all whilst speaking absolute gibberish.

She sees me smiling at her and she can't bear it. 'Mummy, don't look at me!'

'OK.' I look around her room instead, where I see a plethora of clothes all over the floor. It's pointless putting her clothes away as, every morning and evening, she takes them all out to decide what to wear that day.

Inca realises the attention isn't on her. 'Mummy, you read it!' She shoves the book into my hands, making the pages ruffle.

'Careful, darling, and yes, of course I can read it.' I once again assume the preferred book-holding position, clear my throat and start my Oscar-winning narration performance.

I am a page in when: 'Mummy, you're not my best friend.' I pause, give her a warm smile and carry on reading.

Inca manages to interrupt every other line in the book: 'Mummy, shut up. Mummy, you smell like broccoli. Mummy, I don't like this book. Mummy, STOP, I don't like it!'

I try to ignore all these irritating interruptions but it comes to a halt when she tries to snatch the book out my hands again, this time ripping a page.

I am officially done. I've spent 15 minutes trying to read this sodding book and instead have been ridiculed.

I close the book. 'OK, that's enough. It's bedtime.'

'I want Daddy to read it!'

Fine with me.

'Daddy! Inca wants you to read her a story.'

'OK, sure.' Jesse is happy to sit on the edge of her bed and pick up the same book.

'I DON'T WANT DADDY!'

Jesse doesn't protest and exits the bedroom as quickly as he came in.

'What was that?' I ask him, as I hover outside her bedroom.

'She wants you,' and off he goes.

FFS.

'Mummy, you read it.'

And we're back to square one. On loop. Finally, Inca is settled and asleep and I emerge from her bedroom looking and feeling violated. Now it's time to settle the boys, and I'm angry Jesse hasn't started this preparation. Instead, they're all in the middle of watching *Wayne's World*.

'Guys! It's time for bed!

'UGH!' 'UGH!' 'UGH!' 'UGGGG!'

Reading with the boys is a lot easier – in some respects. The first story of the evening is usually read with enthusiasm and decorum – I visualise myself on Cbeebies reading the bedtime story that follows *In The Night Garden*. But then they ask for another story, and this time I'm not as animated as before, and I am definitely faster at reading, and deliberately choose a book that is a lot shorter than the one before.

When they ask for a third book, I am reading like the robot, Johnny 5, from *Short Circuit* – turning perhaps three pages at a time.

'Good night, guys. Love you. Sleep tight and no need to get out of bed, OK? OK? OK????'

But inevitably, just when you think you have the all-clear to sit down on the sofa, have a flick of the TV, a scroll of social media and a glass of wine you hear the patter of little feet coming closer to you.

Bollocks.

And the excuses come: 'Mummy, I had a nightmare.'

'But you haven't fallen asleep yet.'

'Mummy, I'm hungry.'

'You just had a banana and you should have had your supper.'

'Mummy, what time is it in Australia?'

'Eh?'

'Mummy, watch ... watch, Mummy ... Mummy ... Mummy, watch.'

Oh, here we go. And once again I am watching.

'Mummy, watch … watch …'

I'm actually intrigued to see what he'll pull out of the bag this time.

He farts and giggles.

'Goodnight, Sonny.' This is said very matter-of-factly. Like it really *is* bedtime and you really *are* staying in bed.

He skips off back to his bedroom happy with his fart and I decide that I may treat myself to a long, candle-lit bubble bath. I am a big fan of bath time for myself – it's like an event. I will soak for a good hour with a book or sometimes watch Netflix on my phone with a glass of wine. It's a time when I tell Jesse I do not exist; however, on occasion, I give him the kids' walk-ie-talkie and when I'm feeling extra queen-like, I will walkie-talkie Jesse to come and fill up my wine glass. He arrives with the bottle of wine, fills it up and looks around the bath-room that has too many lit candles in it for his liking, making a mental note of the ones he'll need to blow out because I'll forget (I can guarantee he's written this in his right of reply). My zen self-care will be temporarily disturbed by his 'quick wee' – a lengthy and musical one with many start and stops of the flow, standing next to me, my eyeline at the exact same level as his urethra … but even this will not stop my bath night date with myself.

'Pull the flush.'

He pulls the flush.

'Put the seat down.'

He does so.

I mean … *why*?

Eyes closed, head back in absolute relaxation in an abundance of candles, bubbles, wine and 'Mum chill' Spotify playlist (check it out, it's great), I really feel a sense of unwinding. I am transported to a time and place where children and adult responsibility don't exist. I think of Thailand in 2004 – a time where I really felt like I found my deeper self: a sense of life and reason accompanied by the debauched throwing back of SangSom buckets at full moon parties with my sister Bonnie and friends. Some of the best days of my life. I smile as I reminisce about these days – but am bought back to reality with a sudden jolt, spilling my red wine over my bubble-bathed breasts.

'Mummy.'

For fuck's sake. He's out of bed again.

'Mummy, what are you doing?'

Before I can even answer, Sonny has blown out the three candles that were next to me and turned on the main bathroom light, which blinds me, and totally brings me back from Haad Rin beach to Surrey.

And the questions come again. But this time I walkie-talkie Jesse, and he comes to put Sonny to bed. Again.

I remember when I was a child I would do the same thing. Bonnie and I shared a room and, guaranteed, Bonnie would always fall asleep before I did – she still does: as soon as her head hits a pillow she is gone – whereas I will stay awake thinking for way too long.

I remember getting out of bed a few times when my mum had some friends over. I heard the clinking of wine glasses, laughter and the song 'Morning Train' by Sheena Easton. I knew I had to go and say hi – it was rude not to, right?

I probably got out of bed one too many times, interrupting Mum and her friends catching up – and back then, they really were catching up: they didn't have WhatsApp or social media to keep tabs on each other as we have today – so when they all got together, it really was precious time. The last thing they needed was a six-year-old continuously getting out of bed and disturbing their precious few hours together.

So Mum gave me a sip of red wine. No need to panic! It was the eighties and anything went – and we all ended up totally fine. I think …

So when Mum gave me a small sip of red wine with her friends, it was fine.

I went off to bed and Mum thought her plan had worked: a hit of red wine would send me into a lovely deep sleep and she could continue her evening with her friends.

Not so much …

Ten minutes after putting me to bed for the fourth or fifth time (maybe even more), Mum and her friends were startled when I starting singing, 'It's a Long Way to Tipperary' at the top of my voice – like the way men roar at football matches. Yup, that was me. I have no idea why I sang this song and definitely don't know why I had the urge to sing it like a football hooligan, but there you are. Was it the wine? Was it the excitement of my mum having a small party downstairs that I wanted to join? Who knows.

Having calmed me down for the nth time, Mum kissed me goodnight, walked over to the door and said the same soothing word she always said just before she walked out of my bedroom: 'Cobblers.'

She had said 'Cobblers' every night for as long as I could remember, and my sister and I never questioned it. We'd say it back too. 'Cobblers, Mummy.'

It was years later, when I realised that cobblers meant 'nonsense', that I confronted my mum and asked her: 'Mum, why did you always say "cobblers" when you put us to bed?'

Mum looked perplexed. 'What *are* you talking about?'

'Why did you say "cobblers" when you put us to bed? Is it because you thought parenting, and putting us to bed, was nonsense?'

Mum paused and had a good think – before her face lit up with a huge smile and laughter. Tears were streaming down her face as she explained ...

Turns out Mum wasn't saying 'cobblers'. She was saying, 'God bless.' Say it a few times out loud and you'll hear how similar they sound.

Mum and I still laugh at this to this day, and we actually now say 'Cobblers' when we end a phone call or say goodbye to each other.

There is a cottage near where I live in Farnham called Cobblers Cottage, and whenever I walk past it I smile to myself and usually end up calling my mum.

The tooth fairy

One time when you can get your kids into bed and to STAY in bed is when they're expecting a visit from the tooth fairy.

I really like playing the role of the tooth fairy – I write letters, sometimes, from the fairy in my smallest handwriting. I do messages like 'Brush your teeth properly' and 'Stop eating sweets'. This doesn't work, of course – the kids just want to know how much money they'll get.

What *is* the going rate for a tooth these days? And what do you do with it when the tooth fairy has made her visit? Sonny lost his first tooth at school and he was so excited about putting it under his pillow. He was so cute, especially as he'd been really worried about losing a tooth, thinking it may hurt ... He came running up to me at the school gates holding it out, and it looked even smaller in his hand than it did in his mouth.

(I couldn't help but think that bastard tooth was the reason for many broken nights' sleep and a copious amount of Calpol and countless dribble-soaked baby bibs. A part of me wanted to bury it as a sacrifice.)

Sonny wanted to make it as easy as possible for the tooth fairy to find, so he drew an arrow on a piece of paper pointing directly to the tooth under his pillow. That evening, when all was quiet, I checked my purse for some money to place under his pillow.

Shit.

I had zero change. Nothing. Absolutely nothing.

'Jesse, have you got any money for the tooth fairy?'

'How much?'

'I dunno – £2?'

'I've only got £20.'

Hmmm, what a predicament we were in. It was too late to go to the shops and break into the £20, and our neighbours would probably be asleep at midnight on a Tuesday, so we had a very difficult decision to make.

Did we:

Not give anything?

Give him sweets instead of money (but we didn't have any sweets).

Give him £20 and make up some bullshit story about the first tooth being more valuable? (What was Basil going to say ...?)

'Mummy, look!'

(Not gonna lie – I was quite happy to hear 'look' instead of 'watch'.)

Sonny was beaming a gappy grin, flapping a £20 note in his hand as he ran towards me.

His older brother was behind him with such a scowl on his face. 'Mum, I didn't get that much from the tooth fairy.'

QUICK! MAKE SOME SHIT UP!

'Yes, you absolutely did, darling, but you don't remember. We put it in your bank account.'

As soon as I said this I regretted it. Why couldn't I just have just stopped at 'Yes, you absolutely did, darling, but you don't remember.' Why??

'Can I please spend it? We want to buy some Lego, don't we, Sonny?'

Now they are both beaming. Great. So that one tooth, which looked like a sucked-on tic tac and is now flushed down the loo, cost me £40. *What on earth?*

One time, when Basil lost a tooth, I totally forgot about being the tooth fairy that night.

'Mummy, the tooth fairy didn't come!'

QUICK! MAKE SOME SHIT UP!

'They don't fly on Sundays, darling. That's their day off.'

Thank goodness it *was* a Sunday and thank goodness children will literally believe anything – apart from vegetables being good for you.

But then the same thing happened the next night.

'Mummy, the tooth fairy didn't come again!'

Q U I C K! MAKE SOMETHING ELSE UP!

'Darling, the tooth fairy won't take teeth that she thinks are too dirty. You must, *must*, MUST clean your teeth a little better. Then I'm sure she'll come.'

The next evening I walked into the bathroom to help assist with tooth brushing when I caught Basil brushing his extracted tooth and not the teeth in his mouth.

'Mummy, I'm making it nice and clean for the tooth fairy.'

'Darling, you need to clean the teeth in your *mouth* – I think that was the point?'

The next morning I excitedly asked Basil if the tooth fairy came.

'Mum, I know it's you who gives the money to us.'

Time for coffee.

Grandparenting

As I mentioned earlier, June is the month of Jesse's birthday (and my mum's), so there are always lots of celebrations and reasons to go out for dinner or drinks. This will of course include a babysitter when Jesse and I go out together.

There is definitely a 'wising-up' evolution when it comes to mothers and handing over duties to the babysitter. With my first child, for example, I actually went to my local art store on the high street and bought a red A3 cardboard sheet and a black marker pen, and charted out the entire day of my baby's routine. There were asterisks on key items like 'Remember to change nappy' and 'He doesn't like wind when in the garden.'

My mum and mother-in-law totally ignored the routine I had spent months getting right, which resulted in my baby not going to bed on time, which inevitably resulted in the baby being overtired and crying a lot and being awake when I got home. PANIC!

'Did you follow the routine, Mum?'

'No, not really ...'

'Did you feed him?'

'Well, he didn't seem hungry, so no.'

LIVID.

'He's seven months old! He can't exactly ask for a ham sandwich with a side of fries – there is a routine there for a reason!'

'Well, in my day, we gave you what we had when we thought you needed it and got on with it. We didn't have all these gadgets and vibrating sleeping doo-dahs. It's ridiculous!'

My mother-in-law once told me, when Basil was teething and he was in a lot of pain and with a temperature to go with it, that Calpol was unnecessary and I was 'just tranquilising him'. Jesse had to remind her that he remembers having Calpol until he was old enough to open it himself. It's funny how our mothers 'know best' because they parented thirty-plus years ago. I had to hide in the bathroom and sneak in some Calpol, hoping that Basil would easily take the Calpol syringe (does anyone throw these away? I must have about two dozen of them). My secret Calpol mission failed miserably when Basil wriggled out of my arms and spat out most of the Calpol, which went all over his clothes and mine. What was worse was that I didn't know how much Calpol he had taken so I was then in the predicament of do I go again, or leave it? (I usually go again and end up googling 'Calpol overdose', then see 'liver failure' coming up on my phone screen and wonder if a quick trip to A&E is worth my while.)

Then I discovered you can double drop with Nurofen for Children. It felt like a euphoric moment, knowing there was more help at hand. (Top hack if your kids absolutely hate taking the syringe of medicine – cut the back of a juice box out and place something the size of a shot glass at the bottom of it, with the medicine in it. Then put the straw in it and offer the juice box to the child as normal (you hold it, though). The child thinks they are drinking a sugary drink and the parents are giving their child a dose of medicine – everyone wins!

I digress – as I was saying, regarding babysitting … the first child had an A3 red sheet blu-tacked to the kitchen wall with intricate instructions, and a tray with everything that might have been needed on it, from wipes and nappies, to a thermo-motor, a change of clothes, Calpol and Nurofen, teething granules, Vicks VapoRub (even though the baby was totally well) and I even drew a diagram of where to place the cuddly toy in the cot. I had everything there, JUST IN CASE. I added the number of the restaurant on the off-chance my and Jesse's phones didn't have any reception, and I had a security camera in the baby's room with the app on my phone so I could watch everything at home if I wanted to.

Second child I had some Calpol on standby, and pointed out where everything was, just in case.

By the time my third baby came along, when the babysitter arrived you'd see a Louise-shaped hole in the wall as I made a quick exit out of there. If anything happened they had my number.

To all the parents that have four or more children, I'd love to know if you're more relaxed the more children you have!

Solo nights out

Jesse has been pretty relaxed throughout our entire parenting journey so far – apart from the £445 *Little Mermaid* shark issue, and mess in the car, and perhaps the kids being fussy eaters. Jesse is pretty chilled when it comes to being a dad. He doesn't stress about getting them to school on time, and when he is late he shrugs it off. He doesn't feel the need to get the kids into bed at bedtime, and will often offer watching *Mandolorian* or *Wayne's World* with the boys at their actual bed time, which drives me mad (but the boys love it).

In fact, Jesse has a great knack for keeping the kids awake when they need to be asleep. When I put them to bed it's very chilled. Screens are off 30 minutes before lights out, we read, and the energy is low and tranquil. And when Jesse is out for the night or back from work late, and I am in sole charge of putting the kids to bed, I can manage to get them down sometimes a good 40–45 minutes earlier, and have a peaceful evening. Until, of course, Jesse comes home from the pub and makes the most ridiculous amount of noise that is comedy gold when you compare it to how I come in from a night out.

I'll go first.

When I come home, I'm very aware the house is asleep. After all, the last thing you want to do is wake up sleeping kids when you've had a few glasses of wine and actually all you want to do is sleep. As soon as I reach the front door I become the quietest being alive. The keys are pulled from my bag to open the front door so slowly and quietly that I don't even disturb the fox across the road that is rummaging through my neighbours' food bin. I tell myself I'd be a really good burglar as I open and then close the door behind me, making sure the latch closes with only the smallest of 'click' sounds. I tiptoe down the hallway and place my bag and keys on the hallway table, shushing myself as I go along. Before heading upstairs, I usually decide to get a glass of water and, once again, expend a lot of effort to make sure I am so quiet that even when I turn on the kitchen tap the flow of water is only just above a trickle. I accidently kick a kid's toy on the way to the stairs and freeze as a deafening, over-enthusiastic singing voice comes from my toddler's pull-along car. I shudder and quickly glance up the ceiling to check if I have woken the children, and turn off the singing car. All is safe, so I creep up the stairs making sure I step over the third one up that I know has a creak in it.

This quiet procedure continues until I'm washed and tucked into bed, happy and content that I managed to keep everyone asleep.

And now Jesse. For starters, he'll be laughing to himself way too loudly outside the front door as he reads WhatsApp messages from the people he's just been on a night out with, and this wakes me up immediately. He opens and closes the front door like it's Saturday afternoon, with absolutely no appreciation of the fact that it's the middle of the night; then burps as he walks down the hallway, followed by some other gross man noises, slamming his keys down on the hall table as he passes it. He too wants to get a glass of water before bed and

I can hear his every move downstairs. Cupboards are opened and slammed closed, and glasses are chinked around. The kitchen tap is on full throttle and even from my bed I can tell he hasn't turned it off properly.

LIVID.

He too will manage to kick some loud and infuriating toy, yet he will LEAVE IT ON. I hear various noises repeated over and over whilst Jesse returns to his WhatsApp chat and continues to laugh over the noise of the toy, followed by the heaviest footsteps up the stairs. Finally, he barges into our bedroom, full of joy. 'Oh, hi, you're still awake.'

'I am now,' I say, through gritted teeth.

Jesse, feeling the vibes from the pints at the pub, ejects himself out of his jeans and pants, which are left on the bedroom floor perfectly intact, like a fireman's overalls ready to jump into in case of an emergency. The time he spends doing a wee should actually be in the *Guinness Book of World Records*. And, just before jumping into bed, he will usually give me a naked willy shake, where he flaps his willy from side to side making small slap noises against his body. If I'm lucky, he'll tuck his willy in between his legs and pretend he is a woman.

Who said romance is dead?

I guess he's really enjoyed his 'Dad Week'.

July

End of the school year

Ah, the last month of the school year. With summer loom-ing, there is a buzz and anticipation in the air.

The summer holidays have their pros and cons.

In a mere few weeks the school uniform laundering, school run, homework, school trips, school projects, PTA meetings, packed lunches, full water bottles, reading log books, after-school activities and school WhatsApp chats will come to a sudden halt – a time of quiet that excites you. And you really feel like you need this break. All the parents and carers seem more chilled at the school gates – perhaps it's because we're in the warmer months and most people at the gates are looking extra cool in their sunglasses and summer wear. There is more camaraderie between parents as we all agree that the year has flown and that we should all meet up for end-of-year drinks.

As it's the end of term, the kids are coming home with all sorts of school books and drawings they've done over the school year. Sonny wanted to show me every single item of work he'd done straight away when I picked him up, but I thought to myself that it was at least refreshing not to hear 'Canihaveasnack' immediately on him seeing me.

(I can safely say that the majority of this artwork ended up in the bin.)

Yes, summer – even the teachers look more chilled. The same goes for my toddler's nursery school teachers, and they don't even break up for the summer.

I am so, SO thankful for nurseries staying open basically all year apart from Easter and Christmas. It costs a fortune, is basically a second mortgage (come on, UK, wake up to this scandal) but I am thankful for their opening hours.

'Inca's mummy – can I have a word?' My daughter's key worker beckoned me over and I braced myself for what was about to come. 'I have a funny story to tell you.' She smiled.

Oh, thank goodness. I was worried that it may have been more 'penis talk'.

I took a breath and settled in for this funny story, as Inca came running towards me, beaming with absolute joy.

'Sorry if this sounds a little rude, but I had to tell you.'

Oh God, here we go. I smiled on the outside and wondered if my worried fake smile was obvious. I was pretty sure she was going to mention the word 'penis'.

'Inca told me today that you have a very big vagina.'

Cue pelvic floor exercises.

'Ha ha, that's funny – and quite spot on. I have pushed out three children, after all. Inca basically walked out of my vagina and was the only child I didn't need stiches with.'

I had taken it too far. The childless, 20-year-old nursery teacher didn't need to know this information, and I sensed she was now the one who was fake smiling on the outside.

And yet I didn't stop.

'You know, it actually feels like your baby is coming out of your bum and not your vagina when you give birth. Like a really big poo.'

STOP TALKING.

'You know, I did poo, too, when I gave birth. But I didn't realise and blamed Jesse for doing the most awful farts.'

LOUISE. STOP TALKING.

'My vagina is fine, though – considering it's taken an absolute battering. I don't know why people say "grow some balls" when they need to be brave. Balls shrivel when they're cold … vaginas are incredible. I actually think if men had uteruses they'd brag about them down the pub.'

Inca's key worker was backing away, looking slightly disturbed by my unexpected vagina chat, and glanced to a child – any child – to suddenly need her attention and stop this hideous conversation.

TIME TO GO.

School sports day

July also presents the school sports day, which is always a great way to allow your competitive side to shine on through, isn't it? We loudly encourage our children to race, shouting from the sidelines very embarrassing mum cries, for all to hear, whilst our kids pretend they don't know us.

'Go, Basil!!! Come on, Basil!'

Basil was mortified and ignored me as I jumped around like a middle-aged and very uncool cheerleader.

I made a mental note that I needed to buy a better fitting bra, wear a Tena Lady, and put in my contact lenses. It was a really sunny day and I didn't own a pair of prescription sunglasses – I thought I'd be OK just winging my eyesight on a day where you actually have to look out for your child and cheer them on. There I was jumping up and down, flailing my arms in the air and shouting my son's name to COME ON, only to realise I was shouting at someone else's child. And I only came to this conclusion when I remembered I had sent Basil in wearing his tracksuit bottoms and not shorts (couldn't find them during the morning rush to get ready) – so Basil was pretty much the only kid on sports day with legs covered in navy blue. I felt a little sheepish knowing I had been hollering at someone else's child, and tried to style it out by getting out my phone and looking at my emails. Naturally I was told off by a teacher with a wagging 'no phones, please – focus on your child' finger.

Yes, I'm trying to focus!!!

I saw an email had come in: 'TV commercial confirmed – shoot this Thursday.'

YES! I had been waiting for this confirmation and was so excited that it had arrived. I decided to read the rest of the email later and to ignore the embarrassment of coaching a child that wasn't mine.

I spotted Basil as he lined up for the 100m sprint. This was a race I was very good at, at school, so I was positive Basil would do well.

You watch your kid race with such pride – regardless if they're first or last, or if you have a good eyesight – they are in it and, more importantly perhaps, you made it there despite your work commitments. Hurrah!

Last year I was torn between work and sports day, and I had decided to leave halfway through it. I managed to grab Basil's attention across the field to let him know I was leaving, and he just nodded in a very cavalier manner.

Was he upset I was going? Was he going to race again? Did I really need to go?

Cue the mum guilt.

I had got as far as the school gates when the mum guilt started to pull at my heart strings … I made a U-turn and came back to the field, only to watch my son do nothing else but play with his mates while more experienced athletes stepped up to run.

I was trying to get Basil's attention just to let him know I was still there. The waving of the hands over my head had no luck. I had to get his attention.

Then the headmistress walked onto the field and took up her position by the pupils, who were all sitting crossed-legged on the grass in their designated team area wearing either a red, green, yellow or blue sash. She bought her loudhailer to her mouth: 'It's now time for the parents' race!'

Oh, crap – this is it, isn't it? This is how I can get Basil's attention so he knows I am still here for him.

The shite we do as mothers.

I started to eye up the other mothers around me, sniffing them out, wondering if they were a faster runner than I was. I was convincing myself that 'I AM A FAST RUNNER' – I was the fastest girl in my primary school, and the second fastest in my secondary school – *I've got this. I have still got it.* I may not have sprinted for a good 26 years but how hard could it be? It was probably just like riding a bike. For crying out loud, I had given birth three times.

I CAN DO THIS.

I confidently walked up to the start line and immediately felt a pang of fear. *Why am I doing this again? Does it really matter that Basil doesn't know I'm still here? The mothers seem to be very pally with each other – when did I miss out on all the parenting banter? Maybe I should unmute my school WhatsApp chats. I think I need the loo. Oh god, I'm wearing flip-flops. Should I take them off? Would I look too competitive if I do take them off? Have I got time to google Princess Diana when she ran and won the race in Prince William's sports day to see if she took her shoes off?*

No one else was taking their shoes off so I decided to also keep mine on. I took a deep breath and told myself that I was a good mum for getting involved and, really, what was the worst that could happen?

Well.

I didn't win. But I did feel like I won the 'losing dignity' game: my pelvic floor gave up halfway through the race; my right flip-flop broke; and Basil did see me as I ran past him shouting his name and still waving at him – and he decided to ignore me.

I couldn't believe how breathless I was at the end of the race: bent over, palms on my thighs, trying to catch my breath and trying to give the impression that I was OK even when my back went into spasm.

Why do we do this to ourselves again? Ah, yes, the children. Basil's eyes had followed me without any emotion as I ran that 100 metres. I should have just left when I had the chance.

When I collected Basil at the end of the school day, the first thing he said to me after 'Canihaveasnack?' was, 'Mum, please don't wave your hands up in the air and call my name again – it's embarrassing.'

A little part of me died. ('I pushed you out of my body – I made you, and yet you're telling me I'm embarrassing?') I *was* a little hurt, but also understanding. I remembered how embarrassed I used to be of my mum for just walking down the street. I used to deliberately walk six paces behind her to make out I was walking alone. Now when we walk down the street, I link her arm with mine and hold her hand at the same time. I guess we all go through these embarrassing moments …

Speaking of embarrassing – that TV commercial I mentioned earlier in this chapter —? Well, I finally read the email and I was to shoot a fashion TV commercial. I was thrilled – the shoot dates were before the end of the school term. I could make it work, hurrah!

On the call sheet there was something written in large, bold letters: *DO NOT BE LATE – WE ARE ON A VERY TIGHT SCHEDULE. I REPEAT, DO NOT BE LATE!*

I'm a very punctual person and had no doubt that I would be there on time. I take pride in always being early or on time for things. Even now, as a parent, I am always on time – even when I'm caught on the way out of the front door and realise the baby has just done a poonami and needs changing immediately, I will still be on time. And should I be running a little bit late I will always call and apologise, all the while feeling anxiety creeping into my veins.

On the day of the commercial shoot I decided to drive to the studio. The location was somewhere off the beaten track and I was looking forward to being in the comfort of my own car after the shoot and not having to wait for an Uber.

I got off to a good start – I used Google Maps on my phone to direct me onto the M25, then the M40 … and … Oh, no. I had missed the turn off the motorway and now Google Maps had added an extra 20 miles and 45 minutes due to traffic. HOW COULD I BE SO STUPID! I was panicking. I may hate being late, but to have had a call sheet that explicitly told me not to be late too …?

I lost it. What on earth should I do???

I decided the best thing would be to call the client – not the production team (like a normal person), but the client. The top dog of the brand who's spending a shitload of money on the commercial. Surely she would understand and be cool with me.

I found Erika's number on the call sheet and called her as I slowed down to a standstill on the motorway.

It rang. No answer. Voicemail.

'Hi, Erika, it's Louise – the model for today's shoot. I'm so sorry but I'm running a little bit late. You see I missed the turning off the M40 and now I'm stuck in traffic. I should be with you in about 40 minutes. Again, I am so sorry – I am such a punctual person normally and I hate being late. Sorry again, and I'll be with you shortly.' With a grimace, I pressed the 'end call' button.

My frustration, anger, tiredness and anxiety got the better of me and I needed to let it all out … I began *screaming* at the top of my voice, hitting the steering wheel with such force it started to hurt my hands. 'CUUUUUUNNNNNNTTTTTTT! YOU FUCKING CUNNNNT! THIS IS SO SHIIIIIIITTTTTTTTT. FUCK OFFFFFFFFFFFFFFFF. ARGHHHHHHHHH! CUNNNTTTTTTTTTT!'

Oh, that felt better.

I grabbed my phone to call my sister.

Wait, what?

The line was still open. I hung up the phone … then thought of my potty mouth episode. As it all dawned on me, I started to feel a little sick. I'd managed to call the main client and scream down the phone, calling them a cunt and to fuck off.

I was mortified. Beyond mortified.

What did I do now? Call her back? Call my agent, explaining? Hope that the ground swallowed me up and spat me out into another universe? How could I have been so careless???

Arriving at the studio, I'd never felt so sheepish walking into a room in my entire life. Not only was I late to the shoot, but the boss had heard a side of me that should always stay private. Unless she thought I had intended to speak to her that way …?

Oh gosh, this is awful.

I had no idea who Erika was when I arrived and quickly asked a runner who to look out for. She pointed over to a very angry-looking woman, who saw me at the same time.

She's coming over. Oh, shit.

'Hello, you must be Louise?' Erika held out her hand to shake mine, and I reciprocated.

'Hello, yes. Erika?' I played it cool.

'Yes, that's right.'

'I'm sorry I'm late – I missed the turning and —'

'Yes, don't worry. I got your message.'

Shiiitttttttttttttt.

And then we both did the classic British demeanour thing and decided to ignore the elephant in the room.

I can confirm Erika did not book me again, and that this is possibly the most embarrassed I've ever been – apart from uploading my vag-ie to Facebook. I now *always* check to see that my phone is off when I am in the car, just in case of another outburst at someone else's expense.

End-of-term parent drinks

Before schools break up for the summer, there are usually some form of end-of-term drinks with the other parents in the class. Usually, the majority of people can go – including the dads! Hurrah! A time for the dads to all get involved and meet each other, too.

It's a bit like taking your child to a play date: I find myself saying the same things to Jesse before we arrive at the party: 'Please be good, don't embarrass me, and it's Emma and David's party.'

Getting parents together that doesn't include queuing up to collect your child after school is a whole new experience of meeting people. It's the new and improved version of the same person you usually see at the school gates, but this time we are all chatty – we have wine and gin, we gossip about the teachers, we laugh and we think, 'Actually, you're really cool and I'm so pleased I met you.' And all the men behave themselves too – no cornflake game at this party, thank goodness. We all congratulate ourselves for surviving another school year and towards the end of the evening I realise that, next year, I *really* want to be on the PTA and blurt it out like word vomit so that I cannot take it back, as once you offer your service to the PTA it's very hard to take it back.

Shit! I cannot, just CANNOT take anything else on. My mind is already too full, cluttered with all the daily shite I have to remember. I definitely find my mind seems to have tabs open, like a computer, and some need to be shut down before I can focus on other tabs, otherwise there will be a malfunction.

This happened recently in Sainsbury's …

Too many tabs open

I was with the kids doing a quick shop for supper that evening – you know, the usual fish fingers, sweet potato fries that are disguised as real chips but which I already know are only going to be prodded with forks, and some peas that I also know I'll be on hands and knees picking up off the floor later on.

Whilst at the self-service bagging area I received a very important phone call from my agency. I had been waiting to hear from them if I was being confirmed for a shoot in Cape Town – a shoot I really wanted – when that robotic voice of doom informed me I had an 'unrecognised item' (even though I am very familiar with my Villa Maria Marlborough Sauvignon Blanc white wine) in the bagging area. I was trying to hold a professional conversation with my agency, whilst shushing my kids who were telling me ON LOOP and tapping my arm at the same time there was something wrong with the machine, and trying to grab the attention of a Sainsbury's member of staff, who seemed to be helping everyone else apart from me.

Too many tabs open.

My agency told me, 'Please don't be disheartened but they have confirmed another model. Another blonde. It's crazy because you look alike but she is more flexible ... she doesn't have kids.'

My heart sank.

I didn't get the job.

I didn't get the job because I have children.

I've been in the modelling business for 25 years and over these years I have learnt how to handle rejection. As a model, you are rejected around 85 per cent of the time; learning this from my early teenage years was tough – especially when navigating an eating disorder too – but by my late twenties I was a pro at accepting rejection: I knew it wasn't personal, it was business.

But *this* rejection felt personal. They had presented my motherhood status as a form of weakness, or as seeing me as unfit for the job.

It was around this time that I decided to start an Instagram page. I had seen the power of social media and how you can use it as a platform to really market yourself or your business, and also realised I would be taken more seriously if I had an account. I decided to call my page 'Mama Still Got It' and honestly felt a pang of embarrassment when I did. What would people think? But I was sick and tired of the stigma that can come with being a mother within the work place, and how we are pushed out as if we are damaged goods. I wanted to make a stand for myself and other woman that, regardless of our age or profession, we have still got it – and that no one should tell us differently. I decided to talk more openly about being a mother and a model in my forties. It was time to stand up for myself and my career.

Don't get me wrong, though – I was terrified and doubted myself on a weekly basis. *What if it's shit? What if I don't get heard? What if people think I'm full of myself? What if I don't get anywhere?* And then I thought: *What if it takes off? What if I can actually make other mothers out there feel better about themselves?*

What if I can actually make a career from this? What if I can one day write a book on this ... I've learnt that being around my kids when I receive negative news is the best company I can be in. Sounds crazy, especially as I was deep in the stress zone of trying to buy food and the kids were talking at me and breaking out into a floss fight (this is where they floss, then decide to push each other to the floor and repeat) but I didn't want my kids to see me upset – the most important thing to me in my life is my family. If they are happy I am happy. And they were happy. Are happy.

I put on my positive hat, took a deep breath, paid for the food that had now been 'recognised' by the Sainsbury staff member and went on my way – but still with way too many tabs open in my mind. I think one of our (mother) superpowers is how much we can do with one hand behind us, not looking at where that hand is, when we're in the car.

We were in the car on the way home from Sainsbury's when Sonny wanted me to attach a piece of Lego to the work of art he was creating in the back seat.

'I'm driving at the moment so it's a bit tricky,' I said to Sonny, but he didn't give a crap whether I was driving or mid bungy jump – he wanted my help NOW.

As we all know as parents, trying to defuse any stressful situation is better than letting it drag on, because the kids WILL NOT STOP asking you to do something.

So: eyes ahead on the road, right hand on the steering wheel, left hand behind me in a position that would have made a contortionist proud, I managed to fix a Lego design that I hadn't seen yet.

Other examples include opening a packet of crisps, separating two kids, putting a shoe on, wiping faces and taking jumpers off.

Finally, it was quiet again and I was in deep thought about work, house, kids, play dates, birthday parties, dentist appointments, school uniform, etc when my son piped up again:

'Mummy, Mummy, watch!'

'Mummy can't watch right now, darling. I'm driving.'

'Mummy, watch!'

'I need to keep my eyes on the road but we'll be home in five minutes.'

'Mummy, Mummy, Mummy, watch!'

'Not right now, my love.'

'Mummy, watch.'

I decided it was best to ignore him – I even turned up the music in the car, which made my eldest son Basil sit up, because he wanted to play a song he liked on my phone, that connects via Bluetooth to the car:

Basil: 'Mum, can I have your phone?'

Sonny: 'Mummy, watch.'

Basil: 'Phone, please.'

Sonny: 'Mummy, Mummy, watch this.'

Basil: 'Mum! Where is your phone?'

Sonny: 'Mummy, watch! Mummy, watch!'

Inca: 'PENIS!'

THAT IS IT. I AM *DONE*.

I pulled over and found myself yelling at all three of them. 'Basil! No! You can't have my phone! Inca, stop saying "penis", and Sonny, WHAT IS IT?'

There was a short pause, and then: 'Sorry, penis,' said Inca, and we all fell about laughing.

And that's the thing about kids: with the summer holidays and August around the corner, it's going to be tough. Mentally, physically and spiritually exhausting. But at any given time you can appreciate the madness and instead of trying to not step in the puddles, we can learn how to dance in the rain.

It wasn't until I got home I realised I had left my shopping at the self-service counter. Too many tabs open.

School's out for summer

OK, brace yourselves, because this is going to be a bumpy ride. Schools are out – we are officially in charge and take full responsibility of our children 24/7 for six whole weeks ... which I find hilarious. How on earth am I in charge of small people? HA!

Before we dissect the turbulent month of August, I have some of my own rules over the summer holiday period that have taught me to stay that extra bit cooler in the long hot days ahead:

1. If your child gets wet at a swimming pool, hot tub, or splashed with a hose pipe, there is no need to give them a bath that evening.
2. Say yes to 'CANIHAVEASNACK'. With all the snacks in the day, this will result in a meal. Job done.
3. Pay them to wear sunscreen.
4. When they say 'Mummy, watch' let them know you are watching so they don't repeat themselves over and over and over ... and over.
5. Move the hands on the kitchen clock forward 90 minutes. When it's 9 p.m. it looks like it's 10.30 p.m.
6. Embrace the chaos – it doesn't matter if your house is mess.
7. Drink that wine and gin.
8. It's OK to be on screens if it gives you some breathing space. Just make sure they're not googling 'girls' bums'.
9. Try to enjoy it as much as you can – not long from now, they'll be grown up and won't want to hang out with you at all. And guess what? We'll miss it (apparently).

So, now that we have cemented the basic mothering rules/ needs over the summer holidays, let's dig in deeper and really talk about those oh so *special* days off.

At-home days

Installing a paddling pool in the garden is a tell-tale sign that holidaying with small children is a stress and that these summer months will be long and relentless. One time, Jesse and I spent a good 30 minutes filling up the paddling pool using the hose with cold water but adding hot water from the kettle, running back and forth from the kitchen to the garden to make it more bearable for the kids to sit in. It was quite the operation, which was abruptly aborted when a potty-training Basil decided to take an adult-sized turd in the pool, making all other kids run a mile and refuse to get back into the pool. And if it's not poo, it'll be mud, grass, wee, food, toys that aren't supposed to go in water, my clothes, my sunglasses or my mobile phone – followed by children confusing the paddling pool with a trampoline. Bouncing on the side of the paddling pool walls and stepping on them to get in and out of the pool seems to be a favourite pastime for my boys, alas making the padding pool deflate and us parents have to blow it up again – and refill it again. It's quite the chore and inevitably at some point will be punctured along the way. From clean paddling pool to muddy plastic carpet in the garden. Every year without fail.

Theme parks/days out

Shortly after the schools break up for the summer holidays, we all kid ourselves into thinking we're going to have the best six weeks off together, as a family. We're going to have the best fun and not worry about work – until, of course, work is knocking at your door and you find yourself answering emails in the line queuing up for Legoland whilst sounding incredibly enthusiastic about a ride that you have no idea the name of or what it involves, but you're in it for the long haul because YOU ARE A JUGGLING, MULTI-TASKING QUEEN.

'Mummy, Mummy, watch.'

'Mummy! Mummy! Watch!'

'Mummy, watch.'

This was followed by a tugging at my arms that made me drop my phone mid email 'please can we revert to this tomorrow' type of crap. I retrieved my phone, trying my best to show by my clown-mime facial expression how happy I was to be there and what on earth did my kids want me to bloody watch now?

Then I saw it. The ride I was waiting in line for.

At first glance it scared the shit out of me. At my age I cannot stand rides that are too fast and spinny – they genuinely make me feel sick.

'Why don't I watch you guys on this one and I can film you and send it to Daddy?'

Ah, yes, Daddy who is working from home without any interruptions and managing to have Teams meeting video calls with his IRL background, rather than my green screen of balloons that hides the fact I am indeed not at home.

I found myself getting plugged into a ride where I had to straddle a horse and sit there, hardly able to breathe, because I'd anxiously pulled the bar into my body way too much just in case I was to fall out. I felt utterly sick to my stomach.

I thought it would be best to distract myself on this ride by once again checking emails and replying as much as I could, blocking out the idea that I was about to be flung through the air on a tiny horse, not being able to breathe.

My boys beside me were loving it. They were embracing all of the excitement and reassuring me it would all be OK. My, oh, my – what a role reversal: my ten year old telling me it was all OK and to enjoy it.

And what was the worst that could happen, really?

Well, I'll tell you. Throwing up a little bit in your mouth and having to swallow it as your plunged through the air deafened by the screams of ecstatic children including my own, once again telling me to watch.

I had visions of Jesse casually enjoying a nice email day without having to swallow any of his own vomit, and I promised myself when I got home that I would have some quality time to myself.

Once home and after briefing Jesse on the afternoon I had had, and that I very much needed some time to answer emails without throwing up or screaming, I was granted this wish and Jesse let me crack on whist he 'babysat' our children.

And yet there was no peace. I may have been locked away in another room away from the kids and Jesse, but I could hear the utter madness that was unfolding from behind the door. Noises that sounded like they are definitely trying to kill each other and wrecking the entire living room, into the bargain.

I couldn't focus on my work at all. Instead, I was sitting at my laptop, fingers poised over the keyboard about to type, but all I could think was: 'WHAT IS THAT NOISE AND WHERE IS JESSE?' (I actually think Jesse may have been in the same room

Inca screaming at Jesse, by Basil.

as them but he's so much more chilled than I am – so chilled, that he may as well be asleep at times.)

'Babes, I can't hear myself think!' I text him and, 30 seconds later, the sound volumes have decreased to a normal level. Hurrah.

And then something that brings such joy to my ears happens:

'Daddy, Daddy, watch.'

'Daddy, watch.'

'Daddy, Daddy, watch!'

'Watch!'

'Watch!'

'Watch!'

'Daddy, Daddy, watch!'

'Daddy, *watch*!'

'FOR CHRIST'S SAKE JUST WATCH THE CHILD!'

Another text to Jesse.

It was quiet again for a moment and I settled into some work with one eye on the laptop and one ear on the door, and for the millionth time I wondered if this was what all mothers do when they try to work with kids at home.

I heard Sonny ask Jesse a question.

I heard Basil ask Jesse a question.

And both had the same answer.

'Ask Mummy.'

LIVID.

The boys came bounding into my office full of beans and joy, asking me what came first – the chicken or the egg.

August

Taking your family away on holiday in August is quite something, isn't it? I think it's best if I first start by saying that *nothing is ever as good as it seems or as bad as it seems.* I like to remind myself of this as I start to get over-excited about the idea of having a family holiday abroad, with high expectations of it being the best holiday ever. My imagination takes over and I visualise us as a family together, all peaceful, all laughing around a table watching the sunset, playing a game of Uno as my husband and I share a loving look whilst sipping a piña colada as the children read their books and then tell us they're tired.

If this is what your holidays are like, then congratulations – you have won in life. One day this will be my reality holiday – when the kids are older, perhaps, and I don't have to run around after a toddler. (And I bet I'll miss the chaos!)

Holidays with young children

Going on holiday with small children is quite possibly one of the most stressful things we can do as parents. Maybe it's just us, or maybe it's because my daughter is trying to keep up with her two older brothers; either way, going on holiday with a toddler is, from beginning to end, just one long war between parent and toddler that generally no one wins – it's a constant uphill battle.

Packing

Packing for a holiday? May as well be moving house. All the paraphernalia to remember to pack with a baby … and the more children you have, the more you have to pack. Naturally I am the one that does ALL the packing (and unpacking) in our house. My husband is perfectly capable but he's very much a last-minute Larry and if I left it up to him we would always be late – and, as we know, aeroplanes don't wait for anyone.

One time, I wanted to put more faith in him and give him the benefit of the doubt, so I decided to sit in the passenger seat (metaphorically speaking), and let Jesse decide when was a good time to leave the house and have enough time to check in, go through security and find our gate etc. (I can feel the anxiety rise when I write this.)

Please note that the following travel anecdote is 100 per cent accurate – and something that will never happen again.

We had a flight at 6.31 a.m. from Gatwick (yes, please note that extra minute – why it was there, I have no idea), which meant we had to wake the children up at 2 a.m. or something ridiculous, which as you can imagine was the battle already lost. Three children moaning, complaining – the smallest one had a total meltdown and refused to get dressed, doing the raised arm/body flop when I tried to pick her up.

There was a TV commercial some years ago about a family going to Disneyland. In this 'real' commercial, the parents wake up their children (small children, I may add) and they all smile, hug each other and set off on their holiday so perfectly behaved and happy. Naively, this was how I had imagined this particular morning to play out.

By the time we were all in the taxi going to the airport, my husband and I were not talking to each other. By this point, the kids had figured out we were going on an aeroplane and became excited puppies, bouncing around in the back – without the bumper seats that I had especially asked my husband to mention when ordering the cab. Grr. So now the children were using their seatbelts as a sling shot for absolutely anything they could find in their perfectly packed (thanks to me) backpacks, and arguing about who was going to sit next to the window.

My husband bravely broke the silence between us: 'Have you packed toothbrushes?'

Er, yes, you twat. I'd packed literally everything and then some, for the 'just in case' incidents.

'Yep,' I responded shortly, not making eye contact.

A few minutes passed.

Here he goes again.

'Have you packed the kids' goggles?'

FUCK OFF AND MAYBE ASK ME WHEN WE ARE IN THE HOUSE WHILST I AM PACKING, AND NOT IN THE TAXI ON THE WAY TO THE AIRPORT, YOU UTTER BELL-END.

'Yes, of course.'

I could feel there was more coming from him and I reminded myself to take some deep breaths. I could feel word vomit rearing its ugly head …

'Have you pa —'

'YES, JESSE!!! I have packed *everything*! That is why I spent all yesterday afternoon making sure we were all packed and have absolutely everything. I have packed it *all*, and you would know that if you had helped me do it!!!'

'Well, I packed too …'

'For yourself! YOURSELF! And it took mere *minutes* because all your laundry is clean and put away for your convenience, and who did that???'

'Mummy, watch.'

'Not *now*, darling.'

'Mummy, Mummy, watch!'

'Mummy, watch!'

'Mummy —!'

For the first time in the taxi, I moved my gaze to my child sitting next to me, to see what utter shit he was going to pull out of the bag this time.

He went cross-eyed, stuck his chin out and made a noise like a constipated monkey.

I actually broke into laughter and, for a moment, felt like I was looking forward to our holiday. I gave Jesse a smile that said: 'Let's reset.'

That's the thing about kids – they can either ignite or defuse a situation very quickly. I was very grateful for Sonny asking me to watch him at that particular moment.

Did you see Prince Louis at the 2022 Platinum Jubilee celebrations, when he was messing around and pulling faces at his mother, the then Duchess of Cambridge? Mothers everywhere rejoiced – we could all relate.

Airport rage

When we arrived at the airport I was aware that we were already cutting it quite fine timewise, and we still needed to check in. We got into the queue to talk to a machine, which looked like it was on its last legs, that would assist us with our luggage.

And that was when my toddler decided to run riot.

I didn't mind at first – she had energy to kill before we boarded our flight, and I smiled at other mothers doing the same thing with their small children. For a moment we felt as one, as if we were in a toddler travel club and it was OK if your kid was running around like a lunatic. But when it was our turn to arrive at the ticketing machine to check in our luggage, this was when my toddler decided to turn into the Tasmanian Devil and make life extremely difficult for us.

We did our best to contain Inca's behaviour, whilst talking to a machine that acted like it was from the eighties (in a non-cool way). And we decided, after she had managed to deliberately kick the computer from inside my grip, that we had better put her in her pushchair.

You've probably noticed when toddlers are in such a state of 'I don't give a fuck' that trying to get them into their push-chair is something of a mind, body and soul challenge. They tend to brilliantly demonstrate the meaning of rigor mortis as you try to calmly put them in their seat, their little bodies turning into a plank of wood that makes it almost impossible to plug them into their pushchair as they scream at you, slap you and throw whatever they are holding at you. If you're lucky, you'll get the bonus back-bend too. But you *will* win this fight – you have to. Even though it will zap all your patience and dignity in public.

I'm pretty sure bystanders used this performance as a form of contraception. (There was apparently once a TV commercial by Durex, that was banned. It showed a toddler having a full-on tantrum in a supermarket aisle. The scene continued long enough for it to be uncomfortable viewing, and then the text appeared on the screen: 'Wear a condom.' Genius.)

So as I was rugby-tackling my daughter into her pushchair and dodging her slaps, my other two boys and Jesse were getting all the luggage on the belt for it to be whisked away to

the plane. Finally, the machine stopped, bleeped and spat out
our boarding passes. Hurrah, we were off!

Noticing the time, I was starting to get the panic on. The
plane had started to board and we still hadn't made it through
security. I could feel my anxiety levels start to rise as I began a
small jog to the security gate, pretending to be such a fun mum
that I was enjoying the running.

I wasn't in the slightest. I was cursing my husband under my
breath and myself for not remembering to wear a Tena pad in
my knickers. But I reassured myself that I'd be fine – it was only
a small jog …

When we reached the security point, our boarding passes,
that had been given to us by the oldest computer I'd ever seen
moments earlier, came up as VOID.

The security guard immediately thought we were dodgy and
asked us to step aside.

'We just got them!' I explained. 'We're going to miss our
flight!'

'Who gave these boarding passes to you?' asked the guard,
who had now summoned someone else on her walkie-talkie.
The commotion had started a stir behind us as people looked
up from their phones to see what all the fuss was about, camera
phones at the ready in case we'd do something whacky and suit-
able for a TikTok video.

'We got them from YOU! At this airport! We're going to miss
our flight – please let us through!'

The VOID boarding passes were passed around four
people of authority, and luckily we were told they were fine …
hurrah!

I thought nothing of the VOID boarding passes and continued to mentally prepare for the next stage of our journey.

You do not want to be behind a family when going through
security. What will take two minutes for a single person will

usually take about half an hour for a family of five, due to the amount of paraphernalia we need to take out of the bags to go through the x-ray machine; the baby food that needs to be checked; the milk that needs to be thrown away or drunk extremely quickly, usually by myself; the pushchair that needs to be folded up, meaning taking the toddler out the pushchair that it has taken so long to get her into, putting it through the machine, making sure the toddler walks through the security machine alone without running off or kicking off, putting said toddler back into the pushchair and going through the same drama as before.

And guaranteed our bags are always stopped for extra checking due to the rogue pouch of organic fruit purée I forget about at the bottom of my bag.

We made it through security and had minutes to get to our gate. I was back to being in a mood with Jesse, who seemed completely oblivious of the time we *didn't* have as he casually walked through the airport to the gate – like a teenage sloth. I think he deliberately walked slowly to make a point – or to royally piss me off.

'What gate is it?' I asked Jesse.

'575.'

Oh, good – the gate that was the furthest away in the entire airport. We may as well have walked to bloody Spain! We all started to lightly jog, much to my toddler's delight as she was back in the pram, thinking it was a fun game. She looked back at me to see if I too was enjoying this as much as she was. Little did she know I was ever so slightly starting to pee myself, and my 'glow' was turning into a full sweat-on. But she was happy, thank goodness.

'Mummy, watch.'

Mummy, Mummy, watch …!'

At this point I was so not in the mood to watch anything

apart from the ticking clock and where the gate was ... but it continued from behind me:

'Mummy, watch!'

'Mummy, you're not watching!'

Jogging with a backpack-covered pram, a sweat-on and a pelvic floor that was severely testing me, I managed to look at my son behind me, to once again see what he was doing that he so desperately needed to show me at this particularly stressful moment.

Nothing.

Absolutely nothing.

He was just jogging behind me doing nothing, but this was something I had to watch him do. I congratulated him on his ability to keep with me, which was more than I could say for Jesse, who was still lagging behind us, looking at his phone and not worried at all about getting to the gate.

After what felt like an eternity we got to the gate. I was delighted to see that nobody had started to board and we were indeed there in plenty of time. Cross, though, that the 'FINAL BOARDING' message on the screens at the airport was in fact a lie.

My husband walked up to us in the departure lounge about five minutes later with a chilled demeanour and a round of bottled waters from the vending machine along the way.

'Where was the emergency?' he asked, smirking.

I wanted to hug him and slap him in the face at the same time.

We off-loaded all the bags from the pram, closed it up and I took a deep breath. We had made it. I wandered around, walking after my toddler, thinking it was good for her to work off some (more) energy before we boarded the plane. The boys were already on their fully charged tablets, Jesse was on Twitter and I felt my sweaty brow start to cool down. I was very grateful for the water Jesse had bought just moments earlier.

Families were called to board first so we took advantage of this and headed to the front of the queue with boarding passes in our hand – totally forgetting the VOID situation.

The ground staff scanned our boarding passes and looked puzzled. *Oh, here we go again*, I thought. 'We were given these boarding passes from this airport,' I offered up, before the person doing the scanning started to question them.

'No, you're at the wrong gate. This is a TUI flight – you're flying with EasyJet.'

FUUUUUUUCCCCCCCCCCKKKKKKKKKKKKKKKKKKKKKKKKKK!
Panic.

Jesse and I looked at each other.

'RUN!'

For the first time in our relationship, Jesse actually ran to get somewhere on time – something that made my stress levels go through the roof as I now knew *he* was worried. He took Basil with him, and the pram. There was no time to think – it was just GO!

I scooped up my two-year-old, three bags and told my six-year-old to stay close to me. I ran, but I had absolutely no idea where I was going. I'd lost my husband and my eldest son, I had no idea what our flight number was, or our gate number, and I was literally beyond a mess.

Jesse called me and I managed to answer and speak with my phone lodged in between my right ear and my shoulder as I ran back into the main terminal concourse.

'We're gate 95.'

'Gate 95??!!! Are you kidding me??? FOR FUCK'S SAKE, JESSE!'

He hung up and I realised there was no time to have an argument but continued to run with my head at the 90-degree angle required to balance my phone on my shoulder, my toddler on one arm and the three bags on my other.

Ah, the toddler … it was at this moment that she decided she wanted to do a poo.

My head cocked to the right, I managed to side-eye her on my left and tell her it wasn't the best time and that we had a plane to catch. By this point, my light jog had upgraded itself into a heavy sprint, and my sweaty brow had turned into a full-on wet face that even my eyebrows were struggling to control. Beads of sweat marinated on my mascara, causing my eyes to sting. My pelvic floor had left the building entirely: I had fully wet myself.

Of course, this wasn't OK with her so naturally Inca had a meltdown, pushing herself away from me, kicking, slapping and shouting. Somehow managing to add extra body weight to herself, she slid down the left hand side of my body. She was clinging on to my leg and I was still managing to run.

'Mummy, put her in the pram,' gasped Sonny. Ha! The pram! *I would do anything right now for that pram …*

I decided I should let her run, so I placed Inca on the ground, put my phone away and offered her my hand. She refused to take it, expressing this by stamping her foot on the ground, clasping her hands together and pouting angrily. Turning around, she started to run in the other direction … It took all my strength and patience to pick her up and start running again.

The gate was FAR AWAY. I was running past other gates with families looking happy, ready to board their flight without any stress. I could feel the weight of them all watching me as I ran past with a screaming toddler who was shouting 'Poo!', and me with a wet patch on my jeans. I cursed myself for drinking that whole bottle of water.

As I ran past the departures board, I noticed it said 'GATE CLOSED'. Suddenly, I stopped in my tracks and decided to give up. We were never going to make it. I called Jesse to let him know it wasn't worth the stress and drama, but my phone played the 'no reception' card. I couldn't get through to him and had no idea where he was.

It was at this point that my six-year-old said something I will never forget. Sonny is the most positive, optimistic little boy and at this particular moment of admitting defeat, Sonny shone. 'Mummy, you can do this. I believe in you. You can do anything you put your mind to. You are my magic.' (I am actually welling up as I type this.) He spoke to me the way I speak to him. They do listen! This is a memory that will stay close to my heart forever. In the depths of despair and darkness, we found a ray of positive hope. My son really is Sonny by name, sunny by nature.

His words of encouragement were exactly what I needed to hear at that particular time. He believed in me and I didn't want to let him down.

We finally saw gate 95 in the distance. At the end of the terminal's long corridor I could see my eldest son Basil waving his arms in the air: 'MUMMY!!! MUMMY!!! WE'RE HERE!' I felt a sense of achievement and all I wanted to do was run to my son and give him a huge hug.

We made it. I was a train wreck but we made it. Jesse looked me over and had the sensibility not to ask why my jeans were wet or why I had bloodshot eyes and mascara smudges all down my cheeks.

This was not how I had envisioned myself to look when we flew.

Jesse, Basil and Inca all ran to the plane and I fumbled around, trying to find the boarding passes; I decided to keep Sonny with me in case I needed more of his positive vibes.

'These are void,' said the airline staff member. 'I can't let you on the plane.'

Deep breaths.

Deeper still.

Oh, dear. Here she comes ... My inner lioness mother bitch cunt-face had been woken up.

I. LOST. MY. SHIT.

There are only two people on this planet who have seen me lose my shit: my husband Jesse and my sister Bonnie, and they are always shell-shocked after this beast erupts. And now I can count the lady who worked for EasyJet, and Sonny, my six-year-old son.

I can't quite remember word for word what I said, but put it this way – she let us on the plane.

I walked down the aisle looking for my seat number aware all eyes were on me – WE were the late family that had kept everyone waiting. I was also very aware I looked like Alice Cooper with a wet backside. By this point I was not even embarrassed. I had lost all dignity (this usually only happens when you give birth but now, I figured, also when you run for a plane).

I sat down in my seat and couldn't quite believe we'd made it. I was almost in a state of shock. In a trance, I stared straight ahead – I actually don't think I blinked for three minutes. I was soaking wet – part sweat, part piss. And I was *fuming* at Jesse. I couldn't even look at him.

He leaned over and asked: 'Did you pack my toiletries?'

Flight club

When I was in my twenties I travelled around the world on fashion shoots and it was a lot less stressful. One week I'd be in Morocco, the next Thailand, New York, Paris, Bognor Regis ... I was travelling all over the place, and taking a plane was as normal as taking the bus. I became friendly with the British

Airways check-in staff at JFK airport and they would always bump me up to business class on my flights back to London. I once had a date at Heathrow's terminal 3 Costa coffee. I even met a guy on a plane and we ended up dating for a while. I know many models who have met their future partners on a plane – because this is where we always were. But as exciting as it was, I always felt a pang of 'one day' when I would see a family together in the departure lounge, all excited to board their flight. I knew one day I wanted a family of my own to fly on a plane with. I loved the idea of everyone on an adventure together, and didn't ever once think about the stress that can come with it.

Cut to twenty years later, when I was sitting in my urine-stained jeans, hair in frizzy disarray, on edge, unable to look at my husband.

My kids had already asked for snacks, my toddler had figured out how to unfasten her seatbelt, repeatedly open and close the tray table mechanism, and how to kick the seat in front of her. (I was delighted when I saw a small child sitting in front of my toddler – thank goodness it wasn't a grown up.) I had a flash-back to the young, responsibility-free, light-packing single traveller, and I missed her *terribly*.

We taxied to the runway and for the first time in 20 minutes, I glanced over to Jesse to make some sort of eye contact.

He was asleep.

Why, why, *why* does he always fall asleep on the plane when there is still so much parenting to do?

I had a toddler now refusing to sit down and who was trying anything in her power to move away from me. She even managed to slide under her seat and find the life jacket.

'Excuse me, can you please make sure your child is sitting down with her seatbelt fastened? We're about to take off.'

You fucking do it. 'Yes, no problem.' I fake-smiled.

But there was very much a problem, because my toddler wouldn't do what I wanted her to do. And I knew that as soon as I tried to contain her, she would scream at the top of her lungs. And so she does – with my husband still fast asleep across the aisle from me.

With a crash of mum guilt, I realised she was still holding in the poo that she had needed earlier, so I started to mentally plan the escape from our seats to the loo the moment we were allowed to do so.

The twenty-year-old me would always want to stay well clear of any children on a flight. I flew to Cape Town once with a toddler kicking the back of my seat for 9 hours of the 12 hour flight. Generally, I knew if I was near a child on a plane I was in for a rough ride. What a stupid cow I was! How typically selfish of a young, childless person to think about how it would be affecting *me* and not the mother. Today, if I am flying solo for a shoot abroad, I actually really miss my kids not being with me and always want to help other mothers with children when they're having a rough time. I like to reassure them that it's OK if your child is kicking off on a plane – I just wish someone had said this to me when I flew for the first time as a mother.

Basil was seven months old and we went to Thailand for New Year's Eve (I had booked the destination before I became a mother, can you tell?). I vividly remember considering opening the door of the plane when we were 35,000 feet just to escape the utter chaos we had with us. To make matters worse, we had an eye-roller and tutter sitting in front of us, turning around giving us *the eyes* just to let us know we were ruining her flight.

It enraged me. I was doing everything in my power to keep Basil calm and quiet whilst I was in the middle of an anxiety battle, but still she gave me the look of disgust.

It meant war.

I decided I was going to fart on this woman. I'm not sure if you're aware of this, but farts can lose their potency when on an aeroplane – something about the air filter and external air supply – and thank goodness, otherwise the vessel would STINK on long-haul flights. I stood in the aisle with my back to her as I rummaged in an overhead locker, so my bum was pretty much directly in her face. And I let one out. Flying always makes me gassy so I had the perfect guff lined up. Off it went in her direction … she didn't know, but it really did make me smile and reduced my stress levels somewhat. A form of self-care if you will – farting on strangers on the plane. I guess you won't find that in a self-help book.

Later, I was shushing the baby in the gangway where the toilets at the back of the plane are. She came along and saw me waiting in line. She gave me the same disgusted look, and I decided to up the ante. We didn't talk, we just stood next to each other for a good twenty minutes, waiting for the loo. But there wasn't anyone in the loo – I was just outside it shushing my baby – MWWWOOOHAHAHAHAHAHAHAHAHAHAAA! When she eventually figured this out, she gave me the best tut she could muster and pushed her way into the loo.

Moral of the story: don't mess with a mother in despair – we will bring you down.

I have definitely become a stronger, bolder, more defiant person since becoming a mum. I was known as 'Switzerland' BC (before children) – I was always on the fence about most things, and never spoke up or stood up for myself. Now I fart on strangers when they annoy me. Who am I?

One time, whilst flying with my 18-month-old, I needed some milk on the plane, to help soothe him. I had finished breastfeeding and the milk I had had in the bottle ready to go had been taken away from me at security. I had completely forgotten to get some at the airport, but had reassured myself that, once on the plane, I'd be able to get some.

Wrong. The airline we were flying with didn't have pints of free-flowing milk, but had those tiny tubs that you have to rip open and which perhaps gave you a teaspoon full.

I knew it would take a lot to fill up a bottle; still, I knew I could rely on the air stewardesses to provide me with some quality milk tubs to help soothe my toddler.

Wrong. I was sternly told that only one tub per person was allowed on the plane. Panic! I really needed milk, and we had a good 90 minutes left on the plane.

It was time to pull out the motherhood guns. I knew what I had to do …

When the air steward was past my seat and busily attending to other passengers – offering them their tea and coffee with one tub of milk – I headed to the kitchen area at the front of the plane.

Pretending that I needed the loo, I hovered there, my heart pounding so much I could feel the pulse in my neck almost knocking my dangly earrings. I rummaged through the cupboards until I came to a very full drawer of milk tubs. There must have been hundreds in there! I took a full handful and raced back to my seat, terrified of being caught. All of this was done with my baby in tow, as I thought it would be a good idea to use him as bait if I was questioned on what I was doing.

I then spent the next 15 minutes opening and emptying all the tubs into the bottle, hiding all the empty packets in my handbag (that still smells to this day a bit of off milk). But I did it! Another classic example of a mother going that extra mile for her child.

Holi-daze

We landed at our holiday destination, and as soon as we had, questions from the kids came flying in:

'Why do we have to go on holiday?'
'Mummy, do they have ketchup in this country?'
'Mummy, did you know "Spain" rhymes with "pain"?'
'Why have you hired a car?'
'Why is it so hot?'
'Why do I need to wear sunscreen?'
'Mummy, watch, watch, watch! Mummy, watch …'

Silly me for thinking the plane would be the most stressful part of going on holiday with the kids! Being on holiday with young children is parenting to the extreme. It's next-level parenting. We have them all to ourselves for 14 days straight, making sure they don't drown, they stay hydrated, have sun lotion on, wear a hat, don't fight with each other, make sure they are outside most of the time but covered up, not on their screens (otherwise you may as well be at home, as my parenting magazine tells me) and basically have no down-time for yourself until they are all asleep around 10 p.m. because we (the parents) are too exhausted to even think about doing a proper bedtime routine. Hence the rules in the last chapter.

Being in a swimming pool with your small children is very much a love/hate situation. I love that we are all in the water together and making the most of 'our time' together. I often grab my phone and record Jesse in slow motion as he throws Inca up in the air and catches her again – smiles all round. If I were to post this online we'd look like the perfect family on tour. What you *don't* see online is the endless splashing from my kids, who decide to jump into the pool (with flippers on, I may add) next to my head. They resurface as I am still wiping the over-chlorinated water out of my eyes and are up in my face immediately: I can see the reflection of myself in their goggles and wish I had fully taken off last night's mascara.

How you wish you'd had time to get semi-permanent lashes done, or a wax, or even had time to get your eyebrows threaded. My last summer holiday, I basically needed garden shears to get me back on track. I even forgot about my hair colouring appointment before we left to go away. I looked a hot mess when I arrived at the pool: pale body, dark roots, stubble rash around my bikini line area, and I had even managed to mistake my eye mask for bikini bottoms, so I that had to wear my mother-in-law's all-in-one swimsuit from the nineties, which had lost all its elasticity in the bum and boob area. My kids liked to point and laugh, saying I had pooed myself as the material sagged around my backside.

Basil, my eldest, who doesn't quite yet understand his strength, decided to climb up on me from behind, using my shoulders as his platform to raise himself out of the water. This also had the outcome of pushing me down into the water at quite a terrifying speed, and for a moment I felt as though my life was in danger and how much I was *not* enjoying this time at the pool.

I flurried to the surface, feeling my sun-burnt shoulders from where Basil had gripped them. I took a breath and just as I opened my mouth to tell Basil off, I inhaled a good wave of water that Sonny splashed in my face using his flipper. It streamed out of my nose. I officially felt violated.

As I wiped the water out of my eyes and tried to style out the snot that had started streaming down my face, and ensure my boobs were still well and truly contained inside my swimming costume, I was greeted with a wet slap and called 'It!'

Oh, good. We were playing Tag in a pool full of other people who probably didn't want to see a 40-something-year-old running through water with mascara down their face and boobs almost knocking them out. But I play along because I AM FUN and I want my kids to remember me as fun when they are too cool to play with me anymore.

There are moments of utter joy, of course. They don't last long, so when you have a pang of *'This is great!'* LAP IT UP. I know too well that these fleeting moments will come to a standstill, usually when my children (my eldest more than anyone else) slide up to me on the beach and ruin my tranquil moment as I look out to the ocean and watch a beautiful sunset, and say 'Mum, I'm bored. Can I have your phone?'

I read somewhere that we only get 18 summer holidays with our kids. This partly upset me and party filled me with joy. I would love a holiday where I don't have to worry about where they are on the beach, and to be able to totally unwind and relax. I would love to read a book! I have no idea if any parents out there actually have time to read books so if you are reading this right now, BRAVO! You are nailing life! Send me a message on Instagram right now that says 'GREENBUSH' so I know you got this far in reading my book. You rock!

(If you're wondering where 'GREENBUSH' has come from, it is what the kids and I shout at wasps that linger and hover over our food. It generally doesn't work at all but makes the kids feel like they have some sort of control over these pesky bugs. If you were to sit across a restaurant from us, you'd probably think we were all mad shouting 'GREENBUSH' at our plates.)

I decided to try and make this game of 'It' as short as possible by threatening the kids with the word 'ice cream', using it as a ploy to leave me alone and sit still for five minutes. But then I heard my three-year-old ...

'Mummy, Mummy, watch!'
'Mummy, Mummy, watch!'
'Mummy, watch!'

I looked over at Inca, who was happy in the baby pool, all properly kitted up like she was ready for swimming-pool war: the all-in-one suit, the hat that covered her neck, the sunglasses, the arm bands, the goggles, the sunscreen ... I mean, she looked ridiculous, as if she was allergic to water. (When I was a kid on holiday at Inca's age I was pretty much naked – not even wearing sunscreen. Gotta love that eighties parenting.)

I was watching Inca intently to see her do some splashing or jumping or something equally as insubstantial, when she stopped. She's silent. She wasn't doing anything apart from looking totally frozen – she wasn't even blinking, but looking directly at me, her smile starting to fade. *Holy shit, is she having a seizure?* In a panic I started to run to her but then she moved, looking really happy with herself and says, as loudly as possible: 'I did a wee!'

Oh, kill me now.

Camping

But what about those summer holidays that don't whisk you abroad? Camping in the UK is always a great escape and a brilliant idea – until you have a fight with your partner just as you leave after packing up half of your house to build another, temporary home where you're more cramped than you were before, minus the creature comforts. You realise on day two that you don't actually like camping but you do realise it's a great time for the kids to be feral, be free, roam and live like cavemen. And the truth is they do absolutely love it, which means that I love it too (apart from when they are crawling and only want to head towards the fire pit), until that time, when you've returned home and you're back to reality, but have forgotten to brief the kids that they can no longer do wild wees. (On Basil's first day back at school he urinated in his classroom's outside area that had a little stream running through it – and in front of other parents, too. Which, to be fair, cemented a solid relationship with them. Gotta love kids for breaking the ice. Or pissing on plants.)

Camping is obviously about the most out-doorsy holiday experience you can get, but the frustration is that, like a lot of kids, my boys hate sunscreen – especially my eldest. I try my best to make it fun, in any shape or form, but he will still do his best to avoid putting it on. It usually ends in a wrestling match with me pinning him down and smearing sunscreen into his cheeks and nose, or I end up running after him with cream ready in the palm of my hand, ready to slather it on.

'You can only do my arms!'

'I need to do you all! It's for your own protection!' The irony is, I need protection whilst putting on my son's sun protection – flailing arms and legs catch me in areas that will bear a bruise for days.

Sometimes I wonder if it's worth letting the kids actually experience the nasties that could happen if I didn't protect them from all the things I warn them about. Would they learn to apply sunscreen if they got burnt, or would they brush their teeth better if they got awful toothache? Would they get their shoes on quickly if we left for school shoeless?

To the people with older children – DO THEY EVER LISTEN? I often ask myself, or Jesse, or anyone who will listen: When does all this get easier? I'm really looking forward to a holiday that doesn't include mealtimes or sun cream application with meltdowns.

Ferry vs fairy

Last Easter, we travelled to Ireland by car to visit Jesse's family. I was very pleasantly surprised by how enthusiastic Inca was to travel by ferry. Turns out she thought I'd said 'fairy'. Her disappointment turned into a tantrum. But I could sympathise with her on this occasion.

Jesse's Right to Reply

Whoah, whoah, whoah, whoah. Whoah!

OK, let's just take a minute here to reset. Forget everything you just read – here comes the husband with some truth bombs that will introduce you to the *real* Louise.

OK, OK, I *did* read all the stuff written about me and yes … perhaps there are some differences between us that I can try to work on. I do go to the loo longer than Louise does and I do get more sleep than she does, but it's all out of love. The kids want her more than they want me at certain times in the day – isn't that love? And to be honest (and perhaps all dads can agree with me on this) – we are actually envious that the kids go to the mother first. We'd do anything to be interrupted during a luxury poo or be woken up at 4 a.m. with the news that's there's a wet bed that needs changing. Why don't the kids ask for us first?

Just kidding – we are very smug about this and long may it continue.

In the grand scheme of things, and without sounding like I'm weaponising incompetence, is not helping out with Christmas admin or taking a shower at the swimming pool really such a bad thing? In my defence, Louise seems to enjoy all these things. And she has this remarkable habit of saying she's 'fine' when I ask her why she looks like she's chewed on a wasp. After asking three or four times and getting the same answer I can only assume that she is actually fine. Then she won't talk to me for an entire afternoon as I try to decipher her (very good) eye-rolling and huffing and puffing. She gives the big bad wolf a run for his money.

The truth is, I will know that something is bugging her and I've given her three or four chances to let me know how I can help – and yet here we are, ignoring each other in the car on the way to the airport for a nice family holiday. I only asked her if she packed some key items, for crying out loud.

Men are not mind readers. Take note.

If Louise has annoyed or irritated me she'll know about it and it'll be dealt with immediately, whereas Louise will keep quiet and let all her exasperations marinate over a matter of weeks, mocking me in her videos online, and probably with her girlfriends in WhatsApp chats. Then, without any warning, she'll explode into a chorus of mocking madness. She tells me it's a Virgo thing. I beg to differ.

So, back to Louise and a little bit on her/us.

First off, she's not even really called Louise. She must have mentioned it somewhere in here that her birth name is Katherine Louise Spencer-MacCallum? Imagine how much fun it was booking flights for her in the early days of dating, when I didn't know this information. It's not every day you find out your partner's name is something else entirely. When we said our wedding vows, according to Louise we had a 'Ross and Rachel' moment in *Friends*: all my side of the family and my friends gasped when they heard me take 'Katherine' as my wife and not 'Louise'. I mean, what?

Watching Louise write a book has been intriguing. She has kept it at close quarters, perfecting the tilt of her laptop screen to stop me from snooping these past few months. Please also note that, as it turns out, writing a book in a domestic setting is the perfect get-out clause for doing anything:

Me: 'Let's watch a new series/Reply to that urgent email/ Bring about world peace/Pretty much anything I want to do.'

Louise: 'I can't. I'm writing a book.'

Anyway, let's get on with it.

Do you like being spoken to from the next room? Come on over. My wife would be delighted to test the capability of your humble human ears, often through walls and around several corners, and will take offence should you fail to exhibit the hearing capacity of an anxious dog.

Fancy living in a kitchen that resembles Sigourney Weaver's in *Ghostbusters*? Be my guest. Louise will interrupt your methodical food preparation by putting things away that you've just taken out of the cupboard, throw away the white ends of the spring onions and can't walk past a candle without lighting it, leaving it to burn to a cinder unchecked. (Then she'll probably order a takeaway.) We're one step away from eggs jumping out of their box and cooking themselves on the worktop.

Want to see how quickly a home interior can be brought to its knees? Fill your boots. Observe Louise as she actively distributes fragile objects throughout the house at a perfect height for infantile interference: multiple glass photo frames displayed at waist level; delicately poised plant pots on microscopically thin legs; permanent-ink pens a-plenty; and the unsupervised distribution of sticky foodstuffs. It's an absolute free-for-all.

You may be thinking, '*No biggy – just get a good cleaner.*' And you'd be right. Except Louise's idea of a cleaner includes cleaning up before the cleaner arrives because God forbid she could be that untidy! So basically we're paying for a cleaner to come over and clean what Louise has already cleaned.

I knew Louise was the one when she asked which movie star most resembled her and I replied 'Mickey Rourke in *The Wrestler*' and she laughed (google image search it if you don't

know); but really, it's because I felt for the first time that my
friends, family and those around me genuinely liked a prospec-
tive Mrs Boyce more than me! I half joke, but there was
definitely an underlying sense of that, and I'd say that's a good
benchmark for anyone wondering about such a thing.

We met through her brother, George. Myself and my buddy
Edd got chatting to him in a bar in Mui Ne, Vietnam in 2006,
whilst in the midst of backpacking across the world. When you
travel Vietnam you either start at the bottom and work your
way up or vice versa. This means you keep bumping into the
same folk on your way, a kind of game of serendipitous, stoned
leapfrog. This kept happening and we ended up travelling with
George through Laos, ziplining through the jungle into
Thailand, road-tripping the Gold Coast and New Zealand
before one big hurrah in Cusco, Peru.

In all that time he never once mentioned his sister.

But when we got home things took a turn as George ended
up in Louise's spare room in Clapham. The well-told story is
that I blocked her toilet and had to manfully own this unfortu-
nate event by paying for a plumber to fix it. However, I can now
reveal that a little-known but key factor in this traumatic tale is
that George had thrown up in the loo before I got there. The
first plumber who turned up refused to solve it, it was that bad.
(Sadly, however far Louise's star rises, I can't imagine Disney
buying this screenplay.)

George revealed to me one night that, despite this, Louise
was interested in me. I replied with the obligatory: 'But she's
your sister.' He told me it was fine but I'd have to marry her. So,
to cut a long story short: George moved out, and I moved in.

A romantic ritual to any London house move is trying to
secure a parking permit before your car gets towed away from
outside your new home. Upon visiting Brixton's council office I
returned to the flat with permit in hand.

'Did you get a full year permit?' asked Louise.

'No, just a six-month permit. Let's see how things go,' I jested. In that kind of exaggerated truth situation, within six months we were pregnant with Basil, and it was 12-month permits on retainer from then on.

Fast-forward a decade and it's my pleasure to present you with key learnings from my lived experiences with Mama Katherine Louise Spencer-MacCallum Boyce.

Forced sharing

Everyone knows that harmonious living is all about compromise. Our house is no different – I have to compromise heavily to meet Louise's demands.

We're talking about the 'communal' sock drawer, for example. Louise has never bought a pair of actual socks – yet miraculously wears them all the time. It's truly a wonder. That's right, she has rebranded my sock drawer as the communal sock drawer, and withdraws from it with wanton abandon, leaving me with slim pickings to choose from.

And as if that wasn't bad enough, let's consider these actual feet she has. She has chimp feet, surely borrowed from a distant primate in the Spencer-MacCallum bloodline. They're like an extra pair of hands – I swear she can bend her toes back to touch the top of her foot. She can control each toe independently too, splaying them like a cat stretching its paws in all directions. Quite a disturbing sight, and certainly not something you want invading your socks. Sadly at least two of the kids have inherited this trait and I'm afraid to take them to the zoo in case they're not allowed to leave.

Filth is for fathers

Louise is also a consummate pro at Bin Jenga: the art of balancing as much shit as possible on top of a bin instead of tying the bag up and putting it out. And woe betide me if I were to challenge this tick. It's a 'blue job' (meaning a job for a male), or something. Nothing to do with basic hygiene. Sometimes I wonder if she is actively trying to breed fruit flies and save them from extinction.

This extends to the car, of course. AKA our bin on wheels. She feeds the kids more food in our car than anywhere else. It's like a museum of crumbs resting on a bed of congealed, discarded clothing. When I take the car to the car wash, they give me that headshake that says, 'That'll be £10 extra for you – again,' as *I* take the public shaming for the mess.

Unsurprising surprises

As an experienced driver for over 20 years, it's surprising how surprised Louise is when she puts no petrol in the car, yet wonders why the tank is always empty. And her contact lenses always play up when a long journey is afoot, rendering me the designated driver as she spends the journey on Instagram. Then she'll be outraged when, upon arrival, I have the temerity to catch up with my own phone for a couple of minutes before leaving the car. How cheeky I am.

Do you have an ungodly and increasing quantity of cardboard arriving at your house? We do. I get that the boxes take up space, but rather than flatpack them somewhere out of the way, Louise will happily stack them up outside, taunting the elements to do their worst with them. It's just uncanny how they go wet and floppy and dissolve into the ground, every time. What are the chances?

Blaming the kids for things she's done

Any dads who are reading this, watch out for this one. Ever found the hosepipe resembling a spaghetti junction? Extension cord not rewound properly? Phone chargers mysteriously migrating from room to room? Found the peanut butter in the fridge? It was the kids, apparently.

Fake emergencies

Patience is not a strength for my dearly beloved. When there is no actual rush to leave the house – let's say I've got 20 minutes counting to the agreed departure time – Louise will announce there are only 10 minutes left. This is a frequent occurrence whereby a trusty glance at my phone for a time check is not at all required.

Try crossing a road with Louise. To be fair, I have terrible pedestrian discipline and will depart the pavement firmly in the belief that a car will not want to hit me. Halfway across a road, however, my wife will happily drag you back to the pavement should the glimmer of a car headlight appear on the distant horizon. As an adult I should be allowed to cross roads without holding hands, come to think of it.

If you survive crossing a road with her, then have a go at watching a movie with Louise. All concept of enjoying a fictional escape together will soon descend into a hyper-real trauma whereby you're reduced to thinking it's actually happening in real time, and X character did just actually die and it's your fault because you could have done something about it. She will unashamedly google a movie to find out the ending, apprising you of this discovery with an expectation that you will be as equally pleased to find out.

I really don't know why we subscribe to Netflix or Prime. Louise's fear of watching something she won't like forces her into a cultural void of *Seinfeld* and *Friends* re-runs. Sitting on the sofa with her can be a groundhog day existence as you're forced to endure a persistent crime against music: that clunky bassline between scenes of Jerry Seinfeld doing a bad job of not laughing at his own jokes.

Questions she has actually asked me

Can chimpanzees speak English?
Is a humdinger a type of car?
Is the London Eye half-price on a cloudy day?

OK, so I've got all that off my chest. Louise's favourite retort in our argumentative tit-for-tats is always: '*Try giving birth*' and really, it's pointless trying to respond to that. In fact if there were qualifications for arguing I think we'd both be eligible for honorary degrees. But we've always been very good at moving on from disagreements quickly, applying a goldfish-like memory technique to act like it never happened. A tried, tested and recommended formula. Especially when you're just too bloody busy to argue.

It will be of no surprise to reveal that Louise is a natural and fantastically loving mum, who took to the challenge of childbirth with full preparedness (as much as is possible) and poise.

My overwhelming memory of all three of our children being born is of witnessing actual miracles; vivid and unique moments in time which I consciously tried to take in, and thankfully, they're precious seconds that remain clear. Of course I was full of admiration for Louise each time, and especially how she took full control (as much as can be possible) of the process. With Basil it was a home birth and pretty much went to plan. She'll tell you that I went to the supermarket for a big shop as she went into early labour and was at the cheese counter when she called to see where I was, but I didn't hear her complaining about the full fridge we had for the next week ;)

Later that night, with labour in full flow, our midwife gave the heads-up that with one more push she'd be there, and I'll never forget the speed at which Basil shot out and circled the birthing pool. He had an extraordinarily long umbilical cord which, had it been just a little longer, would surely had seen him complete a lap of the pool.

He arrived in the early hours and we woke up a few hours later in a dream-like state. I remember going back into the living room and, to my shock, the birthing pool had deflated, leaving about an inch of clearance before everything started to leak onto the floor. It was effectively a murder scene about to unfold so I frantically bucketed half of it into the bath and dragged the pool into the garden to empty out the other half.

Our love for each other and Basil grew amazingly well that summer, as did our plants in the garden.

When bringing our second child Sonny into the world (his was the diciest birth of all our children), the delivery room had swathes of (incredible) NHS staff coming and going. There was some tension due to Louise's blood loss, so all sorts of nurses and experts were arriving. An anaesthetist was the straw that broke the camel's back when, for the 56th time Louise was met with 'Hi Katherine, I'm Deborah and I'm here to ...' and swiftly corrected with 'MY NAME IS LOUISE!'

Being total pros, the NHS obviously try to keep patients clear on every single development but in her peak birthing mode Louise was clearly having none of it. 'Oh, I'm sorry ...' replied Deborah.

'IT'S NOT YOUR FAULT – MY PARENTS WEREN'T THINKING WHEN THEY NAMED ME' Louise clarified.

For Inca's birth there was some precautionary measures in place, as the doctors weren't quite sure what happened with Sonny. We were grateful to be given a private room overlooking the Houses of Parliament as we arrived at St Thomas's Hospital at the early stages of Louise's labour. This time she was taking the battle to mother nature: she was incredibly prepared, her hypnobirthing recording playing in her earphones and she was completely psyched. Honestly, I wasn't needed at all except to relay updates to the nurses, choose a music playlist (Louise wasn't happy about this) and take pictures.

I'll always remember the surprise on the midwife's face when Louise sent me to tell her it was time, sooner than she was expecting. Afterwards, in her joyous Irish accent she acknowledged Louise's perception with, 'Well – you know your body, don-cha?'

And it was a girl, to top it all off.

Louise had often joked about wanting 'a pink one' and here we were. I remember saying, 'And I'll get to do a father of the bride speech after all!' as the tears flowed.

So there's a snapshot of life with Louise. But let's finish up with looking back at how 'Mama Still Got It' came to be, or as I remember it anyway.

There are good reasons why Louise is still modelling and being booked after 25 years. Let alone the obvious, she's not a diva, and has built up a great reputation for being professional, on time and easy to work with. She is an absolute pro and people like working with her. She saves all her vitriol for me ;) (You're welcome, fashion industry.)

She says herself that she was told never to expect to work again after becoming a mum, which is obviously mental. I remember floating the idea to her of starting a blog and, one day, after I came home from swimming with Basil, she asked me, 'What do you think of the name "Mama Still Got It"?' And mamastillgotit.com was born. Her friends, family and peers didn't know what to make of it all but obviously over time, it's been so impressive to see how her enormous proactivity and reactive, creative instinct has opened up so many avenues and opportunities for her through social media, in combination with her work.

My background is in brand and creative direction so people around us automatically assume it's me doing a lot of the camera work and editing – I can assure you it's absolutely not! Full credit to Louise for growing into a one-woman creative machine. It's been brilliant to see the increasingly positive engagement and feedback she regularly receives. It's getting to the point where on any given day I'll recognise my own short-falls, and suggest she makes a piece on it.

Thank you to everyone reading this who has spurred her on and shared her content with such encouraging advocacy. There's plenty more to come and I can't wait to see where else she takes things.

Lastly, a big thank you to Louise for allowing me a right to reply in this fantastic achievement, her debut book. Congratulations, babe! (I'm getting 10 per cent, yeah?) X

Nana's Still Got It

A grandmother's point of view. By Vanessa MacCallum, mother of Louise, Bonnie and George, and grandmother of six children.

Just when you thought you'd got your life back – mortgage paid, house to yourself, a bit more cash in hand, freedom to become reckless again, rock and roll times (yippee, at last, I've missed you, Wilson Pickett!), it all goes tits-up as your children, thinking they are doing you a favour, present you with their children – commonly known as your grandchildren.

Don't get me wrong ... we actually do crave to fill the void that our children have left – but we never realise the cost, both physical and mental, as well as the burden on our poor ageing knees. Grandchildren are *lovely*. Yes, I mean that. Just one smile excuses all the dishevelment, raised blood pressure and clearing up mashed bananas off the floor.

But there are rules, of course.

The announcement of the pregnancy. Bottle of fizz, phone all your friends, be joyous and genuinely over the moon. How wonderful that we're going to be grandparents, everybody! We are responsible for a new generation. Aren't we clever?

1–6 months. This is easy. They just lie there. They are now on bottles so we grandparents can share in the feeding. We can almost feel the bond opening up before our very eyes, a feeling that can even reduce you to an emotional wreck. You continue to have that bottle of fizz and phone the friends again. Isn't grandparenthood just the best thing ever!

6–12 months. A different matter. This time, you actually need that bottle of fizz for medicinal purposes, and you phone your friends for advice and reassurance. The knees by now have totally given up. But that little smile shines through and all is wonderful again. You have already forgotten the sleepless nights (that's when, as a wonderful parent to your own children, you actually offer to babysit and have your grandchildren stay over); now it's tidying away all those items they invariably want to touch, let alone spending a good chunk of the evening putting all the toy paraphernalia away.

Of course, we don't have childproof houses any more. But why, after having put out sensible play things, do they (girls and boys alike) head for the switch of the oven, or electricity sockets, with such determination and speed? And this is on all fours too (myself included). The speed seems to be faster at my house, more than at their own home, or is that because I am slower? Need to think about that one.

That bond between generations could become a little weakened if not checked but, once again, that smile comes through and our response now says that it's absolutely fine with us to target more electric sockets – be my guest to unplug and detune the TV while you're at it. Let's face it, *Peppa Pig*, *My Little Pony* or *Thomas the Tank Engine* are no match to the really exciting things in life: a big hug, an affectionate kiss and we're off again. Love it!

Of course, it's not just the knees that get a bashing. What about one's back? The bending over is so awkward. One's deportment goes out of the window but as long as our grandchild has a feeling of security, who actually cares what contortions we need to go through? But it's those grandparent versus grandchild rugby tackles whilst changing or dressing that really take their toll. Their parents have the knack, but we the older generation are a bit more hesitant to use our strength. Can you remember this when your children were this young? I'm sure I don't, but there again the memory does have a natural way of obliterating things we do not want to remember. No, seriously, I can't remember my kids challenging me to rugby tackles while dressing them.

12–24 months. As soon as the wee ones start talking – now we have lift-off. It's just heaven. That bond we hoped has been sown and fed in the 1–6 months bit is now beginning to yield its harvest. They call you Grandma (or Nana, Granny or whatever) for the first time, and this is when we actually realise that we ARE grandparents. Getting old. After all, the grandchildren are reminding us of that each time they call you Grandma (or Nana, Granny or whatever) – that you are their grandparent. How did that happen? But it is firmly established – we have a special place in the hierarchy of the family.

2–3 years. This next stage is not so simple. How can a child, who has only lived for three years, be so demanding, and quite frankly premeditatedly devious? And we're expected to fall in with it, keep calm and accept that this is the 21st century.

As we know, one of the most important rules of being a grandparent is to keep your mouth shut (rolling of the eyes might be more acceptable unless a photo is being taken at precisely the same moment of said eye movement. Then it's on Instagram, showing your feelings worldwide, so it's probably back to the preferable option of just keeping quiet). But has the generation between ours and their children completely forgotten, or even remember, the word, 'discipline'? No should mean no! But no! (Sorry about the abundance of the word 'no'.)

Picture this: the grandchild can politely ask for something (a snack, a drink, play date, a new outfit etc) and, if not acceptable, the grandparent politely says 'no', adding some explanation as to why the request was rejected.

Then the tournament begins. Grandchild relentlessly asks again and again. (Would you mind if I put the word 'again' in again?) The politeness turns to tantrum, tantrum turns to tears and in the end we back down just to keep the peace. Grandchild grins and mutters, 'Yes! Knew they'd give in.'

4 years and upwards. Thankfully, grandchildren become far easier to handle and please. In fact, we can learn from them. Every time you see them it's crazy how much they have grown, both in stature and intelligence. And that bond seems to tighten. That bond is cooking.

That bond is *priceless*.

We like to help out. Well, we do ... confess! We even volunteer to be the member of the family who accompanies the grandchild on a nursery school excursion to a children's farm or such like, generously offering our own children a break and, quite possibly, assume we're going to have the time of our life, showing off in front of the mums and dads that 'we don't do age'.

Wrong. The intentions are good but the outcome really isn't as attractive. I mean, there you are, 'midst a handful of 2–3 year olds, yours being the youngest, who couldn't be less interested in historical and/or educational facts, rushing around with the intent to annoy and the only calming element is ice cream or one of his/her favourite biscuits that Mum has packed for the journey (which you tried to locate earlier but the plastic picnic box has been deeply buried in the travel kitbag, or the oversized buggy seems to have been intentionally packed to make it impossible to find. Let alone then open).

My grandchild decided that that day's outing had been personally arranged to test my running skills. With Mum and

Dad conveniently at work, Grandma is the perfect target. And how they can run ...! What a sight! One agile sprinter (Olympics 2030 here we come) at a height of 2'6" running away from a fully grown, 5'9" adult who is reduced to wheezing, hands on hips to illustrate that we are ready for the knacker's yard. The child is triumphant and demands a reward, with absolutely no concern as to the health scare they put me through.

When you get home, when asked how the trip has gone, you lie. You look at your grandchild (who will have no recollection whatsoever of narrowly killing off their grandparent earlier that day) and say it was a wonderful day.

Another occasion when we stupidly volunteer to help out ... the school pick-up, in our own car. Your car is suitably equipped with a child seat – generously donated by your children, how kind – but when it comes to actually using it, the grandchild seems to know better than you how to strap up. They are not amused. And quite frankly nor are we. OK, so I found finding the correct strap for the right connection not as easy as it should be ... but they then look at you as if you're off the planet, and ignore you when conversation starts up.

And it's not just a multitude of straps. The prams today are like tanks. Admit it: oversized wheels, 'multi-position reclining seat' (words taken direct from a pram ad), a four-way suspension system so your child can have a smooth ride, shopping basket, storage space, handbrake etc. No mention of head lights, windscreen wipers or reversing camera as yet, but it's like having a car, as if one day we'll need to have a licence to push these vehicles. Add a child into the equation, throw the shopping into the shopping basket, balance your handbag somewhere near the handles, make sure you remember where you've put the front door keys, and you may as well be taking a combined weight-lifting and memory course. Once again, us grandparents discover muscles that have been dormant for years. Perhaps it's not such a bad thing, really. Not to mention remembering into which pocket you put those wretched house keys.

Is your memory as good today as it was yesterday? How many of you out there will confess to not being able to remember names, or people and places? It can take a couple of hours to click in and then, suddenly, whilst talking about something totally alien and nothing to do with the original conversation, the word/name just spurts out like a burp, as if the word has been hanging around in the mouth waiting for an inappropriate and possibly embarrassing time to come to the surface. The brain has decided to push out the forgotten name/word with no thought for the speaker or the listener.

Anyway, back to grandchildren.

Feeling tired, you suggest that a bit of TV would be a good idea – not for the grandchild, I hasten to add, no – for us. A bit of 'down time' as they say these days. We're all happy to do this.

But then there's the problem of getting to the right 'area' of the TV. It's not just point and click anymore, oh no. Thanks to computer games and pay-per-view and goodness knows what, turning on the TV has become an undertaking worthy of something off *Star Trek*. Thankfully, most grandchildren understand and easily grasp technical ideas, internet problems, resolve glitches etc which we fail to understand. Where did all these scientific, look-no-wires gadgets come from? To be fair, we never had these contraptions, so we shouldn't feel so dinosaur-ish. How many times have we heard, 'Grandma, for goodness' sake, it's so easy – you just delete this, encrypt that (err, excuse me?), save that attachment and there you are ...' (I don't have the heart to tell him I got lost at 'delete'). But *let* them do it for you – they get a buzz because they know something we don't and we equally get a buzz for being looked after in this ever-increasingly technical world. And we love them for it. And, funnily enough, they love us for it too!

So, the TV is switched on, and it's a wonderful feeling to be able to put one's feet up, have a cuppa and just relax ... when suddenly, loud-speaking, fast-talking (are they in fact actually speaking at all or shouting?), distorted-looking danger rodent cartoon characters move around the TV screen at such speed that I can't keep up with the plot. Raised blood pressure time. I know life speeds up as one gets older but this is ridiculous. Whatever happened to such wonderful children's programmes like *Bagpuss* and *The Woodentops*?

We also have a multitude of toys to help us entertain our grandchildren these days. In my day, an old box big enough for two would be fun. Not now. Oh, no. Now we have colour-coded, out-of-tune musical play centres, robotic cop sirens, pop-up-I-don't-know-whats, fangle-dangle what-do-you-call-this-contraption? toys. Plastic rubbish. But, I have to admit, all within the realms of health and safety. I still think an old box is within these boundaries but it's just not acceptable these days. Pity.

Bedtime. (When it comes to bedtime, there are occasions when the grandparent has gone to bed before the grandchildren. Let's face it, our adorable grandchildren can *wear us out*.) How did this come around so fast? Reading a bedtime story is the most wonderful moment of the day, when the grandchild is totally engrossed with every word you say and you momentarily have control, the child putty in your hands. They throw their arms around you and you feel like a million dollars. You sincerely love that child beyond measure and hope that another day will bring about as much muscular pain and exhaustion as the day just gone by – it was worth every second.

Apart from all the frustrations, when it's time to leave and go home, and your grandchild says: 'Why do you have to go,

Grandma?' or 'Why don't you stay over, Grandma?' you actually wonder why, in fact. Your heart says: 'I'll hang around for another couple of hours, because I love you so much,' whilst your head says: 'Don't be daft, haven't you had enough? Think of your knees.'

Invariably the head wins.

Everything is too fast these days ... which means only one thing: we are getting slower. But our grandchildren love us for this. We offer a certain stability, calm and a haven where the grandchild can momentarily visit for a bit of peace, and slow down for a while. It may not last for long but it's there for them. That precious smile and 'Grandma, I love you' says it all.

We live in a fast-moving world: transport, eating, growing up, learning, television etc and sometimes we need to feel that time can stop and we can come up for air. Grandparenthood is a bonafide remedy to this.

Once I started singing 'Let it Be' by the Beatles and was corrected with 'Let it Go' from the film *Frozen*. Bit too close for comfort, word-wise ... grandchildren seem to think that us grandparents don't have a life: 'Grandma, Mummy tells me you went to the cinema yesterday – are you sure you should be out that late?' What? I haven't (yet) got the bottle or heart to let them know what I used to get up to. We may be over 60 but we are sixties chicks, and the grandchildren could learn a thing or two from us. BUT we now have a responsible position in the hierarchy so just 'let it go' and treasure their concerns. Looking back, I think our generation got up to more mischief than the grandchildren do today. Yes, that's certainly true. (And I actually knew the words to both songs and consequently I got a 'smiley face' sticker for being so up-to-date with my choice and expertise of songs.)

Never did we think having grandchildren would be so full of surprises – and mostly all good surprises. I often agree that going to work in the office is the equivalent of having a day's vacation, and very needed. How many of you out there have come home after a day's child-minding and felt like dying for a while, ready to take a week to recuperate, annoyed that you left home wearing your best white T-shirt and returning with a substitute-spaghetti-dinner food-stained T-shirt. Should have worn a plastic coated, fool-proof outfit. Think I might patent this idea.

There's just one more thing. OK, so we've raised our kids; spent years teaching them right from wrong; have the badge to show that we've been good parents and that we possibly (no, undoubtedly) know a thing or two about bringing up a family. There's an unwritten rule, however, in the handbook of grandparenthood guidance ... keep quiet – unless guidance is asked for (bearing in mind it may be 20 years out of date). Don't offer advice or suggest a different way of doing things. Can you not remember our own mothers and mothers-in-law offering advice when it wasn't needed? So this is an important rule and should be adhered to at all times.

So, to sum up ... It's just the most wonderful feeling and experience to be a grandparent, to look after and cherish the grandchildren, to see them change from the scanned hospital photo into proper little people, to see a family resemblance, to melt when they acknowledge your existence, to be proud that your own children have been so clever, etc ... but how nice to give them back! And then the following day, actually ache at not being with them, missing them like hell and enthusiastically making arrangements to meet up again as soon as possible. Human nature – nothing like it. I love it.

I remember saying goodnight to my children: after story time, I'd stand by the door, hand poised over the light switch and say, 'God bless'. Years later, I discovered that my children thought I was saying, 'Cobblers', so I am very careful to say a clear, 'Good night' to my grandchildren.

Grandparent job description
Part-time job: Out of hours work that includes
weekend catering and dormitory organisation.
Cooking skills a plus; diplomacy a must.
No pay, but rewards are endless.

10 useful tips to help with application

1. You will need to excel in the culinary department. You will need to be a details person, in terms of brand of nuggets, the exact shape of chips, and the preferred pattern on the plate on which to serve up these specific items. It will be a sign you've done well if the plate is half empty, and on attaining this you will have passed your probation. (NB: Outright approval is signalled if seconds are asked for, but this rarely happens unless ice cream with sprinkles is on the menu.)

2. Diplomacy is essential when organising sleeping arrangements, particularly for a sleepover. Reverse psychology is thoroughly recommended to convince a grandchild they are in the best and most comfortable bed, whether on the floor, in a bunk or divan.

3. Reading a book at bedtime is highly recommended. You will enjoy the story even though it's been read many times before and the child now joins in, word for word. Animated vocals are fun for both the applicant and the child.

4. You must be prepared to sleep with one eye open, and an ear to the ground, so as to be immediately awake and

alert should any untoward tragedy occur, such as an argument over who has taken the covers, who woke up who, and any fighting amongst siblings.

The reward for this is endless cuddles in your own bed in the early hours of the morning as they descend on you. (NB: This is an important episode, as childhood memories are made of this.)

5. Applicants must appear ignorant from time to time so that said grandchild can boast of his/her knowledge of technology, but at the same time you will need to offer sufficient advice in more down-to-earth matters. A kind of mutual self-indulgence and mutual admiration is recommended – keep silent and just listen (this takes practice).

6. Must be willing to be hated, if only for a while. Deep-rooted rules and manners that are not always gracefully received must be maintained, but not to the extent that might annoy the line managers ('parents').

7. The applicant must also be quick enough to inadvertently (actually deliberately) cheat at board games whilst telling the grandchild that cheating is not acceptable. Sometimes the grandchild needs to lose so that the applicant can prove that losing is just as important as winning. (NB: This can actually be great fun, but practice is advisable.)

8. Must be able to converse thoughtfully and patiently, and be relied upon to mend items, such as sewing back on an ear of a loved cuddly companion, at the same time sounding convincing that all is now better; to reassuring them the repair you did the previous week was perfectly adequate and would have sustained the element of time had they not tried to undo said repair.

9. Must be astute enough to distinguish cries of 'crying wolf' to those of genuine concern, and hear both sides

of the story. Must show no favouritism even though it's
quite obvious what happened and who started it, and
teach the satisfaction of making up.

10. Never report back to the line managers ('parents') of any
mishap, unless hospitals visits are involved.

Please consider the job description carefully, and only apply if
completely sure you can fulfil the requirements wholeheartedly.
No training is given but every applicant should have a heart of
gold and jump at the job. (NB: jumping is not necessary.)

Although this job does not carry any remuneration, it will
be very enjoyable and thoroughly rewarding, with free hugs
for life.

Final Word

There are so many moments we forget about in life – I can't remember what I did on this day 20 years ago, this time last year or last week, for that matter, but life happened and it must have been OK because I'm still here. Certain memories stay tattooed on our brains with detailed precision; we know that it was a moment that moved us, whether it was from joy, fear, love …

One memory that has always stayed with me happened when I was a new mother, and I felt like I was at my lowest ebb. I was tired. Beyond tired. I was a fraction of myself. I was walking my eight-month-old baby around in the pram trying to get him to sleep, shushing his cries and wishing I was somewhere else, when out of nowhere an elderly lady appeared.

She came over to us, took a look at my agitated baby and reached out to touch him. She couldn't quite reach him but my baby stopped crying. She gave him such a beautiful smile, then looked at me. I felt like she could read my soul, that she could feel what I was feeling.

She reached for my hand and quietly spoke. 'Enjoy every moment. Even the bad moments. It won't last forever, then you'll miss it.' And she walked off.

I don't know if she was my guardian angel or just someone in the right place at the right time, but her words moved me. I took her advice on board and have tried to embrace both the good and the bad ever since. Ten years on, the baby in that pram is now old enough to get himself to sleep, old enough to

All you need is beautiful love, according to Sonny.

have a sleepover at his friends' houses and is embarrassed to kiss me at the school gates – and I would do anything to have him back as a baby in that pram and give him a huge cuddle.

Becoming a mother changes the landscape of your heart forever. It is the most overwhelmingly beautiful journey. Even on the most difficult days, feeling a little warm hand slide into your palm as you walk down the street, or seeing a toothless chuckle, can make any stressful day feel that little bit lighter. And when your kids tell you they love you, it makes everything worthwhile.

I wouldn't change it for the world.

Breathe.
Listen.
Laugh.
Love.
Repeat.

Now, it's back to September, and we do it all over again. Who's ready? Let's *do* this!

Thank You

A few mentions to those who made this book come to life:
Firstly, I'd like to thank YOU, the person holding this book (or listening to the audiobook). Thank you for your support and for taking the time to pick up this book and read my words, you absolute legend.

Thank you to Katya Shipster and all the team at HarperCollins for giving me this wonderful opportunity to write a book and for having faith in me to write it! I hope I've done you proud ... can we do another one?? I already miss our mammoth WhatsApp chats and emails about bringing this book to life. What a journey it's been, and I'm so thankful for my words, memories and secrets being printed. I think ...

Thank you, Angharad Marsh, Marnie Toocaram, Anna Shillinglaw, Blaise Kelly and all at MiLK for your management, guidance, and confidence in me. You guys are amazing, and I'm so grateful you took a chance on your first 'mummy blogger' and continued to keep me on your books as a model. Turned out alright, didn't it, eh?

Thank you to the 'Pennies' ... Bebe, Jessie, LA, Laura, Sarah and Tamara. Solid, real, authentic friendships that started when I was 13 years old and will carry on forever. Thank you for all the laughs, the copious amounts of WhatsApp messages on a daily basis, for demonstrating the real meaning behind 'women supporting women' and for always being there when I'm not feeling my best. We raise each other up and this, my *dear* friends, is gold. I am so thankful for you all.

Thank you to all the wonderful mothers I have met on my parenting journey – from everyone in the 'Drinkies' WhatsApp chat including Anna, Alice, Regan, Kristen, Joanna, Helena, Charlotte, Nicola, Lisbeth, Lucy, Claire; to the new parents I've met at my new school, especially Laura, Sarah and Jess. The best thing about parenting (apart from having children) is who you meet along the way at the school gates and play dates. I'm so grateful we're on this journey together!

To my friends I don't see enough of because of life and motherhood: Cat, Harriet, Vicky, Philippa, Sophie, Cottaging lot and Jenny. We need to hang out soon please! And to the incredible women I've met on Instagram who have now become friends for life – special mention to Erna aka @mercer7official (follow her for fashion).

Massive thanks to Jesse's side of the family: Brenda, Geoff, Sue, Garrett, Ben, Rosie, Kate, Andrew and Gabriel for being such great in-laws and always being there for us. We appreciate you more than you'll ever know.

To Zoran, Alex, Steve, Jessie Burn and little baby Max – I adore you all.

Thank you to my sister Bonnie and brother George for always, ALWAYS being silly with me, always laughing with me, and always having my back and supporting me. Bonnie, you are my best friend and I'm so happy you've been on this journey with me ... the good, the bad and the ugly. Thank you for agreeing to be in my silly videos and forever looking out for me. I absolutely love that our kids were born at the same time. I've loved becoming a mother with you – Olivia and Sam, I love you, guys! George – thank you for going travelling, and randomly bumping into Jesse five times around the world, so that he turned into a husband with whom I have three beautiful children. And sorry for terrorising you when we were kids – I didn't realise how much Bonnie and I did until writing this book. (It's very funny, though.) Thank you for your ongoing support and love and random funny TikTok links at midnight. Bonnie and George – you have always been the wind beneath my wings. More than you know. I am blessed to have siblings as best friends. Pub?

To my mum, Vanessa, for being my rock, my inspiration, my home. Your support, your grace, your wisdom, your optimism and your sense of humour is priceless and has made me the woman I am today. I absolutely adore you. Thank you for being so hands-on with the kids – we are all so grateful for you. Thank you for contributing to this book – I love hearing your comical side of your parenting/grandparenting journey. You are definitely a Nana Who's Still Got It!

I'd like to thank and mention my Dad who passed away from MSA three weeks before Inca was born. I wish so much he had met her – I can imagine hearing his infectious loud laugh from all the stories I would have told him. I know he'd be proud of me, my brother and my sister and his six grandchildren.

To my husband, Jesse. I fucking love you. More than I probably tell you. I'm so pleased you baby-trapped me (ongoing joke) and decided to spend your life with me. Thank you for your unconditional, continuous love, support and laughter. Having children together has been one hell of an adventure and I can't wait to make more memories with you. Jesse, you believed in me even when I didn't believe in me, helping me grow into who I am today. You've seen me at my lowest and helped me become the woman I am. Thank you for accepting me as I am – warts 'n' all. You have no idea how much I love you. You are the perfect choice for my first husband.

To my three beautiful children: Basil, Sonny and Inca. Thank you for picking me to be your mother, thank you for being you, thank you for teaching me what patience and unconditional love means, thank you for all the laughs, the cries, the melt-downs and looking for heart-shaped rocks wherever we go on walks (they're my most valuable possessions) and never, ever stop being unapologetically you. I hope you read this book if you ever become parents, and perhaps you'll see similar stories in here that you can relate to your journey. Thank you for your understanding when Mummy had to shoot off to finish writing this book and I missed story time ... I will make it up to you. Snack? You guys are utterly brilliant. How lucky am I to get to love you every day. You are my magic.